THE HEALER-PROPHET

William Marrion Branham
A Study of the Prophetic
in American Pentecostalism

[Reprint edition]

THE HEALER-PROPHET

William Marrion Branham
A Study of the Prophetic in American Pentecostalism

Reprint edition with a new preface
and a foreword by David Edwin Harrell, Jr.

by C. Douglas Weaver

MERCER UNIVERSITY PRESS
Macon, Georgia   2000

ISBN 0-86554-710-6   MUP/P211

CONTENTS

FOREWORD

A widespread healing revival erupted in the American pentecostal sub-culture in the aftermath of World War II. Stirred as this isolated group was by thousands of reports of marvels and miracles, no one could have predicted that fifty years later millions of people around the world would be flocking to revivals remarkably like those that swept the United States in the late 1940s and early 1950s. American pentecostals believed they were witnessing a powerful moving of the Holy Spirit, but when outsiders periodically noted the massive healing services conducted by a coterie of talented independent evangelists, they generally ridiculed and caricatured the revivalists and their extravagant claims.

In hindsight, it is clear that the events of those years were consequential indeed. As it gained momentum and visibility, the post-World War II pentecostal revival persuaded many mainstream Protestants to rethink their views on the gifts of the Holy Spirit and to join pentecostals in praying for a new outbreak of God's miracle-working power. By the 1960s what had begun as a spontaneous panpentecostal revival spilt over into Protestant denominations and the Roman Catholic Church. A booming charismatic movement in the last third of the twentieth century altered the religious demography of the world. At the end of the twentieth century, scholars estimated that as many as half of the Protestants in the world were aligned loosely with the pentecostal/charismatic movement. At present, the movement remains vibrant and expansive. In the United States, huge independent megachurches boasting 10,000 to 25,000 members have arisen in nearly every American city. By the 1990s, however, the cutting edge of the revival had moved into the developing world where pentecostal-type denominations flourished and huge throngs assembled to seek healing and miracles. Indigenous evangelists in Latin America, Africa, and Asia replicated and surpassed the mighty works of the American pioneers of the 1950s. In addition, tens of millions of Roman Catholics embraced the gifts of the Holy Spirit in the Catholic Renewal Movement after tongues-speaking revivals broke out on the campuses of several Catholic universities in the early 1960s.

Pentecostalism was a strongly missionary movement from its beginnings in the early twentieth century, and the message spread around the world in the decade following the famous Azusa Street meeting which began in Los Angeles in 1906. Nonetheless, before World War II, pentecostalism was largely confined to small, bickering sects that appealed mostly to the down-and-out. But by 1945 American pentecostalism was poised for an era of expansion. A new generation of believers filled pentecostal churches, and they were led by a new generation of leaders. This new generation of denominational leaders was less dogmatic and sectarian than the founders of American pentecostalism, and they initiated a panpentecostal rapprochement symbolized by the founding of the Pentecostal Fellowship of North America in 1947. After World War II the churches seemed ready to lay aside their quibbling and unite all those who embraced the baptism of the Holy Spirit in common cause. Furthermore, many of the pentecostal churches in the postwar years had attained a new respectability. Congregations were bulging with workers who had steady jobs and who yearned to gain the respect of their fellow Christians. In short, pentecostal churches emerged from World War II with a new economic capability and a newfound sense of pride. Finally, the postwar generation that filled the pentecostal churches yearned for a new outpouring of the miracle-working power of God. They had heard from their grandparents and parents tales of mighty miracles, and they waited on the Lord for a fresh outpouring of the Holy Spirit in their time. Out of these new theological and sociological realities, and out of this gnawing sense of anticipation, the postwar healing revival was born.

At this auspicious movement in the history of American pentecostalism, first a trickle, then a deluge of gifted and audacious evangelists seized the moment to capture the spiritual and organizational leadership of a spontaneous revival. Based mostly on their claims to God-given powers to bring healing to the sick, in the late 1940s these evangelists began holding huge panpentecostal crusade across the South, then the nation, then the world. For nearly two decades, in auditoriums and tents, they healed the sick, raised the dead, and preached the full gospel message of Holy Spirit baptism. For a few months at the beginning of the revival, the pentecostal churches embraced these self-proclaimed anointed messengers, sensing that the revival was from God. But as the evangelists's claims became more extravagant, and as their financial appeals became more self-serving and extreme, the churches backed away from the revival. As a result, the evangelists established independent ministries. Some of these ministries, most notably Oral Roberts, built financial empires larger than any pentecostal denomination. In the long run these independent organizations exercised a powerful influence on the expansion of pentecostalism around the world. It was the independent ministries, more than any other single force, that exported the message of God's miraculous power to the masses in the Third World.

The independent pentecostal ministries of the post-World War II period changed and evolved through the years. In time, organizational skills became more important to an evangelist's survival than spiritual gifts; teachers took precedence over healers; and, with the advent of television, entertainers reached more people than the mystical and charismatic preachers who had dispensed healing under the tents in the 1950s. These new breeds who sustained the pentecostal/charismatic expansion in the last quarter of the century owed much, however, to the first generation of independent ministers who had begun the revival.

Today, millions of charismatic Christians around the world know the names of the celebrities of the early healing revival, such as Oral Roberts, and of later television evangelists, such as Jimmy Swaggart. They are less likely to know William Branham's name. But in the 1950s Branham's name was on the lips on nearly every pentecostal. It was spoken with reverence and awe; it was a name that bespoke powerful miracles and supernatural happenings. It may properly be said that Branham initiated the healing revival in 1946, though surely the times were ripe in the pentecostal subculture for the outpouring of supernatural claims that followed. Oral Roberts began his independent ministry a year after Branham. Roberts and the stream of evangelists who heard the voice of God calling them to a ministry of healing in the decade after 1946 always deferred to William Branham as the first of the modern prophets of God. It was Branham who had unleashed God's miraculous powers in the postwar period.

The story that C. Douglas Weaver tells, then, is one of riveting interest to those who trace their religious roots to the post-World War II craving for an outpouring of the Holy Spirit. It is a fascinating, unlikely tale of triumph and disappointment. Branham was enigmatic and controversial at the height of his career, and he became more ethereal toward the end of his life. Weaver tells the Branham story fairly and dispassionately. Indeed, he writes with a rare and admirable degree of sympathy for his subject. As a result, his book will help outsiders understand the making and functioning of a prophetic personality in the pentecostal subculture.

Because of his limitations as an organizer and promoter, or, as his followers believe, because of his integrity and calling, Branham soon found himself in the backwash of the revival that he had initiated. Under these circumstances, as Weaver points out, Branham became more and more unorthodox in his claims and teaching. But if his following became narrower, it also became deeper. Before his death in 1965, he had assumed the dimensions of a cult figure.

In the aftermath of Branham's death in an automobile accident, thousands of his followers believed him to be a Messiah-like figure; others believed him to be a special prophet to his age. His thousands of recorded sermons were transcribed and treated as scripture. Around the world, several hundred thousand people separated into "Spoken Word" churches. This process, which is carefully traced by Weaver, illustrates another of the lasting legacies of the great healing revival—the creation of new religious groups. The healing-revival movement has long since fragmented, leaving in its wake scores of independent institutions and new coalitions of churches. Branham's followers were the firstfruits of this creative ferment.

So, read on. This is a story well told and truly worthy of reading. Much of what has happened in the pentecostal/charismatic world in the second half of the twentieth century owes something to the startling reports and wondrous claims that echoed from the Branham healing campaigns of 1946 and 1947.

2000   *David Edwin Harrell, Jr.*
                                              Auburn University

PREFACE TO THE PAPERBACK EDITION

Participants of the Pentecostal/charismatic tradition in American religion sometimes call the development of Pentecostal denominations during the first half of the twentieth century the "first wave" of the Holy Spirit's renewal and restoration of primitive (first-century) Christianity. A "second wave" occurred with the advent of the charismatic movement in the 1960s. Charismatics affirmed pentecostal theology that advocated the use of all of the gifts of the Spirit (speaking in tongues, divine healing), but these believers generally maintained their ties to nonpentecostal denominations. In the last two decades the charismatic movement has spawned a "third wave" that gives added focus to the restoration of primitive Christianity. Independent ministries advocate the restoration of prophets and apostles, signs and wonders, as well as spiritual gifts, a gospel of prosperity, and spiritual warfare.

Readers of American religion need to take another look at the ministry of William Branham, for in this thriving subculture of contemporary independent charismatic religion, Branham's legacy is alive and well. Because of his role as divine healer turned prophet, the major emphasis of this thematic biography, Branham has been called the "principle architect of restorationist thought" for the "new charismatics" (Michael Moriarty, *The New Charismatics*, Zondervan, 1992). Popular "restoration prophets" Bill Hamon and Paul Cain, for example, cite Branham's significant influence upon their ministries. These men, among others, have spread Branham's legacy into charismatic groups like the Kansas City Prophets and the Vineyard Fellowship. The Toronto Blessing and the Brownsville Revival, revivals that have attracted national attention for their controversial emotional practices, include a focus on apostles/prophets that find root in

Branham's teaching about an end-time prophet. Even the most popular contemporary television healing evangelist, Benny Hinn, frequently endorses the ministry and teachings of Branham. For an uneducated "Holy Ghost" independent preacher and healer, Branham's influence amazingly endures.

In the book, I briefly described Branham's legacy upon his closest followers at the time of his death in 1965. After Branham's death, his family and followers developed numerous independent congregations known as the "Message." Branham is acknowledged at minimum by "Message" believers as the "end-time prophet" whose "message" is the Word of God "in its purest form." Branham's sermons have obtained scriptural status for most followers as the infallible "voice of God" to the Bride of Christ before the Second Coming of Jesus. Voice of God Recordings in Jeffersonville, Indiana is led by Branham's son, Joseph, and has developed an aggressive missionary program to send tapes and written sermons throughout the world. These missionary efforts continue to expand. From 1986 to 1996, for example, more than fifty million Spoken Word sermon booklets were printed. In 2000, Branham's "message" is currently being translated into forty-three different languages. Mission efforts are growing on every continent. "Message" believers have established 1,600 churches in Latin America but the most active agenda is in Africa, where churches and libraries exist in twenty-six nations.

Like most new religious movements, the "Message" has typically developed some structure and organization. As the "end time" extends itself chronologically, believers nevertheless maintain a sense of eschatological urgency with their aggressive missionary program because of their faithfulness to Branham's message of restoration. Persons interested in the development of new religious groups will also benefit from analyzing the influence of Branham.

I am very grateful that Mercer University Press has recognized the value in publishing this study of William Branham in an accessible paperback edition. Special thanks to Editors Marc Jolley and Andrew Manis for their efforts. I have always been indebted to David Harrell for his encouragement and enthusiasm about my study of Branham. Harrell's foreword is a superb concise analysis of the legacy of the post-World War II healing revival.

November 2000   *Doug Weaver*
                                                          Vidalia, Georgia

ACKNOWLEDGMENTS

This book began as my dissertation at The Southern Baptist Theological Seminary in Louisville, Kentucky. In my study of the history of Christianity, I am indebted to Dr. Bill Leonard and Dr. E. Glenn Hinson. Both professors have a teaching ministry that combines a deep faith commitment with expertise in the historian's craft. Having had the opportunity to be their student and colleague, I am grateful for their friendship, their encouragement, and their model for teaching and studying church history. In the writing of this work, I am especially thankful to Dr. Leonard for his commitment of time, his interest in the project, and his patient, skillful guidance as a supervisory professor.

Words of deep appreciation must also be given to Dr. David E. Harrell, Jr. The acknowledged expert on healing and charismatic revivalism in American religion, Dr. Harrell read the manuscript twice and offered suggestions regarding its revision. I am most grateful, moreover, for his initiative in recommending the manuscript for publication.

This project could not have been thoroughly researched without the assistance of William Branham's followers in Jeffersonville, Indiana. Paul Branham and Mindy Quick, employees of the Voice of God Recordings, Inc., provided me access to all of Branham's taped sermons. Cheryl Losh, secretary of Spoken Word Publications, did the same with the printed sermons. Special thanks go to Billy Paul Branham, executive-treasurer of the Branham Tabernacle. In addition to providing resources, he always had time to answer my questions. Branham's followers extended to me their unreserved cooperation and friendship. Enough cannot be said about their sincere, warm Christian spirit.

Many other persons have contributed to this book. I am thankful to the librarians at The Southern Baptist Theological Seminary and The Holy

Spirit Research Center, Oral Roberts University, for providing research materials. Dr. Paul Chappel of Oral Roberts University offered bibliographical insights and helped arrange important interviews. The personal insights of Robert Moore, a former follower of Branham, were indispensable to understanding the beliefs of Branham's current disciples. Dr. Grant Wacker of the University of North Carolina read the manuscript and offered helpful suggestions regarding its transformation from a dissertation to a book. I am also grateful to Mrs. Johnnie Sherwood, who typed the manuscript, and Mrs. Nina Wilburn, who proofread the final copy and helped prepare the index.

My wife, Pat, has provided her unbounded love and support throughout the completion of this project. Finally, I must remember Aaron whose first four years of life have provided me with never-ending joy. It is to my wife, son, mother, and the memory of my father that I dedicate this work.

INTRODUCTION

The dynamic growth of Pentecostalism in the twentieth century is a major feature of the contemporary religious scene. An integral element of the history of Pentecostalism is the contribution of the healing revivalists; from its origins divine healing was an important part of the Pentecostal movement.

Healing revivalists like F. F. Bosworth emphasized that deliverance from sickness was provided in the atonement of Jesus Christ. Physical healing was therefore the privilege of all persons who evinced the necessary faith. John T. Nichol, a prominent historian of Pentecostalism, suggests that the efforts of the healing revivalists to meet the physical needs of the people have facilitated the conversion of many followers to the Pentecostal faith.[1]

Healing revivalism, according to David E. Harrell, Jr., erupted in 1947, and continued unabated until 1958. Harrell contended that 1958 was the transitional point when the healing revival was transformed into a broader, charismatic revival in which healing played a major, but not dominant, role. In contrast, charismatic revivalism gave more emphasis to all the gifts of the Holy Spirit.[2]

Harrell asserted that the healing revival produced two "giants"—William Branham and Oral Roberts. Branham is acknowledged as the leader and pacesetter of the revival. Whereas Roberts readily adapted and sus-

---

[1]John T. Nichol, "Pentecostal Churches," *Encyclopaedia Britannica* (15th ed.), *Macropedia,* 14:31.

[2]David E. Harrell, Jr., *All Things Are Possible: The Healing and Charismatic Revivals in Modern America* (Bloomington: Indiana University Press, 1975) 8.

tained his leadership in the transformation of healing revivalism to the broader charismatic revivalism, the less sophisticated Branham was not as widely successful, and his popularity eventually declined. He became increasingly exclusivistic, and given to the doctrinally bizarre. In his last days, Branham's followers placed their leader at the center of a Pentecostal personality cult.

Today, Branham's role in Pentecostalism and American Christianity is largely unknown to those outside the Pentecostal tradition. One observer eloquently describes the lack of knowledge concerning Branham.

> Fame above all things is fleeting, a flame that dies quickly no matter how brightly it flares for the moment. Probably no single figure in the Pentecostal movement illustrates this fact better than William Marrion Branham. . . . In the days of his prominence, the 1950s, what Spirit-filled believer did not know his name? Yet today, we may wonder, what believer does?[3]

This study is an attempt to examine Branham's role in American Pentecostalism and its significance for understanding one important subgroup of religious America. The biographical aspects of the work will focus primarily on Branham's significance to the Pentecostal movement. The thematic perspective of the book, however, will be to analyze Branham as a Pentecostal "prophet." My thesis is that the controlling identity for the ministry of William Branham is that of "a prophet to a generation."[4] By analyzing Branham's "prophetic" identity, and the effect it had on his ministry and the ministry of his contemporaries, one can draw some conclusions concerning the prophetic element as a model for continuing revelation in Pentecostalism.

In order to analyze Branham from the perspective of a Pentecostal "prophet," definitions of Pentecostalism and prophet must be offered as preliminary considerations. The Pentecostal movement emerged out of a deepening of the spiritual life within the Holiness movement at the end of the nineteenth century. The "theological roots of Pentecostalism"— salvation through Jesus Christ, the baptism of the Spirit, divine healing, and the belief in the physical second coming of Christ—were widespread in Holiness circles. Moreover, reports of persons speaking in tongues

---

[3]Robert Price, "Branham's Legacy," unpublished paper, 1. This paper is scheduled to be published in the neo-charismatic journal, *Pneuma*.

[4]Harrell, *All Things Are Possible*, 25.

increased in the late nineteenth century.[5] When in 1901 the Holiness preacher Charles F. Parham proclaimed that speaking in tongues was the evidence of the reception of the baptism of the Holy Spirit, the Pentecostal tradition was born. As an organized movement, however, Pentecostalism emerged on the world scene in 1906 during the now-famous Azusa Street revival in Los Angeles. Led by one of Parham's black converts, William Seymour, the belief spread quickly throughout the United States and beyond that speaking in tongues was "a sign of Baptism in the Spirit for the individual, a sign of the Second Pentecost for the Church, and a sign of the imminent second Coming of Christ."[6]

Larry Hart, a theology professor at Oral Roberts University, insists that, despite the diversity of doctrine and practice of the various Pentecostal groups, a central concept or experience unites the movement— the baptism in the Holy Spirit with the accompanying evidence of speaking in tongues.[7] This post-conversion religious experience corresponds, Pentecostals believe, with the first outpouring of the Holy Spirit upon Jesus' disciples at Pentecost, as recorded in Acts 1:12-2:4. Moreover, Spirit baptism becomes an entrance to a miraculous Christian life-style such as the earliest Christians possessed. The nine gifts of the Spirit catalogued by Paul in 1 Corinthians 12:8-10, (especially tongues and healing) may be received by the Spirit-baptized believer. In other words, gospel primitivism has been restored. In addition to Pentecostalism's three cardinal emphases of the baptism of the Holy Spirit, speaking in tongues, and spiritual gifts, Pentecostalism may be placed within the Fundamentalist-Holiness branch of Protestantism with its stress on biblical literalism, conversion, moral rigor, and dispensational eschatology.[8]

Branham's understanding of his own "prophetic" role developed solidly within the Pentecostal context. Branham was ordained a Baptist minister, and he always declared that his Branham Tabernacle in Jeffersonville, Indiana, was nondenominational. He eschewed allegiance to any denomination, and contended that his church was not an organization but

---

[5]Donald Dayton, "Theological Roots of Pentecostalism," *Pneuma* 2 (Spring 1980): 4, 20.

[6]Robert Mapes Anderson, *Vision of the Disinherited: The Making of American Pentecostalism* (New York: Oxford University Press, 1979) 4.

[7]Larry Douglas Hart, "A Critique of American Pentecostal Theology" (Ph.D. diss., Southern Baptist Theological Seminary, 1978) 96.

[8]Ibid. See also Nichol, "Pentecostal Churches," 30.

a fellowship that had no membership rolls.[9] Branham, nevertheless, gradually adhered to all the basic tenets of the "full gospel." A primary theme of his teaching was the Holy Spirit baptism, and he acknowledged tongues to be an attribute of the Spirit.

Throughout his healing campaigns, Branham described himself as a "Holy Ghost Baptist" when that appellation facilitated positive crowd response.[10] Branham aligned himself within the Pentecostal tradition, however. Regarding his independent Baptist heritage, Branham reflected, "I come [sic] out of it so I could be free"[11] in order to claim the Pentecostal experience.[12] He concluded that the "pentecostal Message is the only true Message from God."[13] Moreover, Branham admitted that his healing ministry in America was not effective except among Pentecostals.[14] Undoubtedly, then, Branham stands squarely within the Pentecostal tradition.

A voluminous amount of literature has been written in an attempt to understand the nature of the prophetic element in the Judeo-Christian tradition. For the purposes of this study, however, several dominant characteristics can be suggested that will help to understand Branham's claim to a "prophetic" identity.

W. Sibley Towner contends that "there is really no way of talking about what the term [prophet] meant or means absolutely, but only about how it has been used."[15] Towner suggests that four criteria were used in the Old Testament communities in order to judge a man's right to prophetic accolade—style, rhetoric, constituencies, and message. First, the prophet exhibited a certain flamboyance of style with the utter conviction that the words he spoke were not his own, but God's. Concerning rhetoric, the prophet "would speak as a prophet should speak."[16] Prophetic

---

[9]William Branham, "Zacchaeus," sermon delivered and recorded in Bangor ME, 17 May 1958.

[10]Idem, "Resurrection of Lazarus," sermon delivered and recorded in Erie PA, 30 July 1951.

[11]Idem, *Conduct, Order, Doctrine, of the Church,* 2 vols. (Jeffersonville IN: Spoken Word Publications, 1973-1974) 1:168.

[12]Idem, "God's Way to Spiritual Unity," *HOF* 24 (June 1957): 19.

[13]Idem, *The Philadelphian Church Age,* vol. 8 of *The Revelation of Jesus Christ* (Jeffersonville IN: Spoken Word Publications, n.d.) 380.

[14]Idem, *Jehovah-Jireh* (Jeffersonville IN: Spoken Word Publications, n.d.) 107.

[15]W. Sibley Towner, "On Calling People Prophets in 1970," *Interpretation* 24 (October 1970): 495.

[16]Ibid., 499.

oracles were introduced with authoritative formulas like "Thus saith the Lord," "Woe," or "Therefore." Third, the prophet spoke within particular institutional contexts; and he spoke to and for particular constituencies. Towner notes that the prophet's disciples, in the end, were the ones who awarded the mantle of true prophethood. Finally, the major criterion in judging a prophet was his message. The prophetic message was consistent and faithful to a limited number of religious themes.[17]

The prophet was able to evince these characteristics because the primary characteristic of his prophetic self-consciousness was an awareness of God's calling. This calling was his divine legitimization, and was usually received by means of a vision, dream, an audition, or mediated through another of God's chosen prophets.[18] In light of this calling the prophet played an integral role in God's revelation to humanity. R. Thomas Schaub asserts that "revelation was a continued dynamic process for them [the prophets] in which they took an active part. They encountered God not only in the word which he addressed to them but in current events of their own day."[19]

On the basis of these considerations, a working definition of a prophet can emphasize the following elements. A *prophet* is a person who, motivated by his conviction of a supernatural calling from God, manifests a charismatic style and an authoritative rhetoric amidst particular institutional contexts. The prophet serves as God's mouthpiece, and his message functions as the word of God to and for particular constituencies. This word is a forthtelling of God's will, and a call of restoration to that will. Foretelling of the future is only a secondary function.[20] In bringing the word of God to the people, this selected vessel is representing a primary method of God's continuing revelation to humanity.

This study represents an analysis of William Marrion Branham as a Pentecostal "prophet." It will examine the way in which that appellation was applied by Branham himself, and by his followers within the Pentecostal tradition. The book is divided into seven chapters. Chapter one is a background study of the prophetic element in the Pentecostal tradition. The prophetic element as a vehicle for continuing revelation in early Pen-

---

[17]Ibid., 497-506.

[18]G[osta] W. A[hlstrom], "Prophecy," *Encyclopaedia Britannica* (15th ed.), *Macropedia*, 15: 62.

[19]R. Thomas Schaub, "Prophets: Past and Present," *Perspective* 12 (1971): 169.

[20]"Prophecy," *Oxford Dictionary of the Christian Church*, ed. F. L. Cross and E. A. Livingstone, 2d ed. (New York: Oxford University Press, 1974) 1133.

tecostalism receives particular attention. The earliest Pentecostals emphasized the revelatory nature of the spiritual gifts. Messages from the Holy Spirit were received through the gifts of tongues, tongues' interpretation, and prophecy. Moreover, the earliest Pentecostal leaders were perceived as channels of continuing, authoritative Holy Spirit revelation. Functioning as prophets for their followers, these spiritual autocrats asserted new, divine revelations, and organized new sects according to directives from God. Pentecostal ideas about continuing, versus biblical, revelation evolved as the movement developed. Dependency upon revelatory messages waned. Nevertheless, an emphasis upon selected prophetic leaders, functioning as vehicles for continuing revelation, is still a possibility in the Pentecostal/charismatic tradition.

Chapters two through six analyze Branham's life and ministry. The second chapter examines his early life up to the time of what he perceived as his dramatic, angelic commissioning. Chapters three and four survey Branham's success in the Pentecostal, healing revival, his views on basic issues in healing revivalism, and the methodology of healing that he employed. Branham believed that his healing gift was founded on his "prophetic" calling. According to the angelic commission, the sick would be healed if they believed that Branham was God's "servant/prophet." When disbelief occurred, misfortune would come to the people. Moreover, Branham believed his chosenness was legitimized by the signs that accompanied the healings. These signs were the vibration of his left hand which enabled him to detect illnesses, and his gift of discernment of the secrets of people's hearts. Finally, in his healing campaigns, Branham believed that he was sent to unify Spirit-baptized Christians.

Chapters five and six deal with Branham's later, radical years, as he attempted to cope with the decline of the healing revival. The evangelist experienced financial difficulties, and increasingly preached controversial doctrine. The "prophetic" revelations included a fierce anti-denominationalism and a vehement judgment against modern culture. Chapter six especially concentrates on Branham's central teaching of his last years—the identity and "message" of the end-time messenger and the necessity of the Elect's heeding the words of this "prophet."

The influence of Branham upon his contemporary revivalists and his followers will be the subject of the seventh chapter. Branham's significance as a "prophet" is further illustrated by the effort of other healing revivalists to claim his "prophetic" mantle for themselves. Moreover, Branham's legacy lives on in the lives of the zealous followers of his "Message." These "Branhamites," or "Message" believers as they prefer to be called, can be found throughout the United States and the world.

Therefore, a brief sketch of the nature of this basically unknown religious movement will be given.

In the conclusion, Branham's ministry will be placed in the broader religious context. Some implications are discussed concerning the prophet as a model of revelation in the Pentecostal tradition. Moreover, Branham's influence upon contemporary Pentecostal/charismatic trends is explored. In addition to placing Branham in the Pentecostal context, his ministry is discussed in the larger prophetic tradition of American religious history.

ABBREVIATIONS

HOF *Herald of Faith*
HW *Healing Waters*
SOF *Shield of Faith*
THM *The Healing Messenger*
TPE *The Pentecostal Evangel*
TSTL *Thus Saith the Lord*
TSW *The Spoken Word*
TVD *The Voice of Deliverance*
TVH *The Voice of Healing*
WWR *World-Wide Revival*

A BRANHAM ALBUM

(All photographs are courtesy of The William Branham Evangelistic Association, Jeffersonville, Indiana.)

Branham baptizing in the Ohio River, June 1933, near Spring Street, Jeffersonville, Indiana. According to Branham, during the baptismal service he received the end-time "message" that would be the forerunner to the rapture. (See pp. 26-29.)

Branham in Houston, January 1950. Perhaps the most famous picture of the healing revival, the light above Branham's head was considered to be a "supernatural halo" indicating the presence of his angel. (See pp. 50, 74-75.)

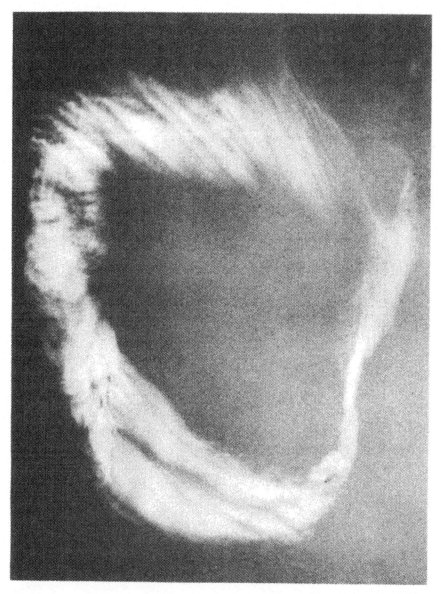

In February 1963 Branham claimed this Arizona cloud was a heavenly constellation of seven angels who informed him to return to the Branham Tabernacle in Jeffersonville and open the seven seals of Revelation. (See pp. 100-101.)

God's presence in the form of the "pillar of fire" resting on Branham's shoulder, March 1964, at Soul's Harbor Temple, Dallas, Texas, the church of W. V. Grant, Sr. (See pp. 74-75, 147-49.)

CHAPTER ONE

THE PROPHETIC ELEMENT
IN PENTECOSTALISM

The distinctive teaching of Pentecostalism—the baptism in the Holy Spirit with the accompanying evidence of speaking in tongues—places the movement at the forefront of contemporary experiential Christianity. Pentecostal scholars concur that Pentecostal theology is "Christ-centered, experience-certified theology."[1] Frederick Dale Bruner, a prominent neo-Pentecostal analyst, observes that

> Pentecostalism wishes, in brief, to be understood as experiential Christianity, with its experience culminating in the baptism of the believer in the Holy Spirit evidenced, as at Pentecost, by speaking in other tongues. The experience with the Spirit should continue, as in the early church, in the exercise of spiritual gifts, privately, and then publicly in the Pentecostal meetings where the gifts have their most significant sphere of operation.[2]

Bruner concludes by affirming that "it is not the *doctrine*, it is the *experience* of the Holy Spirit which Pentecostals repeatedly assert that they

---

[1]William G. MacDonald, "Pentecostal Theology: A Classical Viewpoint," in Russell P. Spittler, ed., *Perspectives on the New Pentecostalism* (Grand Rapids MI: Baker Book House, 1976) 64. See also R. Hollis Gause, "Issues in Pentecostalism," in Spittler, *Perspectives,* 114.

[2]Frederick Dale Bruner, *A Theology of the Holy Spirit: The Pentecostal Experience and the New Testament Witness* (Grand Rapids MI: William B. Eerdmans, 1970) 21.

wish to stress."[3]

The experiential orientation of Pentecostalism lends itself to the concept of a living, dynamic—rather than static—faith. To the Pentecostals, the restoration of apostolic Christianity confirms the truth of one of their favorite scriptural passages, Hebrews 13:8, "Jesus Christ, the same yesterday, today, and forever." This experiential foundation, moreover, serves as the backdrop for the question of the role of the authority of continuing revelation in Pentecostalism. Several issues are pertinent to understanding the function of continuing revelation. The first consideration is the relationship of the authority of God's revelation in Scripture to the authority of one's personal faith experience.

1.

Pentecostals form a consensus in their attitude toward the Bible. Statements of faith declare that "the Bible is the inspired Word of God, a revelation from God to man, the infallible rule of faith and conduct, and is superior to conscience and reason, but not contrary to reason."[4] Exhibiting a fundamentalist perspective toward the Scriptures, Pentecostals often specifically argue for the plenary verbal theory of inspiration of the original autographs. Inspiration is comprehensive, and not applied only to matters necessary for salvation.[5]

Analysts of Pentecostalism concur that the movement is undergirded by a belief in the ultimate authority of the Bible. In theory, God's revelation in Scripture "is a fixed, finished, and objective revelation."[6] Moreover, the Pentecostal method of biblical interpretation is often a biblicism that rejects any historical and critical understanding of the Bible. The modern Biblical methods of higher criticism are seen as tools that mythologize the supernatural, and consequently—Pentecostals aver—destroy faith in the inspiration and authority of the Bible.[7]

---

[3]Ibid.

[4]Carl Brumback, *Suddenly . . . from Heaven: A History of the Assemblies of God* (Springfield MO: Gospel Publishing House, 1961) 356.

[5]Walter J. Hollenweger, *The Pentecostals*, trans. R. A. Wilson (London: S. C. M. Press, 1972) 291. See also Nils Bloch-Hoell, *The Pentecostal Movement: Its Origins, Development, and Distinctive Character* (New York: Humanities Press, 1964) 214.

[6]Cecil M. Robeck, "Written Prophecies: A Question of Authority," *Pneuma* 2 (Fall 1980): 26.

[7]Larry Douglas Hart, "A Critique of American Pentecostal Theology" (Ph.D. diss., The Southern Baptist Theological Seminary, 1978) 99-100. See also Hollenweger, *Pentecostals*, 291-92.

Many non-Pentecostals, particularly those espousing a Protestant fundamentalist perspective, have vehemently criticized the "supposed" fundamentalist view of the Bible. The crux of their attack is that the Pentecostal emphasis of experiential faith denies the ultimate authority of the biblical revelation. Being guided by a subjective human-centered theology, individual experience becomes more important than doctrinal agreement based on the propositional authority of the Scriptures. In essence, Pentecostal theology is dependent more upon experience than upon Scripture.

Critics charge that, for the Pentecostal believer, "the experience validates itself."[8] The believer testifies to an experience, and then attempts to construct a framework of doctrine to justify it. In addition, a biblical hermeneutic results, in which "experience is needed to verify and to confirm Scriptural teaching."[9] The fundamentalists repudiate this experiential criterion by countering that "objective truth is the test of experience, and that is found only in the Bible."[10]

Much of the fundamentalist critique is based upon the concept that God's revelation and the gifts of the Spirit ceased with the post-apostolic era.[11] Yet more sympathetic analysts, both Pentecostal and non-Pentecostal alike, would agree that there is sometimes a tension between the authority of one's personal experience and the authority of the Bible. Pentecostal theology affirms that Scripture has authority over experience. The Bible is the absolute criterion for verifying the validity of one's experience. Nevertheless, Pentecostal theologians warn against "the dangers of an emotion- and experienced-centered theology."[12] Moreover, they admit that in practice "the Pentecostal tends to exegete his experience,"[13] and that continuing revelation is sometimes put on the

---

[8]John MacArthur, *The Charismatics: A Doctrinal Perspective* (Grand Rapids MI: Zondervan, 1978) 59. For a discussion of Pentecostals as fundamentalists see Hart, "Critique," 98-100; Hollenweger, *Pentecostals,* 291-307.

[9]Thomas Bird, "Experience over Scripture in Charismatic Exegesis," *Concordia Theological Quarterly* 45 (January-April 1981): 5.

[10]Ronald E. Baxter, *Gifts of the Spirit* (Grand Rapids MI: Kregel Publications, 1983) 19.

[11]The cessation of gifts was first argued by Augustine. The nineteenth-century evangelical, B. B. Warfield, popularized the view in writings such as *Miracles: Yesterday and Today.*

[12]Gause, "Issues," 114-15.

[13]Gordon D. Fee, "Hermeneutics and Historical Precedent—A Major Problem in Pentecostal Hermeneutics," in Spittler, *Perspectives,* 122.

same level as the Bible. According to Charles Farah, Jr., professor of historical theology at Oral Roberts University, "Wherever the Spirit bursts forth in new power there is always the danger that continuing revelation will take precedence over Scripture."[14]

Pentecostals clearly affirm the infallibility of the biblical revelation and its ultimate authority. At the same time, the experiential nature of faith emphasizes the authority of the present activity of the Holy Spirit. Consequently, the potential is obvious for continuing revelation to acquire a prominent position within the Pentecostal tradition. This is possible, in part, because of the Pentecostal's emphasis on the gifts of the Spirit, the most visible manifestations of the Holy Spirit's activity.

2.

The conviction that the activity of the Holy Spirit is the same today as it was during the apostolic era undergirds the Pentecostal belief that the gifts of the Spirit should have an integral role in the life of the Christian. Pentecostals believe in the reality of all the charismatic gifts of 1 Corinthians 12-14. Yet, the sensational gifts of tongues, with or without interpretation, prophecy, and healing have gained ascendancy in practice. The other less remarkable gifts are usually discussed only briefly, and are consciously little practiced. Therefore, the gifts of tongues and its interpretation, and the gift of prophecy serve as the best tests for the concept of continuing revelation by the present activity of the Spirit.[15]

Among the gifts of the Spirit, speaking in tongues (glossolalia) has always held the foremost position, but especially during the origin of Pen-

---

[14]Charles Farah, Jr., "A Critical Analysis: The 'Roots and Fruits' of Faith-Formula Theology," *Pneuma* 3 (Spring 1981): 17. According to Richard Quebedeaux, neo-Pentecostals (charismatics) have subordinated the authority of the written Word to the "authority of the living, 'dynamic' Word of God made known through the present activity of the Spirit itself." See Richard Quebedeaux, *The New Charismatics II* (San Francisco: Harper & Row Publishers, 1983) 132. Pentecostalism is often discussed in terms of classical Pentecostalism and neo-Pentecostalism. The latter term refers to the expansion of the Pentecostal movement—which began in the 1960s—beyond the limits of mainline classical Pentecostal denominations into other Protestant bodies and Catholicism. Hence, a neo-Pentecostal is a Spirit-baptized Christian who usually remains in his or her non-Pentecostal denomination. Throughout Quebedeaux's book, minor differences are noted between classical and neo-Pentecostal Christians. On the themes discussed in this chapter relating to continuing revelation and Scripture, authors from both groups are in basic agreement. Therefore, classical and neo-Pentecostal sources are occasionally cited.

[15]Bruner, *Theology*, 138-39. A discussion of healing is not included here because the gift is not considered one of the communicative gifts. See also Bloch-Hoell, *Pentecostal Movement*, 142.

tecostalism, when the movement was referred to as "the tongues movement."[16] Every believer, Pentecostals taught, would speak in tongues subsequent to his reception of the baptism of the Holy Spirit. Early in the movement, however, speaking in tongues—as the "initial evidence" of the Spirit's reception (Acts 2:4)—was distinguished from tongues as one of the gifts of the Spirit (1 Cor. 12:30). Those believers who possessed the gift would continue to speak in tongues after the initial sign of the Spirit's reception. Consequently, speaking in tongues is still the central feature of Pentecostalism, being valued as "the highest prized [gift] and even the normative social behavioral pattern."[17]

A representative Pentecostal definition of speaking in tongues is "the power to speak supernaturally by the Holy Spirit, in a language not known to the one possessing the gift."[18] Opinion is divided among Pentecostals concerning the human/divine interaction in the gift. Donald Gee, a leading European Pentecostal, argued that the Holy Spirit inspires the utterance that comes from the depths of the human spirit. To speak of the Holy Spirit as speaker, however, is misleading.[19]

Many Pentecostals, nevertheless, interpret tongues in terms of the Holy Spirit taking over and completely controlling the process. Ralph M. Riggs asserted that tongues, as a sign of Holy Spirit baptism, "is God's method whereby the Holy Spirit may possess men completely and be able to control them."[20] Moreover, an early Pentecostal journal exclaimed that "it is not ye that speak but the Holy Ghost . . . when singing or speaking in tongues, your mind does not take any part in it."[21]

---

[16]Bloch-Hoell, *Pentecostal Movement*, 143.

[17]Martin Marty, "Pentecostalism in the Context of American Piety and Practice," in Vinson Synan, ed., *Aspects of Pentecostal-Charismatic Origins* (Plainfield NJ: Logos International, 1975) 214-15.

[18]Howard Carter, quoted in Bruner, *Theology*, 144. Whenever the nature of speaking in tongues is discussed, a major topic is whether the sounds uttered are simply unintelligible speech, or a language previously unknown to the speaker. Practically all Pentecostals describe tongues as a language. For a positive assessment see Carl Brumback, *"What Meaneth This?" A Pentecostal Answer to a Pentecostal Question* (Springfield MO: Gospel Publishing House, 1947) 109-15.

[19]Donald Gee, *Concerning Spiritual Gifts* (Springfield MO: Gospel Publishing House, 1949) 58-59. See also R. Hollis Gause, *Living in the Spirit: The Way of Salvation* (Cleveland TN: Pathway Press, 1980) 84-85.

[20]Ralph M. Riggs, *The Spirit Himself* (Springfield MO: Gospel Publishing House, 1949) 94.

[21]Robert Mapes Anderson, *Vision of the Disinherited: The Making of American Pentecostalism* (New York: Oxford University Press, 1979) 12.

Besides serving as the "initial evidence" of the Spirit's reception, speaking in tongues had other functions in early Pentecostalism. Messages in tongues were used to identify marriage partners, or to provide answers for other important decisions of daily life. Primarily, the utterances of tongues were regarded as speech in foreign languages (xenolalia) and thus provided the key to foreign missions. Many Pentecostals believed that their initial experience of tongues was accompanied by a divine call to become missionaries. Based upon the preaching success of the apostles on the day of Pentecost (Acts 2), early Pentecostals went to Africa, China, Japan, and other fields in order to preach to the heathen in their own languages. While some missionaries reported successes, the disillusionment of failure resulted in the acknowledgment that some tongues speaking was not xenolalia.[22]

The chief purpose of the gift of tongues is private prayer. The gift also has a public worship function, serving "as a means to communicate directly to men."[23] As a function of the church, speaking in tongues is supposed to be accompanied by the gift of interpretation. Because speaking in tongues was defined solely as xenolalia by the earliest Pentecostals, the gift of interpretation was not common at the outset of the movement. Only after the acknowledgment that some tongues speaking was not xenolalia—combined with pressure from critics to conform to the biblical pattern of 1 Corinthians 14:5—did the use of the gift of interpretation increase.[24]

The gift of interpretation is considered a miracle of revelation from God. Interpretation is defined as "the supernatural showing forth by the Spirit of the meaning of an utterance in other tongues."[25] The gift is a supernatural interpretation and is rarely a literal translation of speaking in tongues. Carl Brumback contended that

> like tongues . . . interpretation does not originate in the mind of the believer but in the mind of the Spirit of God. Even the words themselves are the result of an immediate inspiration of the Spirit, rather than a calm

---

[22]Bloch-Hoell, *Pentecostal Movement*, 87.

[23]Brumback, *"What Meaneth This?,"* 304. Donald Gee, one of the most cautious Pentecostal leaders, was an exception since he viewed the purpose of tongues as almost exclusively devotional. See Donald Gee, *Spiritual Gifts in the Work of the Ministry Today* (Springfield MO: Gospel Publishing House, 1963) 68.

[24]Bloch-Hoell, *Pentecostal Movement*, 145.

[25]Harold Horton, *The Gifts of the Spirit* (Springfield MO: Gospel Publishing House, 1975) 147-49.

selection by the interpreter. In this respect, interpretation of tongues bears a resemblance to the manner in which the infallible Word came into being.[26]

The method the speaker employs often facilitates the conviction that the interpretation is an authoritative and direct message from God. Interpreters testify to the inspiration of the utterances because the content of the interpretation is unknown when they begin their pronouncements. Moreover, the interpreter's message is often given with Jesus or the Holy Spirit assuming the role of speaker.[27]

Pentecostals declare that the purpose of tongues and interpretation in public worship is for edification, exhortation, and comfort (1 Cor. 14:3). This biblical passage is specifically describing the gift of prophecy. Pentecostals, however, argue that speaking in tongues—when accompanied by interpretation—is functionally equivalent to prophecy. The difference between the two is simply the way they operate in the assembly. Prophecy is not preceded by tongues because it is a direct revelation from the Holy Spirit spoken in one's own language.[28]

Pentecostal definitions of prophecy reiterate the same themes reflected in the attitudes toward the interpretation of tongues. Prophecy is "the voice of the Holy Spirit,"[29] given as "a supernatural utterance, inspired by God, in a known tongue."[30]

In addition, prophecy is often given in the first person, with Jesus or the Holy Spirit identified as the speaker, who pronounces a "thus saith the Lord." The content of the prophecy is not known in advance by the proclaimer, but comes forth by divine initiative as a direct utterance of God. Beyond the distinction in presentation to the worshipers, perhaps the only other difference to note between prophecy and the interpreta-

---

[26]Brumback, *"What Meaneth This?,"* 302.

[27]Bruner, *Theology,* 145. Aimee Semple McPherson testified, "The next morning when a message in tongues was given . . . I yielded to the Spirit, who seemed literally to lift me to my feet and spoke to me in English the interpretation of the message." Quoted in Cyril G. Williams, *Tongues of the Spirit: A Study of Pentecostal Glossolalia and Related Phenomena* (Cardiff: University of Wales Press, 1981) 84.

[28]Riggs, *Spirit,* 165.

[29]Ibid., 153. Many non-Pentecostals identify prophecy with preaching. See Jack W. MacGorman, *The Gifts of the Spirit* (Nashville: Broadman Press, 1974) 84. For a Pentecostal discussion that distinguishes the gift of prophecy from preaching see Gee, *Concerning Spiritual Gifts,* 42.

[30]Bloch-Hoell, *Pentecostal Movement,* 147.

tion of tongues is that, in a calm environment, prophecy predominates, whereas tongues is more prevalent in excited atmospheres.[31]

Expositors of Pentecostal faith aver that the inspired messages given through the gifts of tongues and its interpretation, and the gift of prophecy are subservient to the biblical revelation. True revelation through the gifts must be tested by Scripture, and judged as containing nothing contrary to God's written Word. Modern prophecy does not reveal new doctrine, but edifies the mysteries of the Christian faith with greater clarity and, in doing so, provides reassurance for the recipient.[32] The primary purpose of revelation through the gifts is the bringing of God's message to a specific time and place, as opposed to the abiding and universal role of biblical revelation. One commentator suggests, "Perhaps the most that should ever be said of a particular oracle is 'this is what we believe God is saying at this time in our community.' "[33]

The constant reminders that prophetic announcements through the gifts are subservient to the Scriptures are given, at least in part, by Pentecostal theologians who have always been cognizant of the fact that these utterances are often attributed to the infallibility and authority of biblical revelation by zealous listeners. Many Pentecostal worshipers feel it is a sin to question the belief that these oracles are direct utterances of God. This conviction has occasionally led to the firing of ministers according to prophetic directives.[34]

The dichotomy between Pentecostal praxis and Pentecostal piety is especially seen with reference to the spiritual authority of written prophecies. Cecil M. Robeck proposes that the publication of written prophecies by Pentecostals is evidence that the words of "twentieth century prophets" are held in more esteem than the "inscripturated words of Christ and his apostles."[35] From the outset of the Pentecostal movement, prophecies have been transcribed and published. Early publishers included leaders such as Aimee Semple McPherson, and journals such as the *Weekly Evangel* and *The Pentecostal Evangel,* the official publication of the Assemblies of God. *The Pentecostal Evangel,* for example, published dreams, visions, verbatim prophecies, and interpretation of

---

[31]Bruner, *Theology,* 142. See also J. Rodman Williams, *The Era of the Spirit* (Plainfield NJ: Logos International, 1971) 27. See also Horton, *Gifts,* 159.

[32]Riggs, *Spirit,* 158. See also Horton, *Gifts,* 172-74.

[33]Robeck, "Written Prophecies," 43.

[34]MacArthur, *Charismatics,* 22. See also Gee, *Concerning Spiritual Gifts,* 48.

[35]Robeck, "Written Prophecies," 28.

tongues. The major Pentecostal denominations ceased regular publication of prophetic messages in the early 1920s. Circulation of written prophecies, however, was continued by individuals and smaller organizations such as The Voice of Healing. Even today the practice of publishing written prophecies persists in the Pentecostal/charismatic tradition.

Writing from the perspective that the gift of prophecy is valid today as a message from God to a specific time and situation, Robeck argued that "the ability to test the prophetic word has been impaired once an oracle has been placed in written form and widely distributed."[36] By decontextualizing the prophecies, and often presenting them anonymously, the reader has no effective way to judge their validity by the Bible. Consequently, the potential to elevate and universalize the prophecy is more prevalent. Indeed, though written prophecies are often accompanied by a reminder of the ultimate authority of Scripture, the fervid effort to give mass circulation to contemporary prophetic messages belies that assertion.[37]

In addition to the publication of prophetic oracles, the revelatory authority of the gifts of the Spirit can be seen in the development of Pentecostal sects. One example is the phenomenon described as "The New Order of the Latter Rain." The movement began in Western Canada in 1947, but affected Pentecostals throughout North America as it threatened to "split the Pentecostal Movement wide open."[38] Some Pentecostals, dismayed that the movement was abandoning the emphasis of its origins in favor of barren denominationalism, experienced a new revival of the Spirit. This "latter rain" came to restore the prominence of the gifts of the Spirit once and for all.

Several convictions about the gifts emerged. First, the gifts were conveyed only through the "laying on of hands" by Apostles and Prophets. Second, these leaders were chosen by the prophetic utterances of tongues and interpretation. Third, the prophetic messages of the Apostles and Prophets were considered at least equivalent in authority to the Bible. In reality, the prophetic messages were given priority. One adherent of the movement exclaimed, "We discarded all our former doctrines, and left ourselves open to be taught by the Holy Spirit as the

---

[36]Ibid., 38.

[37]Ibid., 43.

[38]Gordon F. Atter, *"The Third Force": The Answer to the Question So Often Asked . . . "Who are the Pentecostals?"* (Caledonia, Ontario: Acts Books, 1970) 143.

streams of revelation flowed from the glory above."[39] Indeed, some leaders added chapters to the unfinished book of Acts.

The authority of the gift of prophecy was especially noticeable. Often a message would identify an individual by name and give detailed instructions regarding personal and practical matters of everyday living. Marriage partners were occasionally selected by a prophetic, divine fiat. Furthermore, prophetic messages were stenographically recorded, transcribed into written form, and published as authoritative decrees from God.[40]

Initially seen with favor by most mainstream Pentecostals, the excesses of the "Latter Rain" quickly brought the movement into disrepute. By 1955, the movement had ceased to have any sizable impact on mainline Pentecostalism.[41]

3.

In addition to the gifts of the Spirit, the authority of continuing Holy Spirit revelation is vividly evident in the dominant influence of charismatic personalities in the formation and growth of the Pentecostal movement. According to John Thomas Nichol, "from the very beginning Pentecostals associated their introduction to the charismatic experience with the ministry of a certain outstanding personage in their area."[42] In rallying around a spiritual leader, any suggestion of formal organization was vehemently denounced by the earliest Pentecostals because their experience of the Holy Spirit had freed them from dead institutionalism. Inevitably, however, these early Pentecostals had to organize for the sake of efficiency and survival. As a result, various sects formed under the leadership of dominant charismatic figures.[43]

Howard Goss—an early Pentecostal leader who was a disciple of the founding father of Pentecostalism, Charles Parham—observed the strong

---

[39]L. Thomas Holdcroft, "The New Order of the Latter Rain," *Pneuma* 2 (Fall 1980): 51.

[40]Ibid., 50. See also Brumback, *Suddenly*, 333. See also John Thomas Nichol, *Pentecostalism* (New York: Harper & Row, Publishers, 1966) 238-39.

[41]Atter, *Third Force*, 143. In 1916, the Apostolic Faith Church was formed in England. Ministers were called Apostles and Prophets and their messages in tongues or prophecy were considered infallible. See Donald Gee, *Wind and Flame*, rev. ed. (Croydon, England: Heath Press Ltd., 1967) 72-74, 106-108. See also Nichol, *Pentecostalism*, 88-89. Nichol noted that a preoccupation with revelations, visions, and prophetic utterances also characterized the German wing of the Pentecostal movement.

[42]Nichol, *Pentecostalism*, 81.

[43]Larry Douglas Hart, "Problems of Authority in Pentecostalism," *Review and Expositor* 75 (Spring 1978): 251.

allegiances to dominant charismatic figures. Realizing the dangers of such intense loyalty, he made an analogy of early Pentecostalism to the wild Western frontier:

It was obvious that we were almost following the primitive pattern of the Western mustangs which had once roamed the prairies. These creatures grouped themselves into many small bands, each following their own leader, but fighting every other leader as well.[44]

These leaders were held in high esteem by their followers. Frank Bartleman—a contemporary of the prominent midwestern leader, William H. Durham—noted that this leader's "word was coming to be almost law in the Pentecostal missions even as far as the Atlantic coast."[45] Moreover, at camp meetings or conventions of Pentecostals, the followers of a certain leader could be singled out by their mannerisms. Durham's adherents, for example, imitated the head-jerk of their leader as they manifested their revivalistic spirit.[46]

The Pentecostal leaders, being afforded such high esteem, conveyed a spiritual guidance that was authoritative for their followers. Indeed, the authority of these leaders was often autocratic. The black Pentecostal, C. H. Mason—co-founder of the Church of God in Christ—was referred to as the "Chief Apostle," "Bishop," and "Greater than the Apostle Paul." Mason completely controlled the administration of the Church of God in Christ. He retained this prodigious amount of authority from 1907 to 1933 until four assistant bishops were added to meet increasing administrative burdens. His leadership has been described as that of a "benevolent dictator."[47]

The most autocratic of Pentecostal leaders, however, was A. J. Tomlinson, the dominant personality of the Church of God (Cleveland, Tennessee). After joining this group in 1903, Tomlinson immediately assumed primary leadership. His official influence increased in 1907, with

---

[44]Ethel E. Goss, *The Winds of God: The Story of the Early Pentecostal Days (1901-1914) in the Life of Howard A. Goss* (New York: Comet Press Books, 1958) 166.

[45]Frank Bartleman, quoted in Nichol, *Pentecostalism*, 82.

[46]Ibid., 82. He noted that charismatic leaders also dominated the development of European Pentecostalism.

[47]Vinson Synan, *The Holiness-Pentecostal Movement in the United States* (Grand Rapids MI: William B. Eerdmans, 1971) 80. Mason was cofounder—with C. P. Jones—of the Church of God in Christ as a Holiness organization in 1895. When Mason was converted to Pentecostalism, tension arose with Jones, who rejected the movement. The result was a split in their church. Mason, the dominant personality, was followed by a majority of the denomination's membership. The majority of the leaders, however, sided with Jones. See 79-80, 135-36.

his being elected the church's first General Overseer; and he was elected annually until 1914 when he was acknowedged as the General Overseer for life. As the church continued to defer all spiritual authority to Tomlinson, his sense of personal destiny was magnified. He became convinced that God had established him as General Overseer.

Tomlinson increasingly asserted theocratic authority for himself. A power struggle ensued when he sought and failed to gain complete control over the appointment of members to the church's governing council. Amidst the power struggle, Tomlinson was accused of, and then impeached for, misappropriating church funds. Still desiring sole authority, Tomlinson left the church and established the "true" church of God—now called the Church of God of Prophecy.[48]

In exercising their spiritual authority, Pentecostal leaders utilized the belief in the revelatory nature of the gifts of the Spirit to facilitate their claims, support their teachings, and guide their flocks. Charles Parham adapted the newly discovered Pentecostal message to his teaching methodology. He incorporated direct teaching from the Holy Spirit through the gifts of tongues, interpretation, and prophecy.[49] A. J. Tomlinson also utilized messages given in tongues to acquire and retain his authority. When speaking in tongues occurred during his worship services, the autocrat was constantly the one provided with the gift of interpretation. Indeed, Tomlinson had his selection as General Overseer confirmed by tongues and interpretation on three separate occasions.[50]

The most significant facet of continuing Holy Spirit revelation through selected leaders is the central role it plays in the formation of the early Pentecostal groups. The leaders often described the origins of their churches in terms of inspiration and revelation. When the students of the Holiness teacher Charles F. Parham agreed that speaking in tongues was the indisputable proof of the Holy Spirit baptism, he called the discovery a revelation from God.[51] This event is now acknowledged as the founding experience of the Pentecostal movement. C. H. Mason also described his spiritual pilgrimage in terms of divine revelation. Convinced since his

---

[48]Charles W. Conn, *Like A Mighty Army: The History of the Church of God, 1886-1976* (Cleveland TN: Pathway Press, 1977) 158-87.

[49]Goss, *Winds of God,* 40.

[50]Anderson, *Vision,* 156. See also Homer A. Tomlinson, ed., *Diary of A. J. Tomlinson,* 2 vols. (New York: The Church of God, 1949) 1:86-87, 100.

[51]Sarah E. Parham, *The Life of Charles F. Parham, Founder of the Apostolic Faith Movement* (Joplin MO: Hunter Printer Company, 1930) 54. See also Anderson, *Vision,* 55.

youth that "God endowed him with supernatural characteristics that were manifested in dreams and visions,"[52] Mason felt divinely drawn to attend the Pentecostal revival at Azusa Street. This experience—similar to his ministerial call which he asserted came through a vision from God—provided the impetus to transforming the Church of God in Christ from a Holiness to a Pentecostal organization.[53]

The two most outstanding examples of the role of revelation in the formation of Pentecostal bodies are the origins of the Church of God (Cleveland, Tennessee) and the International Church of the Foursquare Gospel. The Church of God traces its roots back to 1886 and a loosely organized group of Holiness believers known as the "Christian Union." The fellowship was reorganized as "The Holiness Church" in 1902; but the vision of being *the* church of God did not emerge until the arrival of A. J. Tomlinson in 1903. Upon investigating the beliefs of "The Holiness Church," Tomlinson climbed to the top of Burger Mountain to pray whether to join the group. While praying, he received an apocalyptic vision of "the Church of God of the last days."[54] This band of believers, he declared, was the true Church of God that was now being restored. As a Tomlinson follower evaluated the revelation, "A. J. Tomlinson was the first member of the Church of God this side of the Dark Age Period."[55] Consequently, under Tomlinson's leadership, "The Holiness Church" changed its name to the "Church of God." Eventually, Tomlinson contended, all faithful Christians of every denomination throughout the world would join forces in the Church of God and the Lord would set up his kingdom, beginning at Burger Mountain and ending in Jerusalem.[56]

The formation of Aimee Semple McPherson's church was also inspired by a special revelation. McPherson, the best known Pentecostal revivalist of her time, began her evangelistic career in 1917 as a member of the Assemblies of God. Branching out on an interdenominational basis, she experienced growing success with evangelistic crusades. In 1921,

---

[52]Klaude Kendrick, *The Promise Fulfilled: A History of the Modern Pentecostal Movement* (Springfield MO: Gospel Publishing House, 1961) 197.

[53]Hollenweger, *Pentecostals*, 482.

[54]Synan, *Holiness-Pentecostal Movement*, 84.

[55]Perry Gillum, quoted in A. J. Tomlinson, *A. J. Tomlinson God's Anointed—Prophet of Wisdom. Choice Writings of A. J. Tomlinson in Times of His Greatest Anointings* (Cleveland TN: White Wing Publishing House, 1970) 1.

[56]Synan, *Holiness-Pentecostal Movement*, 85-86. This exclusivistic view continued until 1937.

while conducting a revival in Oakland, California, McPherson received her revelation of the foursquare gospel. Preaching on the "Vision of Ezekiel" (Ezek. 1:1-28), she suddenly realized the meaning of the four faces of Ezekiel's prophetic vision. According to the revelation, the lion, man, ox, and eagle were symbolic of the perfection of the full gospel of salvation, Holy Spirit baptism with tongues, healing, and the second coming of Christ. McPherson commented,

> A perfect gospel! A complete Gospel for body, for soul, for spirit, and eternity. A gospel that faces squarely in every direction.
>
> ....
>
> In my soul was born a harmony that was struck and sustained upon four full, quivering strings, and from it were plucked words that leaped into being—THE FOURSQUARE GOSPEL!
>
> . . . The term, *Foursquare Gospel,* which the Lord gave to me that day as vividly and fittingly distinguishing the message which he had given me to preach, has become a household word throughout the earth. [57]

Inspired by the revelation, McPherson fulfilled a directive given by God that she was to build a church in Los Angeles. Built in 1923, the Angelus Temple continues to serve as the headquarters of the International Church of the Foursquare Gospel. [58]

In addition to the role of continuing revelation through selected vessels in the formation of early Pentecostal groups, the appeal to revelation by Pentecostal autocrats was an integral element in doctrinal controversies. Revelations were seldom claimed to be entirely new. Rather, the leader's pronouncements were often regarded as fresh insights into the truth contained in the Bible, which had been lost or concealed by God until these last days. The widespread expectations for spiritual authority to be rendered by revelation, however, placed immense pressure on the Pentecostal leaders to claim novel and striking, revelatory messages from God. Howard Goss explained:

> Walking in the light of God's revelation was considered a guarantee of unbroken fellowship with God. . . . Consequently, a preacher who did not dig up some new slant on a Scripture, or get some new revelation . . . was considered slow, stupid, unspiritual. . . . A familiar and most

---

[57]Aimee Semple McPherson, *The Foursquare Gospel* (Los Angeles: Echo Park Evangelistic Association, 1946) 22-23.

[58]Kendrick, *Promise Fulfilled,* 156.

absorbing question when preachers met was: "What new revelation have you received?"[59]

The flood of new revelations, according to Goss, created a mass of confusion within the early Pentecostal movement. Divinely sanctioned pronouncements often gave commands concerning sexual mores. In England, A. E. Saxby organized a universalist sect, named "Ultimate Reconciliation," which denied an eternal hell, and proclaimed the eventual salvation of all humanity.[60] Two revelatory inspired controversies, however, had a major impact on Pentecostalism—the sanctification schism and the Oneness movement.

In incipient Pentecostalism, the Wesleyan view of sanctification as a second work of grace was universally accepted. This was to be expected since most of the earliest leaders had roots in the Holiness movement. In 1908, however, the midwestern Pentecostal autocrat, William H. Durham, denounced the second work theory and promulgated a new doctrine that he called "the finished work of Calvary." Durham, previously an adherent of the Wesleyan view, was convinced the moment he was baptized with the Holy Spirit at Azusa Street in 1907 that he could no longer preach sanctification as a second work. Instead, he could only preach that salvation and sanctification were completed at Calvary. Sanctification, for the believer, was progressive, and not instantaneous.[61]

Durham's revelation was not accepted by all Pentecostals. Some opponents avowed that the Devil had inspired him. One woman related her vision:

> The demons were discussing what to do now that the Holy Spirit had come to the world again. But when at last a very distorted demon said, "I have it, give them a Baptism on an unsanctified life," all the demons roared in approval.[62]

The Finished Work theory spread widely and rapidly, however, and soon was espoused by a majority of Pentecostals. The most significant result was the establishment of a new denomination—the Assemblies of God—by adherents of the new theory.[63]

---

[59]Goss, *Winds of God*, 155-56. See also Anderson, *Vision*, 154-55.

[60]Gee, *Wind and Flame*, 124.

[61]Brumback, *Suddenly*, 98.

[62]Hollenweger, *Pentecostals*, 25.

[63]Anderson, *Vision*, 167-68.

The most blatant illustration of the force of new revelation was the creation of Oneness Pentecostalism, known to its opposition as the "New Issue" or "Jesus Only" movement. In 1913, at a World Wide Pentecostal Camp Meeting in Los Angeles, a well-known Canadian Pentecostal, Robert T. McAlister, preached a sermon in which he declared that the baptismal formula of Acts 2:38 (in the name of Jesus Christ) was to be preferred over the trinitarian formula of Matthew 28:19 (in the name of the Father, and of the Son, and of the Holy Ghost), because the former was the one used by the early Church. McAlister's assertion was interpreted by many as fulfillment of a prophecy that very soon God would reveal something new. The truth of the prophecy was ascertained when John G. Scheppe—having been inspired by McAlister's sermon to undertake an all-night prayer vigil—received the revelation that God demanded every true Christian to be rebaptized "in the name of Jesus" only.[64]

A new movement resulted when McAlister, Glenn Cook, and Frank Ewart agreed upon the necessity of rebaptism. As Oneness leaders administered the new baptismal formula, they were led to develop a theological justification for it. Consequently, a new revelation was given to Ewart, the most influential leader, regarding the Oneness of the Godhead. A unitarian doctrine was espoused that claimed that God is only one person—Jesus. Similar to the patristic heresy of Sabellianism, God had three consecutive modes or offices. The terms, Father, Son, and Holy Spirit were merely titles for the one Jesus. According to Oneness advocates, in the end-time Pentecostal revival, God was restoring baptism in the name of Jesus—the one and only person of the Godhead.[65]

The growth of Oneness Pentecostalism was rapid. It attracted a " 'Who's Who' of early-day Pentecost," and almost destroyed the infant Assemblies of God.[66] After an intense interdenominational battle, however, opponents of the "New Issue" were victorious. Trinitarianism was

---

[64]Fred J. Foster, *Think It Not Strange: A History of the Oneness Movement* (St. Louis: Pentecostal Publishing House, 1965) 9, 51-52.

[65]Ibid., 15-21, 51-53. Oneness Pentecostals saw a new connection between Acts 2:38 and Matt. 28:19. Instead of acknowledging variant formulas wthin the apostolic Church, they announced that the early Church possessed the revelation of the Oneness of the Godhead. In fact, Peter's baptismal formula of Acts 2:38 was in obedience to Jesus' command in Matt. 28:19, since the Apostle knew that the name of the Father, Son, and Holy Spirit was simply Jesus. The loss of this biblical truth was one of the errors associated with the "fall" of the Church into apostate Roman Catholicism, according to Oneness adherents.

[66]Brumback, *Suddenly*, 197.

reaffirmed; and the necessity of "Jesus only" baptism was labeled as baptismal regeneration. Realizing that the Assemblies of God was failing to accept the true revelation, the Oneness adherents left and formed their own denomination—the Pentecostal Assemblies of the World. [67]

* * * * *

The question of continuing revelation is crucial to an understanding of the experiential character of the Pentecostal tradition. Pentecostals advocate a fundamentalist view of the infallibility of Scripture and the ultimate authority of biblical revelation. At the same time, the experiential nature of faith emphasizes the authority of the present activity of the Holy Spirit. Consequently, the belief in continuing revelation by the Holy Spirit—especially in the formative years—assumed a prominent place in the Pentecostal tradition.

The spiritual gifts of speaking in tongues, the interpretation of tongues, and prophecy functioned as a perfect medium for a continuing Holy Spirit revelation. With messages being supernatural in origin, the gifts offered authoritative teachings elevated above, or at least equivalent to, the biblical revelation. New Pentecostal sects also derived their origins from the revelatory nature of the gifts.

The force of continuing revelation in the Pentecostal tradition is especially seen in the spiritual authority of early Pentecostal leaders. These charismatic figures, supported by the allegiance that exuded from their disciples, were spiritual autocrats. They asserted new doctrinal revelations, and felt divinely impelled to organize new Pentecostal groups. Appealing to the continuing revelation of God in their own ministries, these leaders functioned as prophets for their followers. They had been chosen by God, their disciples were convinced, as vehicles of revelation. The leaders would reveal and restore the apostolic faith in the end-time, in preparation for the second coming of Christ.

Despite the prophetic role assumed by the dominant figures of early Pentecostalism, the concept that they were filling a "prophetic office" was rarely emphasized. The belief in leaders serving as vehicles of divine revelation, however, makes the option available for a person to claim the

---

[67]Arthur L. Clanton, *United We Stand: A History of Oneness Organizatons* (Hazelwood MO: Pentecostal Publishing House, 1970) 27-34. Anderson (*Vision,* 181) noted that the Oneness movement did not become unambiguously committed to unitarianism until several years after the conflict within the Assemblies of God. When this occurred, several prominent leaders, who had advocated rebaptism in the name of Jesus, repudiated the movement.

role of prophet. Movements such as the "New Order of the Latter Rain" bear witness to this possibility.

Pentecostal ideas about biblical versus continuing revelation have undergone significant evolution during the brief history of Pentecostalism. As the Pentecostal movement developed from individual sects to general church bodies, the excessive subjectivism has decreased; and the more mature believers have distanced themselves from the dependence upon revelatory messages. The Assemblies of God historian, William W. Menzies, suggested that his denomination demonstrated a developing maturity as early as 1918. Rather than compromise doctrinal integrity by seeking harmony with the adherents of the "Jesus only" issue, the young Assemblies of God insisted upon preserving the biblical doctrine of speaking in tongues as the "initial evidence" of the Holy Spirit baptism.[68] In the 1950s, maturing Pentecostal denominations briefly supported, and then rejected, the healing revivalists for their fanatical excesses. Today, the "traditional and bureaucratic authority" of the major Pentecostal bodies would more easily handle a threat similar to the "naive openness to new spiritual 'revelations' " that was exhibited by the early Pentecostals.[69] One classical Pentecostal theologian has criticized the Neo-Pentecostal (Charismatic) movement for "the tendency of placing revelations on the same level as the Word, or even above the Word."[70]

An emphasis on the belief in continuing Holy Spirit revelation is still a possibility in the Pentecostal tradition, however. While the dangers of claiming the direct voice of the Spirit are recognized,[71] even the most restrained authorities of the movement are willing to risk these dangers in order to have the spiritual gifts which are so highly prized.[72] Moreover, the pronouncements of various nationally known leaders are attributed an aura of infallibility by the Pentecostal/charismatic masses.[73] The Faith/Confession controversy prevalent in the Pentecostal tradition in the 1980s

---

[68]William W. Menzies, *Anointed to Serve: The Story of the Assemblies of God* (Springfield MO: Gospel Publishing House, 1971) 117.

[69]Hart, "Problems," 253.

[70]Ray H. Hughes, "The New Pentecostalism: Perspectives of a Classical Pentecostal Administrator," in Spittler, *Perspectives*, 180.

[71]Donald Gee admitted that "this proneness to undue emphasis upon 'messages' has been a constant danger among new-comers into the Pentecostal Renewal." See Gee, *Wind and Flame*, 73.

[72]Bruner, *Theology*, 143.

[73]Hart, "Problems," 257.

is a primary example. Authoritative new teachings are based on "revelation knowledge," a special revelation received directly from God by those with the necessary faith. [74]

A discussion of the prophetic element in Pentecostalism facilitates an analysis of the ministry of William Marrion Branham. His ministry developed in the Pentecostal context where selected vessels could serve as mediums of continuing Holy Spirit inspiration. In essence, Branham's "prophetic" ministry was a throwback to the spiritual leadership manifested by the earliest Pentecostal leaders. Indeed, the evolution of Branham's "prophetic" identity reveals the extreme possibilities for a vivid belief in continuing revelation through selected vessels, as he became convinced that he was the one and only prophet of the end-time.

---

[74]A fuller analysis of the Faith/Confession movement is reserved for the conclusion.

CHAPTER TWO

THE MAKING
OF A PROPHET

The early life of William Marrion Branham reads like a hagiographical biography of a medieval Christian mystic. Gordon Lindsay, one of Branham's closest associates in the later 1940s and early 1950s, began his sketch of Branham's life by stating:

> The story of the life of William Branham is so out of this world and beyond the ordinary that were there not available a host of infallible proofs which document and attest its authenticity, one might well be excused for considering it farfetched and incredible. But the facts are so generally known, and of such a nature that they can be so easily verified by any sincere investigator, that they must stand as God's witness to His willingness and purpose to reveal Himself again to men as he once did in the days of the prophets and the apostles. The story of this prophet's life— for he is a prophet, though we infrequently use the term—indeed witnesses to the fact that Bible days are here again.[1]

For Branham, his "prophetic" identity was biblically rooted in the con-

---

[1]Gordon Lindsay, *William Branham: A Man Sent from God* (Jeffersonville IN: William Branham, 1950) 11. The reliability of the biographical material should be viewed with caution. As will be demonstrated in this chapter, Branham's autobiographical stories were often embellished, and sometimes contradictory. Other sources, written by his associates or followers, are apologetic and hagiographical in nature. See the bibliographical essay for a listing of the major secondary sources.

viction that "gifts and callings are without repentance" (Rom. 11:29).[2] Later, he remembered his early years as a life of signs and prophecies, the supernatural preparation of God's chosen vessel for a unique "prophetic" ministry. In the foreknowledge of God, before the foundation of the world, Branham was destined to be a prophet. Therefore his whole life, even beginning with birth, gradually revealed for Branham his special "prophetic" calling from God.

1.

Branham was born on 6 April 1909 in a small dirt-floored log cabin near Burkesville, in the eastern mountains of Kentucky. He was born around dawn, and delivered by his grandmother. After the delivery, she opened a window in the log cabin in order to let the morning light help the new parents see their baby. Suddenly, as Branham told the story, "a Light come [sic] whirling through the window, about the size of a pillow, and circled around where I was, and went down on the bed."[3] Neighbors who witnessed the scene were afraid and awe-struck, wondering aloud what kind of child had been born.

David E. Harrell asserted that "William Branham was preeminently the visionary of the healing revival."[4] Indeed, Branham constantly affirmed that this mystical quality was always with him. Not surprisingly, his earliest childhood memory was a vision he had at the age of three. Branham recalled that a "Voice" spoke to him from a tree, informing him that "you'll live near a city called New Albany."[5] True to the vision, Branham noted, his family left Kentucky that same year and moved to Jeffersonville, Indiana—a city within three miles of New Albany, Indiana.

When Branham was seven years old, another significant vision occurred. He later proclaimed that the experience offered a further foreshadowing of the ability to foretell the future by vision. While playing with some friends on the bank of the Ohio River, he had a vision of a bridge extending across the water connecting Louisville, Kentucky, with Jef-

---

[2]William Branham, *Footprints on the Sands of Time: The Autobiography of William Marrion Branham* (Jeffersonville IN: Spoken Word Publications, 1975) 59.

[3]Ibid., 21, 93. Branham's hagiographers constantly embellished his life story. Lee Vayle, for example, stated that the light that appeared at Branham's birth remained for two days. See [Lee Vayle], *Twentieth-Century Prophet: The Messenger to the Laodicean Church Age* (Jeffersonville IN: Spoken Word Publications, 1965) 35.

[4]David E. Harrell, Jr., *All Things Are Possible: The Healing and Charismatic Revivals in Modern America* (Bloomington: Indiana University Press, 1975) 165.

[5]Branham, *Footprints*, 22-23.

fersonville, Indiana. The vision indicated that, during the construction of the bridge, part of the structure would collapse and sixteen men would be killed. Noting the infallibility of his visions, Branham later pointed to the exact fulfillment of the bridge vision. Twenty-two years after the vision, on the spot that Branham claimed, the bridge was built, and the tragedy occurred.[6]

In addition to his visionary experiences, Branham readily remembered God's providential protection of his childhood and adolescence. The sign of light at his birth was soon followed by a manifestation of providential care. When Branham was six months old, he and his mother were stranded for several days in their log cabin during a terrible snowstorm. Food and firewood ran out; and the mother feared that death would result from their isolation. According to Pearry Green, a hagiographer of Branham, a neighbor made his way to the cabin in response to an irresistible supernatural directive; and the Branhams were providentially saved.[7]

The primary purpose of God's providential care was the development of a character of purity for God's chosen vessel. Branham later asserted that God charted his moral course when he was seven years old—only a month before the Ohio River bridge vision. Branham described his father as an alcoholic who operated his own whiskey still. One day while assisting his father at the still, young William heard a noise like a whirlwind coming from a tree. Once again he heard an audible "Voice" speak to him, commanding, "Don't you never [sic] drink, smoke, or defile your body in any way. There'll be work for you to do when you get older."[8] Branham was frightened by the incident at the time, but later realized that this call to purity was part of his preparation for a chosen task.

God's protection of Branham's purity was usually accompanied by the sign of the whirlwind. Branham told a story about his first girlfriend to highlight God's watchfulness. When he was fifteen years old the shy youngster had his first date. To his dismay, the girl began to smoke a cigarette, and asked him to join her. When Branham refused the girl called him a "sissy." His pride wounded, Branham set out to gain peer approval, until God prevented him from compromising his character. Branham described the incident:

---

[6]Ibid., 25.

[7]Pearry Green, *The Acts of the Prophet* (Tucson: Tucson Tabernacle Books, n.d.) 39-40.

[8]Branham, *Footprints*, 24.

She said "Why you big sissy!" Oh, my I wanted to be big bad Bill. . . . I couldn't stand that so I said, "Give it to me!" My hand out, I said "I'll show her whether I'm sissy or not." . . . When I started to strike that cigarette, just as much determined to smoke it as I am to pick up this Bible, see, I heard something going "Whoooossssh!" I tried again, I couldn't get it to my mouth.[9]

Branham also remembered a similar incident with reference to drinking alcohol. Being called a "sissy" by his father for refusing to try some whiskey, Branham grabbed a bottle and lifted it to his mouth. Immediately, the sound of the whirlwind was sent from God to keep him true to his vow of purity.[10]

Branham's inclination toward mystical experiences and his moral purity left him subject to ridicule and misunderstanding by his family and friends. Usually, his visions were attributed to his being a "nervous" child.[11] Other young people, he claimed, often ignored him because of his resistance to smoking, drinking, and dancing.

Branham related one other significant incident that intensified the ridicule and misunderstanding among his peers. As a teenager, he visited a carnival with some friends. One of the carnival fortune tellers/astrologers approached him with the question, "Say, do you know that you were born under a sign, and there is a star following you? You were born with a gift."[12] Branham remarked that the mysterious incident disturbed and confused him. Moreover, Branham was ridiculed by his companions for possessing some unknown gift. In retrospect, he interpreted the event as another sign of his calling. Indeed, Branham disciples explained the incident by citing the Scriptural precedent of the evil spirits understanding the identity of the Chosen Christ before the respected religious authorities. In the same way, the special calling of God had been first recognized by the demonic before Branham understood it himself.[13]

In reflecting back on his youth, Branham judged that it was a "terrible life."[14] He lamented,

---

[9]Ibid., 28.

[10]Ibid., 29.

[11]Ibid., 25.

[12]William Branham, "How the Gift Came to Me," *TVH* 1 (April 1948): 7.

[13]Idem, *Footprints*, 75-78. See also Lindsay, *Branham*, 70. See also Green, *Prophet*, 41.

[14]Branham, *Footprints*, 29.

There was always that peculiar feeling, like someone standing near me, trying to say something to me, and especially when I was alone. No one seemed to understand me at all. . . . I was just a black sheep, knowing no one who understood me, and not even understanding myself.[15]

Exacerbating this "terrible life" was the economic deprivation that the Branham family suffered. His family was the "poorest of the poor."[16] This abject poverty was fueled by his father's alcoholism. Some of Branham's most poignant memories, which undoubtedly captivated his revival crowds with sympathy, touched on his deprived life. Branham related that he often did not have any shoes, and his clothes were usually received from charity. Once he went all winter without a shirt, wearing only an overcoat to school. When it became too warm for the coat, Branham resorted to making a shirt out of a girl's dress. Upon arrival at school, the other children naturally ridiculed him for wearing girl's clothing. Consequently, his humiliation intensified his identity as an unwanted peculiar black sheep.[17]

Yearning for a better life, at the age of nineteen Branham left home for Phoenix where he worked for several years on a ranch, and began a successful professional boxing career.[18] He returned to Jeffersonville, however, when his brother died. In retrospect, Branham contended that the journey out west was his resisting the call of God. Despite the mystical experiences of his youth, Branham had no religious training in his background. Indeed, Branham remembered hearing prayer for the first time at his brother's funeral. Realizing that he did not know God, he tried to pray himself.

Soon Branham's religious quest began in earnest. While working for the Public Service Company of Indiana, Branham had an accident, and was overcome with gas. He entered a hospital, where he claimed to have heard the same "Voice" that spoke to him as a child concerning moral purity. This time, however, the message was "I called you and you would

---

[15]Idem, "How the Gift Came," 7.

[16]Lindsay, *Branham*, 14.

[17]Branham, *Footprints*, 22-23, 101-102.

[18]Branham remarked that he won a local bantamweight championship, winning fifteen consecutive fights. In retrospect, he declared that he gave up boxing for the ministry. See William Branham, "Faith without Works Is Dead," sermon delivered and recorded in Cleveland OH, 22 August 1955. See also William Branham, "Elijah and Elisha," sermon delivered and recorded in Phoenix AZ, 4 March 1954.

not go."[19] Although still not a Christian, Branham asserted that God was calling him to preach, reminding him of special work ahead.

Consequently, Branham's spiritual hunger increased. He started seeking God, and finally received his conversion in an old shed in the back of his house. Again, his experience was confirmed with a sign when a light entered the shed and formed the shape of the cross. After Branham requested further confirmation of God's presence, the light appeared two more times.

Having been converted, Branham visited several churches; but his spiritual yearnings were not satisfied by the staid atmosphere of the established denominations. Finally, he found a small, independent Baptist church which practiced anointing with oil, and he received a total healing from his accident. About six months later, Branham averred, he received the baptism of the Holy Spirit, and accepted the call to preach.[20]

Branham came to interpret his "terrible" childhood as vindicating proof of God's special calling. As he became a leader in the healing revival, Branham believed that in light of his lack of a religious background, God must have ordained his ministry. In effect, the misunderstanding and ridicule of the early years were positively transformed, and assumed spiritual import in Branham's mind. The unusual events, the manifestations of the "Light," and the "Voice" were all foreshadowing signs of a great ministry to come. Indeed, suffering on account of mysterious visions, moral purity, and abject poverty were necessary in order to prepare Branham for a supernatural, "prophetic" ministry to the world.

2.

After accepting the call to preach, Branham was ordained an independent Baptist minister; and he developed a small band of followers. Being supplied a tent, he initiated an evangelistic career with impressive results. The first major tent revival occurred in Jeffersonville during June 1933. Branham later estimated that as many as 3,000 people attended the meetings in a single night. Moreover, at the baptismal service on June 11, which followed the revival, Branham claimed that about 130 people were immersed.

This baptismal service progressively assumed greater significance for Branham, and especially for his followers of later years. Except for the

---

[19]Julius Stadsklev, *William Branham: A Prophet Visits South Africa* (Minneapolis: Julius Stadsklev, 1952) 10-11.

[20]Branham, *Footprints,* 114-16. See also Lindsay, *Branham,* 40-42. See also Stadsklev, *A Prophet Visits,* 10-12.

angelic commission of 1946 that thrust him to the forefront of healing revivalism, the manifestation of God's presence at the baptismal service was second to none in importance for Branham's developing "prophetic" identity. In fact, during the last years of Branham's ministry, the significance of the baptismal experience superseded that of the commission.[21]

Reminiscent of the context of Jesus' baptism, Branham described the incident:

> I was baptizing down on the river, my first converts, at the Ohio River, and the seventeenth person I was baptizing, as I started to baptize, then I said, "Father, as I baptize him with water, You baptize him with the Holy Spirit." I started to—to put him under the water.
>
> And just then a whirl come down from the heavens above, here come that Light, shining down. Hundreds and hundreds of people on the bank right at two o'clock in the afternoon, in June. And It hung right over where I was at. A Voice spoke from there, and said "As John the Baptist was sent for the forerunner of the first coming of Christ, you've got a . . . have a Message that will bring forth the forerunning of the Second Coming of Christ." And it liked to a-scared me to death.[22]

Pearry Green compared the appearance of the light and the voice to the Damascus Road experience of the Apostle Paul. Many of the 4,000 on the river bank who saw the light ran in fear; others fell in worship. Likewise, some heard a voice while others did not.

As a consequence of the confusion, the supernatural import of this event has been downgraded and distorted, according to Green. He contended that the "Voice" from heaven informed Branham that he and his "message" alone would function as the forerunner of the second coming of Christ. The "message" could not be separated from the messenger.[23] From this perspective, some current disciples of Branham assert that God revealed to him in the 1933 baptismal experience the full scope of his "prophetic" consciousness as the *one and only* prophet of the last days. The unveiling of this identity to the people, however, proceeded gradually in "due season."[24]

---

[21]Branham's commission is discussed on 35-37.

[22]Branham, *Footprints*, 71.

[23]Green, *Prophet*, 46.

[24]Statement made by Billy Paul Branham, son of William Branham, personal interview, Jeffersonville IN, 27 September 1984. Green suggested that Branham began to reflect seriously about his unique identity in 1933. A fully developed "prophetic" identity, however, only came gradually, and climaxed in the 1960s. See statement by Pearry Green, interview with David E. Harrell, Jr., Tucson AZ, 27 December 1973. Tape made available by David E. Harrell, Jr., University of Alabama in Birmingham.

That the baptismal experience of 11 June 1933 proved to be pivotal to the "prophetic" identity of Branham is quite evident. As will be noted in chapter six, during the last phase of his life, Branham declared that he alone was given the message that would usher in Christ's second coming. The belief espoused by many of Branham's current followers that he had a fully developed "prophetic" identity in 1933 is not viable. Branham did believe in the idea of a forerunner that would prepare the world for the return of Christ. In his earliest published reference, however, he simply preached an orthodox Pentecostal theme that the forerunner was the restoration of the spiritual gifts to the Church. [25]

Branham did refer to the baptismal experience of 1933 throughout the healing revival of the 1940s and 1950s. The central thrust was that his full gospel message was an essential ingredient in God's preparation for the second coming of Christ. The "Voice" from heaven assured the obscure minister that he had a vital part, but not the only part, in this eschatological preparation. Branham believed that he was but one of many ministers that God had raised to bring forth the rapture, the "catching away" of the Church to meet Christ in the air before the second coming of Christ. [26]

Statements made by Branham's early associates in the healing revival confirm this interpretation that he was but one of many full gospel ministers sent by God to prepare the world for the consummation of the ages. Gordon Lindsay's report of the 1933 baptismal experience referred to the appearance of a "heavenly light." Branham, according to Lindsay, was instructed three times by a "Voice" to "Look up." When the evangelist lifted his head, the "heavenly light" became visible to the

---

[25]William Branham, "Believest Thou This?," *TVH* 1 (August 1948): 3.

[26]William Branham, "Do You Now Believe?," sermon delivered and recorded in Battle Creek MI, 17 August 1952. See also William Branham, "What the Holy Ghost Was Given for," *TSW* 4:3 (n.d.): 36. See also William Branham, *Conduct, Order, Doctrine of the Church*, 2 vols. (Jeffersonville IN: Spoken Word Publications, 1973-1974) 1:166. According to a theory of the end of the world called premillennialism, the rapture is most often viewed as the means to save the Church from the rule of Antichrist, and the accompanying period of tribulation. Subsequently, Christ will return, defeat the Antichrist at the battle of Armageddon, and set up his millennial reign on earth. After an attempted revolt by Satan, there will occur the resurrection of the dead, the judgment, and the creation of a new heaven and a new earth. A minority of premillennialists place the rapture, which is based on 1 Thess. 4:15-17, during or after the period of tribulation. See Timothy P. Weber, *Living in the Shadow of the Second Coming: American Premillennialism, 1875-1982* (Grand Rapids MI: Zondervan, 1983) 11.

people. Significantly, however, this official biography, published in 1950, made no mention of the forerunner prophecy.[27]

Lindsay did connect the forerunner concept with the success of Branham's healing ministry. He noted three separate occasions during Branham's earliest campaigns when the following interpretation of tongues was given by the Spirit:

> That as John the Baptist was sent as a forerunner of the Lord's first coming, so He was sending forth this evangelist and others like him to move the people and prepare them for His second coming.[28]

Lindsay did not make a connection to any previous divine message to Branham, however. Other close friends, even after Branham's claims of identity shifted radically, concurred that along with other healing revivalists, he had assumed a vital role in preparing for Christ's coming.[29]

Branham's personal understanding of the baptismal event at the time of its occurrence in 1933 cannot be ascertained. Perhaps it was simply another mysterious, mystical experience that he did not interpret with any great significance. Perhaps he later embellished the incident by "remembering" the forerunner message when he was achieving success in the healing revival, and the prophetic utterances through tongues acknowledged his leadership role. Whatever the case, 11 June 1933 grew to legendary proportions as Branham's ministry developed.

The month of June 1933 is also pivotal for Branham as the time when he proclaimed his most significant "prophetic" revelations concerning future world events. God revealed to him by continuous visions, Branham asserted, seven major events that had to occur before the second coming of Christ.

---

[27]Lindsay, *Branham*, 43, 71. Similarly, Oral Roberts experienced a revelation that identified his healing ministry with John the Baptist. In the fall of 1948, according to Roberts, God "spoke to my heart and showed me that I would be the John the Baptist to my time in the sense that I would help prepare the way . . . for a great healing to come to the body of Christ." Roberts, as well as other revivalists, believed that the healing revival was a precursor to the second coming of Christ. Unlike Branham, Roberts never developed the idea that he was *the* forerunner to Christ's return. See David E. Harrell, Jr., *Oral Roberts: An American Life* (Bloomington: Indiana University Press, 1985) 87, 149, 447-48.

[28]Lindsay, *Branham*, 105.

[29]Statement by Anna Jeanne Price, former associate of Branham, interview with David E. Harrell, Jr., Shreveport LA, 5 December 1973. Tape available at the Holy Spirit Research Center, Oral Roberts University, Tulsa OK.

The first extant reference to the visions was a sermon preached on 13 May 1956.[30] Subsequently, Branham made periodic references to the prophecies as proof of the infallibility of his God-given visions. From 1960 onward Branham repeatedly asserted that five of the visions had already transpired exactly according to the revelation. He predicted that the last two visions would be fulfilled by 1977. Subsequently, Christ would return.[31]

The first three visions concerned world politics. First, Branham claimed that God revealed to him the successful invasion of Ethiopia by Mussolini. Moreover, the Italian dictator's downfall would eventuate from his own people turning on him. A second vision was that Franklin D. Roosevelt would play a dominant role in causing the world to go to war. America would declare war against Germany and, before ultimate victory, would suffer greatly at the site of a German-built "great wall of concrete," which Branham later identified as the Maginot Line. The third revelation concerned the fate of the three great "isms" of the world scene: Nazism, Fascism, and Communism. Branham predicted that the first two would merge into Russian Communism. The Spirit informed Branham to give the people the following warning: "Watch Russia, watch Russia, the king of the North."[32]

Two other visions, which Branham later affirmed had been fulfilled exactly, involved science and the moral condition of the world. Branham predicted that science would progress, particularly in the realm of manufacturing cars. Automobiles "would constantly begin to shape [sic] like an egg" and they would be run by remote control so that "you won't have to have a steering wheel."[33] Though never specifically naming the model, Branham eventually contended the car was already on the market.[34]

The central thrust of the fifth vision was the moral degradation of women. In the vision, Branham exclaimed, God revealed that the downfall of the American woman began when she was allowed to vote. The vote of women would pollute the nation by electing "the wrong man" for

---

[30]William Branham, "Teaching on Moses," TSW 14:4 (n.d.): 4-5.

[31]The interpretation of the prediction of 1977 by Branham's followers is discussed on 154-55.

[32]William Branham, Is This the Time? (Jeffersonville IN: Spoken Word Publications, n.d.) 9. Branham confused the German Siegfried Line with the French Maginot Line.

[33]Ibid., 9-10.

[34]Branham, Conduct, 2:923.

the presidency of the country. Indeed, Branham felt he was vindicated when Kennedy was victorious in 1960.[35]

Because the first five visions were fulfilled, Branham believed, the last two would assuredly occur. In the sixth vision, Branham saw a great woman rise to power in the United States. This beautiful but cruel woman was not identified specifically by the Spirit, according to Branham. At the time of the vision, and throughout his ministry, however, Branham believed that the woman was probably symbolic of the Roman Catholic Church. Consequently, a constant theme of Branham's whole ministry was that Catholicism was attempting to gain power over the entire world.

The final vision also concerned the fate of America. Branham declared that the Spirit allowed him to view an event just prior to the end of time. The visionary beheld a great explosion that devastated the whole country. Nothing was left standing; only craters and smoking piles of debris remained.[36]

As Branham's ministry developed, the spiritual import of the seven visions increased. A comparison of his descriptions of the predictions reveals Branham's tendency to exaggerate and embellish his actual prophecies. The original prediction regarding Roosevelt simply stated that he "will cause the whole world to go to war."[37] On later occasions, however, Branham contended that he had predicted the election of Roosevelt to four presidential terms. An original prophecy that suggested four presidential terms would have been extraordinary since Roosevelt was still serving his first term in 1933. Naturally, the embellished interpretation has become standard for Branham's followers today.[38] At other times Branham altered the contents of the visions to enhance his "prophetic" authority. Once, he claimed that he knew beforehand that "the wrong person" for the Presidency of the United States would be a Catholic.[39]

The content of the "prophetic" revelations was not especially outstanding. Mussolini did successfully invade Ethiopia in 1935, but he had

---

[35]Branham, *Time?*, 10.

[36]Ibid., 9-11. See also Green, *Prophet*, 47-51. See also William Branham, *The Thyatirean Church Age*, vol. 6 of *The Revelation of Jesus Christ* (Jeffersonville IN: Spoken Word Publications, n.d.) 324-25.

[37]Branham, *Footprints*, 600.

[38]Ibid. See also Green, *Prophet*, 48. See also [Lee Vayle], *An Exposition of the Seven Church Ages* (Jeffersonville IN: Spoken Word Publications, n.d.) 324-25.

[39]William Branham, *Jehovah-Jireh* (Jeffersonville IN: Spoken Word Publications, n.d.) 163.

been planning an invasion since 1932. Predictions regarding presidents and war are not uncommon, particularly during volatile years such as the 1930s. The belief in the advance of mechanical science was little more than common sense. The fulfillment of the egg-shaped car was nebulous; one expositor of Branham's ideas explained that the egg-shaped car would run by remote control "so that people *appeared* seated in the car without the steering wheel" [italics not in original].[40] Most Branham followers of later years simply would not question his authority. Moreover, any critic of the advancement of women through voting rights might bemoan that their new freedom would bring tragic results. The lack of specification of "the wrong person" for the Presidency facilitated an easy fulfillment of the vision. Finally, the prediction of the efforts of Catholicism to rule the world was merely a part of the Protestant aversion to that religious faith.

The actual importance of these seven visions to Branham's ministry is more difficult to ascertain than the baptismal experience. More significant than the nature of the predictions is that Branham believed he had received "prophetic" revelations by vision. Indeed, he immediately transcribed these visions and kept the text in his Bible. Branham's lifelong tendency toward visionary experiences was being incorporated into his ministerial identity. Visions were given a "prophetic" role. In essence, Branham had engaged in his first major act of spiritual authority by way of continuing revelation.

From 1933 to 1946 Branham was the bivocational minister of the Branham Tabernacle in Jeffersonville, Indiana. After the successful revival of June 1933, Branham's supporters had joined together and organized this small independent church. His ministry flourished for a few years but stability was precarious amidst the throes of the Depression. As his lower-class supporters experienced economic despair, Branham preached without compensation.[41] Branham attributed the decline of his church's growth and prosperity to his disobedience to God's calling. He later believed that God's anointing of him left for five years because of his rejection of ministering within the context of Pentecostalism.[42]

Branham's first exposure to Pentecostalism occurred in 1936. While on a vacation, by coincidence he attended a gathering of Oneness Pen-

---

[40][Vayle], *Exposition*, 321. See also J[ohn] R[oyde]-S[mith], "World Wars," *Encyclopaedia Britannica* (15th ed.), *Macropedia*, 12:975.

[41]"William Branham's Life Story," *HOF* 27 (February 1960): 10. See also Branham, *Footprints*, 35.

[42]Branham, *Footprints*, 40. See also Lindsay, *Branham*, 51.

tecostals. He related that, previous to this experience, he had heard of Pentecostals but he understood them to be "a bunch of holy rollers that laid on the floor and frothed at the mouth."[43] He was favorably impressed by the Oneness meeting, however, and was invited to conduct revivals by several ministers who had attended the convention. After serious consideration, he declined the invitations. Branham explained that he was persuaded to avoid the Pentecostals on account of their ignominious social standing.[44] He noted that his mother-in-law was the person who expressed the most vociferous opposition. After hearing about his intentions, she exclaimed:

> Do you know that's a bunch of holy rollers? . . . Do you think you'd drag my daughter out amongst stuff like that. . . . Ridiculous! That's nothing but trash that the other churches has throwed out.[45]

Rejecting ministry among the Pentecostals was the worst mistake of his life, according to Branham. When his wife and daughter died as a result of the 1937 flooding of the Ohio River, Branham interpreted the tragedy as punishment for his resistance to the ministry among the Oneness Pentecostals. In heart-rending fashion Branham testified of kneeling

---

[43]Branham, *Footprints*, 40. Branham's assertion that the "holy roller" caricature was his only previous understanding of Pentecostalism is dubious. Though Branham described the Baptist church to which he belonged as the Missionary Baptist Church (Branham, *Footprints*, 30), the actual name of the church was First Pentecostal Baptist. The congregation was "a Holy Ghost church where they worship God in Spirit and not in fleshly denominations." See *Jeffersonville* (IN) *Evening News,* 10 June 1933, 4:7. The church also had Saturday night "Tarring meetings" for the reception of the Holy Spirit. See *Jeffersonville* (IN) *Evening News,* 5 August 1933, 4:4. The pastor of the church, Roy Davis, asserted, "I am the minister who received Brother Branham into the first Pentecostal assembly he ever frequented." Davis elaborated that he was the first person whom Branham saw anoint with oil and pray for the sick. Moreover, Davis claimed that his home served as the site for Branham's reception of the Holy Spirit baptism. See Roy Davis, "Wm. Branham's First Pastor," *TVH* 3 (October 1950): 14.

[44]Branham, *Footprints*, 35-40, 62-69. Branham often confused dates when he told his life story. On one occasion (63) he said that he attended the Oneness meeting when he was twenty-three years old, however, and this incident occurred after that time (40). Moreover, Branham's memory concerning elements of his life story was often contradictory. Branham declared that he had received the baptism of the Holy Spirit six months after he accepted the call to preach (Lindsay, *Branham,* 41). Yet in his story of the Oneness gathering he remembered how he was impressed with the Pentecostals because they possessed something he did not have—the baptism of the Holy Spirit. The latter incident seems to be an embellishment in order to enhance his relationship to Pentecostals (Branham, *Footprints*, 68).

[45]Branham, *Footprints*, 40.

beside his dying baby daughter, praying for the Lord to save her. He begged,

> Lord, what have I done? Have I not preached the Gospel on the street corners. . . . Don't hold it against me. I never called them people "trash." . . . Forgive me. Don't—take my baby. And while I was praying, looked like a black . . . like a sheet or cloth come down. I knowed He had refused me. [46]

In addition to personal tragedy, Branham's mystical inclination continued to generate tension and misunderstanding in his personal relationships. As the visions increased after he entered the ministry, Branham became alienated from his less enthusiastic, Baptist associates. Roy Davis, the Baptist minister who baptized and ordained Branham, later commented:

> He would always drift out into some sort of conversation which I did not grasp, and later came to disregard as entirely visionary, and finally to dismiss his strange cogitations as useless and irrational. I had been a Baptist preacher for many years, and had been taught to disregard such ideas and concepts of spiritual things as visions, talking with the Lord, and kindred things. Therefore this explains my impatience with Brother Branham. [47]

Branham was especially troubled by the accusation that his mysticism was of demonic origin. Consequently, he sought the assistance of fellow clergy in evaluating the propriety of having visions. Baptist colleagues suggested, however, that the light that appeared at his birth probably indicated the presence of a demon in his life. They further warned Branham to curtail the visionary experiences, or his ministry would fall into disrepute. [48]

By the end of World War II, Branham's days of misery and misfortune began to give way to renewed optimism. In late 1945 and early 1946 the frequency of visions increased dramatically. His followers at the Branham Tabernacle testified that, throughout these early years, many signs and wonders through fulfilled visions accompanied his ministry. They

---

[46]Ibid., 47. Branham (129) claimed that he had prophesied the flood six weeks in advance. See also Lindsay, *Branham,* 52-56.

[47]Davis, "Pastor," 14.

[48]William Branham, "Early Spiritual Experiences," sermon delivered and recorded in Hammond IN, 14 July 1952.

believed that God was preparing their leader for "some special phenomenon."[49]

3.

Contrary to the sense of optimism, however, Branham later preached that he was still bothered by the mystical quality of his life. One day, while home for lunch from his job as a game warden, Branham again heard the whirlwind in a tree. Shaken by its presence, he decided that—once and for all—he was going to come to an understanding regarding his "trances."[50] Having never overcome the fear that his mystical experiences might be from the Devil, Branham left home for a secret hideaway cabin in the woods of Charlestown, Indiana. He informed his second wife that he might never return unless God promised that the visions would never occur again.

Branham spent the afternoon and evening of 7 May 1946 in prayer, in an effort to find peace with God. During the night around eleven o'clock, Branham claimed that he received an angelic visitation. This climactic experience, which Branham avowed was a real event rather than a vision, provided the young minister with his "commission" from God. From that day forward, Branham proclaimed, his "foreordained," unique ministry would be gradually revealed.[51]

Branham shared the story of the angelic visitation and commission throughout the years of his healing ministry.

> Then along in the night, at about the eleventh hour, I had quit praying and was sitting up when I noticed a light flickering in the room. Thinking someone was coming with a flashlight, I looked out the window, but there was no one, and when I looked back, the light was spreading out on the floor, becoming wider. . . . As the light was spreading, of course I became excited and started from the chair but as I looked up, there hung that great star. . . . [it] looked more like a ball of fire or light shining down upon the floor. Just then I heard someone walking across the floor, which startled me again, as I knew of no one who would be coming there besides myself. Now, coming through the light, I saw the feet of a man coming toward me, as naturally as you would walk to me. He appeared to be a man who, in human weight, would weigh about two hundred

---

[49]Lindsay, *Branham*, 82. See also Harrell, *All Things Are Possible, 29.*

[50]Branham, *Footprints*, 72. He noted that at this time he called his mystical experiences "trances." Only later did he understand the concept of a vision.

[51]Ibid.

pounds, clothed in a a white robe. He had a smooth face, no beard, dark hair down to his shoulders, rather dark complexioned, with a very pleasant countenance, and coming closer, his eyes caught with mine. Seeing how fearful I was, he began to speak. "Fear not. I am sent from the presence of Almighty God to tell you that your peculiar life and your misunderstood ways have been to indicate that God has sent you to take a gift of divine healing to the people of the world. IF YOU WILL BE SINCERE, AND CAN GET THE PEOPLE TO BELIEVE YOU, NOTHING SHALL STAND BEFORE YOUR PRAYER, NOT EVEN CANCER."[52]

Branham's immediate response was to try and evade the commission. Like Moses, Branham retorted that he was poor and uneducated; thus, the people would not listen to him or accept his ministry. The angel reassured Branham that God always "speaks through the voice of a man. . . . He don't [sic] use organizations or so forth."[53] Branham described the angel's assurance.

And He said, " As the prophet Moses was given two gifts, signs," rather, "to a-vindicate his ministry, so will you given [sic] two—so are you given two gifts to a-vindicate your ministry." He said, "One of them will be that you'll take the person that you're praying for by the hand, with your left hand and their right," and said, "then just stand quiet, and it'll have . . . there'll be a physical effect that'll happen on your body." And He said, "Then you pray. And if it leaves, the disease is gone from the people. If it doesn't leave, just ask a blessing and walk away."
"Well," I said, "Sir, I'm afraid they won't receive me."
He said, "And the next thing will be, if they won't hear that, then they will hear this." Said, "Then it'll come to pass that you'll know the very secret of their heart." Said, "This they will hear."[54]

Branham was further instructed that his gift of divine healing would be taken to all classes of people, from the poor to kings and rulers. The gift would be available to all persons who would accept his testimony. Moreover, the angel revealed that this unknown minister of a small church would soon stand before thousands in crowded arenas. Through the

---

[52]Lindsay, *Branham*, 77.

[53]William Branham, "The Angel and His Commission," sermon delivered and recorded in Phoenix AZ, 30 November 1947. For an extensive discussion of the supposed similarity between the commissions of Branham and Moses, see William Branham, "Rev. William Branham and the Future," *HOF* 25 (July 1958): 3.

[54]Branham, *Footprints*, 75.

healing signs, God was calling Christians together into a unity of the Spirit. Branham later declared that the angel finished their conversation with the promise, "I will be with you and the gift will grow greater and greater."[55]

In addition to this commission to pray for the sick, Branham asserted that the angel revealed one other important divine message in their thirty-minute conversation—that Branham's commission was one of the signs of the imminent return of Christ. Making no connection with the forerunner message of the 1933 baptismal experience, Branham exclaimed that he was commissioned to tell the people in his healing campaigns that Jesus' coming was near. As Branham's ministry progressed, the link between his commission and the end-time was further embellished. Apparently confusing historical data, he announced that the day of his commission, 7 May 1946, was the same day that the Jews in Palestine signed a peace treaty, and became a nation. According to dispensational premillennialism—the theory of eschatology (last things) to which Branham adhered—the establishment of a Jewish state was a sign of the imminent coming of Christ.[56] Branham, however, came to understand the creation of Israel as vindicating the supernatural aura and eschatological significance of his chosen ministry.[57]

---

[55]"Interview with William Branham," *TVH* 7 (May 1954): 22. See also Lindsay, *Branham*, 79-82. See also Gordon Lindsay, "The Ministry of Angels and the Appearance of the Angel to William Branham," *TVH* 1 (May 1948): 12.

[56]Dispensationalism, a variety of futurist premillennialism was developed by John Nelson Darby of England in the 1830s and became popular in the United States after the Civil War. C. I. Scofield, one of Darby's American followers, helped popularize dispensationalism in the notes of his *Reference Bible*. This theory divided biblical and subsequent history into eras, or dispensations. Each era marked a change in God's method of dealing with humanity. Dispensationalism is characterized by a strict literalism of biblical prophecy. Futurist prophecies will take place among the Jews in the "last days" while the Christian Church will experience a "pre-tribulation" rapture before the reign of Antichrist. See Weber, *Living*, 16-24.

[57]Branham, *Conduct*, 1:47-48. See also Lindsay, "Ministry of Angels," 3. See also "The World in Prophecy," *TVH* 1 (August 1948): 8. The state of Israel was established 15 May 1948. No significant event occurred on 7 May 1946. See Y[ehuda] S[lutsky], "State of Israel," *Encyclopedia Judaica* (1971), 9:358, 364-65. Other healing revivalists linked the eruption of the healing revival with the restoration of the spiritual gifts. Concurrently, God was restoring the land back to his natural children, the Jews, as he was restoring the spiritual gifts to his spiritual children, the Christians. David Nunn and W. V. Grant asserted that the greatest influx of Jews to immigrate to Palestine occurred in 1946-1947. Significantly, the authors noted, William Branham and Oral Roberts both received their divine commission at this time. See David Nunn and W. V. Grant, *The Coming World-Wide Revival* (Dallas: W. V. Grant, n.d.) 22-23.

When Branham returned home and informed his congregation at the church about the angel's visit, the people fully accepted the revelation. His previous visions had come to pass, they were convinced; and this divine message would also. The stage was set for the dramatic rise of William Branham as the pacesetter of a worldwide healing revival.

* * * * *

Branham's experience of the angelic commission would change his life from that of an anonymous, small-town, independent Baptist minister to an internationally known faith healer. Consequently, Branham remembered, and thus reinterpreted, his early years as a life of signs and prophecies, and supernatural preparation of God's chosen vessel for a unique "prophetic" ministry. Indeed, as Branham's claims of identity evolved radically in his later years, he applied certain biblical prophecies to his own ministry. Branham affirmed that, before the event of his commission, he already understood his Scriptural identity.[58] To acknowledge Branham's transformed autobiography, one does not necessarily imply that Branham engaged in intentional historical deceit. On the contrary, Branham's conviction that he was a unique prophet became so pervasive that he evidently understood the increased importance of earlier events as a faithful and correct rendering of his life story.

Subsequent to the angelic commission of 7 May 1946, Branham preached that he was ordained by God to a unique mission. He noted that God's timing was perfectly biblical. Like the prophets of the Bible, Branham was commissioned at the age of forty.[59] Consequently, he reinterpreted his "terrible" childhood and adolescence as divine preparation for his chosen ministry.

According to the Branham autobiography, the year 1933 was the pivotal year in the making of the end-time prophet. The baptismal service of 11 June 1933 was always special to Branham. His ministry received publicity when some newspapers carried the story of an appearance of light at the baptismal waters of the Ohio River.[60] This experience, however, was transformed into the event that revealed Branham's identity

---

[58]William Branham, "The Trial," *TSW* 12:2 (n.d.): 14.

[59]William Branham, "What Is That in Your Hand?," sermon delivered and recorded in North Hollywood CA, 20 November 1955.

[60]Lindsay, *Branham*, 71. I have been unable to locate the newspaper article. Branham's followers in Jeffersonville do not have a copy. Lee Vayle suggested that one of Branham's former acquaintances might have destroyed much of Branham's personal files. See Letter received from Lee Vayle, 4 May 1984.

as the forerunner of the second coming of Christ. Moreover, in 1933, Branham offered predictions of seven future world events. These prophecies revealed Branham's willingness to claim divine inspiration for his visions. Indeed, Branham's persistent tendency toward visionary experiences in his ministry would become the primary vehicle for manifesting an authoritative spiritual leadership.

At the time of the angelic commission, Branham did not perceive himself as *the* end-time prophet. Nevertheless, he was equipped with many elements necessary to acquiring a "prophetic" role in the context of Pentecostalism. Undergirded by a sense of moral righteousness and personal deprivation, Branham desired to be wholly dependent upon God.[61] He believed that he had experienced God's special presence in a light, voice, and whirlwind, and had received direct communication with Him through visions. The visionary's followers believed that he was being prepared for a special ministry. When Branham received his angelic commission, he forged ahead into a unique ministry of healing—the perfect medium for God to speak through a prophet, and continuously reveal His ways.

---

[61]The deprived background was characteristic of the early leaders of Pentecostalism. See Robert Mapes Anderson, *Vision of the Disinherited: The Making of American Pentecostalism* (New York: Oxford University Press, 1979) 104.

CHAPTER THREE

BRANHAM AND THE HEALING REVIVAL, 1947-1955

Twentieth-century healing revivalism found its basic roots in the American and European evangelical tradition of the nineteenth century. The post-Civil War Holiness movement with its emphasis on Christian perfection—the "entire sanctification" of the believer from inbred sin—especially contributed to the rise of the "faith cure" movement.[1] Al-

---

[1]The Holiness emphasis upon Christian perfection is rooted in the teachings of John Wesley. According to Wesley, Christian perfection was not sinless perfection, but was a perfect love of pure motives and desires. This second blessing could be received instantaneously; but Wesley emphasized growth in grace before and after the experience. The American Holiness movement, which developed out of Wesley's Methodism, modified his emphases amidst the revivalistic context of the frontier. Like conversion, the second blessing of sanctification was promised as an immediate event. For Wesley's views, see Albert C. Outler, ed., "A Plain Account of Christian Perfection," *The Journal of John Wesley* (New York: Oxford University Press, 1964) 251-70. See also Harold Lindstrom, *Wesley and Sanctification* (London: Epworth Press, 1946) and John L. Peters, *Christian Perfection and American Methodism* (New York: Abingdon Press, 1956). For surveys of the Holiness movement in America, see Melvin E. Dieter, *The Holiness Revival of the Nineteenth Century* (Metuchen NJ: Scarecrow Press, 1980), Charles E. Jones, *Perfectionist Persuasion: The Holiness Movement and American Methodism, 1867-1936* (Metuchen NJ: Scarecrow Press, 1974), and Vinson Synan, *The Holiness-Pentecostal Movement in the United States* (Grand Rapids MI: William B. Eerdmans, 1971).

though the belief in the doctrine of "faith cure" or divine healing was rejected by some in Holiness circles, many prominent teachers developed the idea that Christ's atonement provided for an instantaneous experience of physical healing, as well as the instantaneous second blessing of "entire sanctification."[2] By the end of the nineteenth century, divine healing was taught, and "faith cure" services were held in much of the Holiness movement.[3]

The most effective propagandist of divine healing before the advent of Pentecostalism, however, was John Alexander Dowie. The healing exploits of his independent ministry became known to millions throughout the world, and led to the creation of the utopian community of Zion, Illinois. In 1890, Dowie formed the International Divine Healing Association, the first organization in America to be dedicated exclusively to the message of divine healing. The evangelist was sympathetic to holiness teachings; but his organization's sole emphasis on healing was evidence that the "faith cure" phenomenon was extending beyond the parameters of the Holiness movement.[4]

When Pentecostalism appeared at the beginning of the twentieth century, the doctrine of divine healing was one of the primary theological roots derived from the Holiness tradition.[5] Moreover, "it was the faith healing movement which provided the miraculous atmosphere of 'signs and wonders' necessary to make the gift of glossolalia acceptable to the multitudes."[6] Charles F. Parham had a ministry of healing as a Holiness advocate, and continued the healing emphasis after "founding" the Pen-

---

[2]Donald Dayton, "The Rise of the Evangelical Healing Movement in Nineteenth Century America," *Pneuma* 4 (Spring 1982): 7-15.

[3]Idem, "Theological Roots of Pentecostalism," 2 (Spring 1980): 16-17. Prominent Holiness teachers who adopted the belief in divine healing included R. A. Torrey, A. J. Gordon, A. B. Simpson, Andrew Murray, R. Kelso-Carter, William Boardman, and Charles Cullis. Cullis was the most influential advocate of divine healing. For an in-depth analysis of the divine-healing phenomenon in the nineteenth century and its European antecedents, see Paul G. Chappel, "The Divine Healing Movement in America" (Ph.D. diss., Drew University, 1982).

[4]Chappel, "Divine Healing," 284-300. See also Dayton, "Rise of Evangelical Healing," 17.

[5]Dayton demonstrated that the doctrines of salvation, Holy Spirit baptism, divine healing, and premillennialism were taught in the post-Civil War revivalistic and Holiness traditions. Only the connection of the baptism of the Holy Spirit and speaking in tongues remained for the emergence of Pentecostalism. See Dayton, "Theological Roots," 3-21.

[6]Chappel, "Divine Healing," vii.

tecostal movement with his assertion that speaking in tongues was the sign of the baptism of the Holy Spirit. Moreover, the pivotal 1906 Azusa Street revival included manifestations of healing.

As the Pentecostal movement developed, healing revivalism flourished. Healing revivalists such as F. F. Bosworth, John G. Lake, Thomas Wyatt, and M. B. Woodworth-Etter organized independent ministries, and earned national reputations in the 1920s while preaching in Pentecostal circles. Some evangelists, like Raymond T. Richey and Aimee Semple McPherson, were even identified with particular Pentecostal bodies.[7] With the flamboyant and controversial ministry of McPherson, healing revivalism peaked.

The triumphs of the 1920s were followed by a decline of fervor during the years of the Depression. Financial difficulties debilitated the touring healing ministries. Furthermore, the 1930s witnessed friction between Pentecostal groups. A paucity of cooperation eventuated that gave rise to a psychological defensiveness. David E. Harrell elaborated that the "pentecostal psyche had already been dealt a crushing blow in 1928, when a national fundamentalist organization refused to admit pentecostal churches."[8]

Immediately after World War II, this psychological defensiveness gave way to a mood of optimism within the Pentecostal movement. Calls for a renewal of the gifts of the Spirit were increasingly heard. The Assemblies of God historian, William Menzies, suggested that

> the tendency in groups like the Assemblies to curb the sensational, to place supernatural manifestations in an orderly context, did not satisfy all comers, especially in the restive years after the war. Perhaps the restrictions imposed by the war years built up an appetite for the sensational in a sizeable proportion of the Pentecostal following.[9]

Conducive to this yearning for the gifts was the emergence of a more cooperative mood among Pentecostals. A new generation of believers, not limited to the lower class, was less stringent concerning doctrinal difficulties. By 1946, rallies of Pentecostals from different denominations became common in cities across America. Moreover, Pentecostals began participating in some national and international ecumenical organizations

---

[7]David E. Harrell, Jr., *All Things Are Possible: The Healing and Charismatic Revivals in Modern America* (Bloomington: Indiana University Press, 1975) 13-16.

[8]Ibid., 18.

[9]William W. Menzies, *Anointed to Serve: The Story of the Assemblies of God* (Springfield MO: Gospel Publishing House, 1971) 330.

such as the National Association of Evangelicals. David J. duPlessis, commonly called "Mr. Pentecost" for his unparalleled contributions to international Pentecostalism, attributed the reemergence of healing revivalism in 1947 to this new ecumenical spirit.[10] Harrell has cogently summarized the Pentecostal situation in the mid-1940s:

> And so, the times were ripe. Pentecostalism had become affluent enough to support mass evangelism. It had become tolerant enough to overlook doctrinal differences. Convictions were still deep enough that there was a longing for revival. As the older generation thrilled to memories of the miracle ministries of the 1920s, the young yearned for a new rain of miracles.[11]

The only problem that remained was the absence of leadership. With the death in 1947 of two early giants, Smith Wigglesworth and Charles Price, the old era of healing revivalism was gone. Both men, however, had predicted a future revival that would be far greater than anything in the past. Indeed, for the new group of deliverance evangelists the timing of the movement's eruption was controlled by the providence of God.[12] Evangelist David Nunn later "revealed" that 1946 was "the year of preparation. God gave the truth of fasting national publicity through Franklin Hall's preaching . . . which is vital to having God's power."[13] Jack Moore, one of Branham's first campaign managers, "believed God was going to offset man's development of the atomic bomb with his own spiritual bomb."[14]

Participants in the healing revival regarded William Branham to be the initiator of the spiritual explosion. The sudden appearance of miraculous healing campaigns, one leader asserted, "was a reaction that the Lord had done for this one man."[15] The revival began, Gordon Lindsay wrote,

---

[10]John T. Nichol, *Pentecostalism* (New York: Harper & Row, Publishers, 1966) 210. See also Harrell, *All Things Are Possible*, 19.

[11]Harrell, *All Things Are Possible*, 20.

[12]Gordon Lindsay, "The Story of the Great Restoration Revival," *WWR* 10 (March 1958): 4. See also "Ministry of William Branham Spearheads This Last Day Move of God," *TVH* 10 (October 1957): 22.

[13]David Nunn, "God's Order of the Day . . . Revive, Restore, Reap!," *THM* 1 (August 1963): 2.

[14]Statement by Anna Jeanne Price, former associate of Branham, interview with David E. Harrell, Jr., Shreveport LA, 5 December 1973. Tape available at the Holy Spirit Research Center, Oral Roberts University, Tulsa OK.

[15]Ibid.

with the angelic visitation to Branham.[16] As the revival grew with astonishing numerical success throughout the world, Branham was universally acknowledged as the pacesetter, "the father" of this last work of God before the second coming of Christ.[17]

1.

The Sunday evening of Memorial Day weekend, 1946, Branham shared with his congregation at the Branham Tabernacle the story of the angelic commission. During the service Branham received a telegram from a Oneness Pentecostal minister, Robert Daugherty. Having exhausted the aid of physicians, Daugherty requested that Branham come to St. Louis to pray for his sick child. When Betty Daugherty was healed, Branham's unprecedented healing ministry had officially begun.[18]

Upon leaving St. Louis, Branham promised the Daughertys that he would return for a revival. In June, he returned, and held a twelve-day meeting with preaching and praying for the sick. Immediately, Branham received an invitation for a revival in Jonesboro, Arkansas. While in Jonesboro, Branham acquired his first campaign manager, W. E. Kidson. Kidson, a prominent Oneness pioneer and editor of *The Apostolic Herald,* led Branham on a tour of small Oneness churches. Suddenly, Branham's gift of healing was enhancing his reputation. Testimonies of healing abounded, and even a resurrection was reported in one meeting.[19]

When Kidson relinquished his campaign duties in order to return to his own congregation, Jack Moore and Young Brown of Shreveport, Louisiana, assumed the campaign responsibilities. After having Branham in his Shreveport "Jesus only" church, Moore was convinced "that Jesus of Nazareth had passed our way in His servant." Moore further suggested that Branham's "ministry seemed to bring our Lover Lord closer to us . . . than anything had done before."[20]

---

[16]"Conference with Brother Branham," *TVH* 2 (January 1950): 2.

[17]"A Letter from J. Mattsson-Boze," *Pentecost* 17 (September 1951): 13.

[18]Gordon Lindsay, *William Branham: A Man Sent from God* (Jeffersonville IN: William Branham, 1950) 82-87. See also William Branham, *Conduct, Order, Doctrine of the Church,* 2 vols. (Jeffersonville IN: Spoken Word Publications, 1972-1973) 1:150.

[19]Harrell, *All Things Are Possible,* 30. See also Lindsay, *Branham,* 88-93. Oneness Pentecostals had recently reorganized as the United Pentecostal Church. For information on W. E. Kidson, see Arthur L. Clanton, *United We Stand: A History of Oneness Organizations* (Hazelwood MO: Pentecostal Publishing House, 1970) 49.

[20]Lindsay, *Branham,* 103-104.

Branham's new ministry continued to attract attention. *Time* magazine cited a June 1947 campaign in Vandalia, Illinois. According to a UPI press release, the town of 5,800 citizens swelled by an additional 4,000 sick persons. Most were blind, deaf, or lame. The town's three hotels were overflowing. Benches were converted into makeshift beds and many visitors slept on the ground. Branham was definitely creating a sensation.[21]

In the spring of 1947, Branham made a tour of the western states. During the trip, Moore introduced Branham to Gordon Lindsay, an Assemblies of God minister from Ashland, Oregon. After witnessing the miraculous aura surrounding Branham's services, Lindsay was convinced that an unprecedented move from God had begun. In fact, Lindsay believed that Branham's ministry was the key to the revival that Pentecostals were seeking.[22]

The coalition of Moore and Lindsay was indispensable to Branham's continued success. Lindsay, "the most talented promoter of the early years of the revival,"[23] was impressed by Branham's humility and desire for unity. Lindsay agreed to open the doors for Branham's ministry beyond the restrictive boundaries of the Oneness movement, into the larger full gospel circles. Branham, who recognized his own lack of organizational skills, was especially excited. This new opportunity to expand his ministry to all peoples was a fulfillment of his angelic commission.[24]

The first "union" campaign involving both Oneness and trinitarian Pentecostals was held in the northwestern states and Canada during the fall of 1947. These "inter-evangelical" services consciously avoided doctrinal controversies, and consequently experienced unbridled success. They were lavishly described with praise and adulation.[25] Cities were made "God-conscious" as they witnessed their greatest religious meet-

---

[21]The brief *Time* article concluded, "As each patient walked or was carried past, Branham prayed over him, felt him to see if he vibrated with demons. When the last hallelujah had died away and the collection had been taken, one young man announced that he had flung away his hearing aid." See "Self-styled Healer in Vandalia, Ill.," *Time* 50 (14 July 1947): 20. See also Theodore Graebner, *Faith Healing: A Study of Its Methods and an Appraisal of Its Claims* (St. Louis: Concordia Publishing House, n.d.) 3.

[22]Gordon Lindsay, *The Gordon Lindsay Story* (Dallas: The Voice of Healing Publishing Co., n.d.) 141.

[23]Harrell, *All Things Are Possible*, 32.

[24]Lindsay, *Branham*, 117-18.

[25]Ibid., 123-26.

ings ever.[26] According to reports, 1,000 to 1,500 were often converted in a single revival service.[27] A summary of the campaign in Vancouver epitomized the adulation heaped upon Branham. W. J. Ern Baxter, a Canadian minister who joined the Branham team, wrote that healings were so numerous the final tabulations would only be known in heaven.[28] Indeed, Branham declared that 35,000 persons received healing during the first year of his ministry.[29] Everyone involved with the reemergence of healing revivalism concurred with Lindsay that the "manifestation of God in signs and wonders" in Branham's ministry "exceeds anything" any previous healing evangelist had ever achieved.[30]

Riding the crest of success in "union" meetings, the Branham team desired a channel for increased publicity. Previously, the only published advertising that Branham had received came from Kidson's Oneness magazine. An "inter-evangelical" approach was now needed, according to Lindsay. When Kidson declined to participate in such an endeavor, the creation of a new journal eventuated.[31]

The original intention of the Branham party was simply to publish one issue of a magazine. The goal was to better introduce Branham to the Pentecostal masses.[32] The response was so overwhelming, however, that the first issue was reprinted several times.[33] Consequently, a monthly publication, *The Voice of Healing*, was born. Gordon Lindsay and Jack Moore were named the editors, and Branham was listed as the publisher. Founded upon the belief that "the ministry of healing was God's

---

[26]"Eighteen Days of Branham Meetings in the Northwest Yield Great Results," *TVH* 1 (April 1948): 2.

[27]Jack Moore, "Message from the Co-Editor," *TVH* 1 (June 1948): 5.

[28]"Eighteen Days," 2. In 1975 Baxter became a leader of Christian Growth Ministries, a group responsible for the "shepherding" controversy in charismatic renewal. Critics charged that the shepherds, "God-commissioned elders," were assuming authoritarian control of their followers' spiritual and personal growth. See Richard Quebedeaux, *The New Charismatics II* (San Francisco: Harper & Row, Publishers, 1983) 138-42.

[29]William Branham, *Footprints on the Sands of Time: The Autobiography of William Marrion Branham* (Jeffersonville IN: Spoken Word Publications, 1975) 177.

[30]Gordon Lindsay, "An Appraisal of the Branham Campaigns," *TVH* 1 (April 1948): 5.

[31]Lindsay, *Branham*, 128.

[32]Statement by Anna Jeanne Price. Price, the daughter of Jack Moore, was heavily involved in the production of the journal.

[33]"Branham Party News," *TVH* 1 (May 1948): 6.

chosen method of reaching the multitudes," the "inter-evangelical" journal became the exclusive publicity organ of the Branham campaigns.[34]

Branham's striking success came to an abrupt halt in May 1948, just as he was gaining worldwide recognition. The evangelist had to cease his ministry because of physical exhaustion. From the outset, the rigors of the revival trail had adversely affected Branham. When the ministry was originally confined to Oneness churches, he put no time restrictions upon his services. Often he would pray for the sick until one or two o'clock in the morning. In a year's time, Branham's weight dropped forty pounds.[35] After Moore and Lindsay became Branham's organizers, steps were taken to limit the time allotted for prayer to one hour or less each evening. Moreover, requests were made to leave Branham alone at his hotels in campaign cities.[36] In meetings just prior to leaving the field, however, Branham was "faltering and staggering from intense fatigue."[37]

The evangelist's condition was later described as a nervous breakdown or nervous exhaustion. Branham explained that the Mayo Clinic told him "you'll never be entirely over nerves because of your father's drinking."[38] Nevertheless, Branham later blamed his campaign managers for the illness. They had allowed him, Branham complained, to dispense healing too long each night.[39]

The devotees of healing revivalism were dismayed at Branham's announcement. Oral Roberts, who entered a ministry of healing one year after Branham, issued a call for prayer that Branham's health might be restored.[40] Some feared the worst, spreading rumors that Branham was dying of ulcers.[41]

---

[34]"Evangelical Policy of the Branham Campaigns," *TVH* 1 (April 1948): 1. *The Voice of Healing* was begun a few months after Oral Roberts's *Healing Waters*. See David E. Harrell, Jr., *Oral Roberts: An American Life* (Bloomington: Indiana University Press, 1985) 149.

[35]"Brother Branham Takes Extended Rest," *TVH* 1 (July 1948): 1. See also "Special Notice," *TVH* 1 (June 1948): 1.

[36]"Instructions for Those Who Live at a Distance from the Branham Meetings," *TVH* 1 (April 1948): 5.

[37]Del Grant, "Branham is Back," *TVH* 1 (January 1949): 3.

[38]Ibid.

[39]Branham did not identify the campaign managers. See William Branham, "Where I Think Pentecost Failed," sermon delivered and recorded in San Francisco CA, 11 November 1955.

[40]"Prayer for Rev. William Branham," *HW* 1 (July 1948): 8.

[41]Grant, "Branham is Back," 3.

Lindsay was especially saddened by Branham's decision. He had procured numerous attractive invitations for campaigns all across the country. Moreover, Branham informed Lindsay and Moore that the publication, *The Voice of Healing,* was their total responsibility. Lindsay felt deserted at this decision. [42] He continued to publish the journal, however, and expanded the coverage to include other deliverance evangelists. [43] Later, Lindsay interpreted Branham's illness as part of God's plan.

> Perhaps in the providence of God, He was permitting Brother Branham to leave the field for a season so that others would feel the responsibility to help carry the torch of this great ministry. [44]

After just six months of retirement, Branham returned to the rigors of healing revivalism. Perhaps motivated by the sudden proliferation of successful, competing evangelists, Branham declared that he had received a miracle of healing. [45] His reappearance was greeted with great enthusiasm. Evangelist Del Grant exclaimed,

> Brother William Branham of Sign Gift Divine Healing fame is back on the field again. Back in the harness for God! Back on the firing line for Jesus! [46]

Branham announced that he welcomed the arrival of other evangelists to the field of healing revivalism. At the same time, he predicted that his own ministry would become even greater. [47] Some claimed that Branham was critical of *The Voice of Healing* coverage of other revivalists. [48] Upon his return to the campaign trail, Branham was still featured in *The Voice of Healing.* Less than two years later, however, Branham criticized the journal for becoming a massive financial organization. This de-

---

[42]Statement by Gordon Lindsay, interview with David E. Harrell, Jr., Dallas TX, 27 July 1972. Tape available at the Holy Spirit Research Center, Oral Roberts University, Tulsa OK.

[43]"The Policy of the Voice of Healing," *TVH* 1 (July 1948): 6. See also "Special Message from the Editor, Gordon Lindsay," *TVH* 1 (March 1949): 2.

[44]Gordon Lindsay, "The Story of the Great Restoration Revival, Part III," *WWR* 11 (May 1958): 4.

[45]"Word from Bro. Branham," *TVH* 1 (August 1948): 1. See also Harrell, *All Things Are Possible,* 33-34.

[46]Grant, "Branham is Back," 1.

[47]"Conference with Brother Branham," 2.

[48]Statement by Anna Jeanne Price.

plorable condition, Branham bemoaned, hindered his ability to follow the Lord Jesus' leading for campaign decisions.[49]

Branham's first major meeting after his absence took place in January 1950 in Houston, Texas. The Branham team, now including the revered deliverance evangelist of the 1920s, F. F. Bosworth, attracted crowds of 8,000 in a single service.[50] The revival gained headlines in the Houston papers. W. E. Best, pastor of Houston Tabernacle Baptist Church, debated Bosworth regarding the biblical justification of faith healing. The debate occasioned a round of fisticuffs in the audience.[51] Yet the debate is most remembered for its place in the Branham legacy.

Best had hired two photographers to take photographs during the debate. All the negatives turned out blank except for the only picture taken of Branham. The photograph revealed "a supernatural halo of light over his head."[52] The Branham team immediately secured scientific proof that the picture was authentic. Branham, upon hearing about the photograph, calmly responded that similar incidents with a supernatural light had previously occurred in his ministry.

For the rest of his life, Branham regarded the picture as a divine vindication of his ministry. He asserted that the "Angel permitted me to have his picture taken with me."[53] This was the first time in history, Branham declared, that a supernatural being was photographed.[54] As Harrell suggested, "the photograph became perhaps the most famous relic in the history of the revival."[55]

In April 1950, Branham—accompanied by Moore, Lindsay, and Baxter—made the first healing tour of Europe by an American deliverance

---

[49]William Branham, "Three Witnesses," sermon delivered and recorded in Erie PA, 28 July 1951.

[50]For a biography of Bosworth see Eunice M. Perkins, *Fred Francis Bosworth: His Life Story* (Detroit: Eunice M. Perkins, 1927).

[51]Louis Hofferbert, "Pastor Vs. Faith Healer Tonight," *The Houston Press,* 24 January 1950, A1: 1-6. See also Louis Hofferbert, "8000 Hear Faith Healer, Pastor Debate," *The Houston Press,* 25 January 1950, A1: 1-6.

[52]"God Vindicates Branham in Houston by Most Amazing Photograph Ever Taken," *TVH* 2 (March 1950): 1.

[53]William Branham, "God in His People," sermon delivered and recorded in Little Rock AR, 27 February 1950.

[54]William Branham, *The Revelation of the Seven Seals* (Tucson: Spoken Word Publications, 1967) 56.

[55]Harrell, *All Things Are Possible,* 35. The photograph is a part of the design of Harrell's book.

evangelist. The campaigns in Finland and Norway were triumphant, more than 7,000 persons often in attendance. Opposition from the state church and secular press, the Branham team felt, only accelerated attendance and enthusiasm. The tour achieved worldwide recognition. Donald Gee— editor of *Pentecost,* the voice of international Pentecostalism—reacted favorably. Indeed, Branham believed his commission was being vindicated since his ministry was now reaching all "the peoples of the world."[56]

Branham conducted other successful overseas campaigns. A South African campaign occurred in 1952. Some considered this revival "the greatest outpouring of the Holy Ghost that that country has ever seen."[57] Gordon Lindsay suggested that the altar call of 30,000 in Dunbar was the largest of its kind in history.[58] Branham supporters were so pleased with the campaign that a book entitled *William Branham: A Prophet Visits South Africa* was soon published. Again, the ministry of Branham received international acclaim. Even the normally cautious Gee received "an impressive number of entirely separate testimonies from reliable eyewitnesses" concerning the "miraculous results" of the campaigns.[59]

Another overseas tour took Branham to Portugal, Rome, and India in 1954. In 1952 Branham had experienced a vision that dealt with a significant future campaign. According to the vision, Branham would speak before 300,000 "Indians" in a single service. For the next two years this vision constantly fed Branham's desire for a greater ministry. When a campaign meeting in India finally materialized, the deliverance evangelist felt a sense of vindication. Indeed, by 1954 Branham contended that his converts totaled over one-half million.[60]

Branham's final, major overseas tour occurred in 1955. Sponsored by Minor Arganbright, a vice-president of the Full Gospel Business Men's

---

[56]W. J. Ern Baxter, "This is Finland," *TVH* 3 (May 1950): 1. See also "William Branham in Finland," *Pentecost* 12 (June 1950): 15. See also W. J. Ern Baxter, "Seven Thousand Fill Finland's Largest Auditorium for Evangelistic Divine Healing Campaign Conducted by William Branham," *Pentecost* 13 (September 1950): 8-9.

[57]Joseph D. Mattsson-Boze, "Editorial Insert," *HOF* 32 (May 1964): 3. Donald Gee cited a report of F. F. Bosworth about the South Africa campaign to point out the tendency of deliverance evangelists to exaggerate their claims for the sake of propaganda. See Donald Gee, *Wind and Flame,* rev. ed. (Croydon, England: Heath Press, Ltd., 1967) 242-43.

[58]"An Interview with Evangelist William Branham," *TVH* 6 (March 1954): 2.

[59]"In the Mouth of Many Witnesses," *Pentecost* 19 (March 1952): i.

[60]Branham, *Footprints,* 236-39. See also "Branham Preaches in Shadow of Vatican," *HOF* 21 (October 1954): 6.

International, Branham successfully toured Switzerland and Germany. In its account of a meeting at Lausanne, Switzerland, *Voice*—the official organ of the Full Gospel Business Men's International—reported another occurrence of the "supernatural light" surrounding Branham. Moreover, a photograph of the event made the cover of the journal. [61]

From 1946 to 1955, Branham's popularity on the revival circuit was sustained. The Branham team changed from time to time, particularly after Lindsay began to work with other evangelists. [62] Despite the influx of revivalists on the scene, Branham remained very influential among the devotees of divine healing. It was not until the fall of 1955 that Branham experienced financial difficulty in his meetings. During that crisis period, the radical shift in Branham's ministry took root.

2.

Several factors contributed to taking Branham to the pinnacle of success. The dynamic revival trio of Branham, Bosworth, and Baxter was a highlight of the early years. Moreover, the effective leadership of Lindsay, Moore, and his daughter Anna Jeanne skillfully publicized Branham as "a man sent from God." Indeed, when Lindsay's book, *William Branham: A Man Sent from God,* was released in 1951, the first edition was exhausted in four months. [63]

An element that especially attracted a wide range of Pentecostals was the campaign emphasis on the unification of Spirit-filled Christians through a conscious avoidance of doctrinal conflict. The personal friendship between Moore and Lindsay was a crucial factor in initiating "union" meetings between "Jesus only" and trinitarian Pentecostals in the beginning of the healing revival. [64] When Lindsay became swamped with campaign invitations for Branham, preference was given to cities where a majority of the resident Pentecostal ministers were willing to cooperate as sponsors. [65] The Branham campaign issued a policy statement regarding the conscious avoidance of doctrinal issues. Except for "the great evangeli-

---

[61]"Concerning Photograph on Front Cover," *Voice* 3 (September 1955): 3. See also "Branham Meetings in Germany and Switzerland," *Voice* 3 (September 1955): 3-11.

[62]Harrell, *All Things Are Possible,* 57. Lindsay organized the disparate healing revivalists into a loose fellowship called The Voice of Healing. Branham often spoke at convention meetings.

[63]"Books Written or Published by Gordon Lindsay," *TVH* 4 (June 1951): 16.

[64]Harrell, *All Things Are Possible,* 31.

[65]"Branham Party News," *TVH* 1 (April 1948): 4.

cal truths of Salvation, Divine Healing, the Second Coming of Christ, and the Spirit-filled life," the *Voice of Healing* reported,

> doctrines that are peculiar to one denomination, or involve thee [*sic*] mysteries of Divine Sovereignty, or which concern formulas of water baptism are to be avoided in the meetings, and not to be identified with it afterwards.[66]

The phenomenon of "union" meetings was prophetic, according to Gordon Lindsay. The ecumenism facilitated the creation of a unity of the Spirit between Christians.[67] Furthermore, Lindsay suggested that Branham was peculiarly suited to achieving an ecumenical spirit. Speaking at a convention of deliverance evangelists, Lindsay opined,

> When God was looking for a man to spear-head this revival he didn't choose a brilliant man or a college professor who would be smart enough to start something for himself, He . . . found a humble unassuming person, an uncolored type of John the Baptist, who in his simple, unlettered manner knew only to preach the gospel and obey God's orders, seeking favor with no man.[68]

Branham reiterated his concern for spiritual unity throughout the peak years of healing revivalism. Motivated by his angelic commission to minister healing to all peoples, the deliverance evangelist asserted that the millennium would come if the Pentecostals would cease fighting with each other.[69] Such bickering was the only reason the second coming of Christ had not occurred.[70] Accordingly, one of the purposes of the Branham campaigns was to facilitate ecumenicity. Branham said that he would go to a meeting of any group and declare "we are brethren."[71]

Branham understood the necessity of avoiding doctrinal conflicts if "union" meetings of the various Pentecostal groups were to be successful. He explained to his church in Jeffersonville that "if you'd tramp on

---

[66]Ibid.

[67]Lindsay, "Appraisal," 6.

[68]Gordon Lindsay, quoted in Anna Jeanne Moore, "Convention Diary, Account of Three-Day Meeting of TVH December 11-13," *TVH* 4 (February 1952): 2.

[69]William Branham, "Everlasting Life—How to Receive It," sermon delivered and recorded in Jeffersonville IN, 31 December 1954.

[70]William Branham, "For Him Will I Accept," sermon delivered and recorded in Hammond IN, 18 July 1952.

[71]"Evangelist William Branham's Message to the Church, Installment I," *TVH* 7 (October 1954): 13.

people's ecclesiastical teaching, it'll make the ministers keep the people away. . . . "[72] According to Branham, such a limitation was one reason why he consented to associates handling the bulk of the preaching duties. He was satisfied with simply emphasizing the subject of divine healing. Furthermore, Branham believed that doctrinal agreement was not necessary for the ministry of healing to flourish. Asserting that Christians should be able to "disagree a million miles on theology," Branham declared,

> if you'd ever break down your walls, let this one be this and that one be that, whatever you are that doesn't matter. But when you can put your hand in your brother's hands and call him your brother and we're working for one cause, that is the Kingdom of God. If it ever gets to the point where I couldn't put my arm around any brother that's working for the Kingdom of God and recognize him as my brother, I feel I'm backslid.[73]

God did not put his endorsement upon one particular church, but He revealed that the pure in heart would see God.[74] "It's Christ's way you must follow. It is not the Methodist, Baptist, Presbyterian, Pentecost [sic] way," Branham preached.[75]

In a rare reference to the particular beliefs of the various Pentecostal groups, Branham pointed out the spiritual disadvantages of theological tensions. He commented:

> I have nothing against any organization but it becomes a political warfare among the people. . . . When I was here before, the Oneness sponsored my meeting and the other group wouldn't come. This time it is exactly the opposite—threeness is having it . . . threeness or fiveness, I don't care what you believe in brother . . . it ain't what you believe, it's who you believe, Jesus Christ, that's important. Let the fellow believe whatever he wants to about it. These things don't amount to very much anyhow. Be brothers, have fellowship with one another.[76]

---

[72]William Branham, *Israel and the Church* (Jeffersonville IN: Spoken Word Publications, n.d.) 67.

[73]Branham, "Where I Think Pentecost Failed," recorded.

[74]William Branham, "Why I am a Holy Roller," sermon delivered and recorded in Chicago IL, 30 August 1953.

[75]William Branham, "God's Way That's Been Made for Us," sermon delivered and recorded in Jeffersonville IN, 10 January 1950.

[76]William Branham, "Works That I Do Bear Witness of Me," sermon delivered and recorded in Phoenix AZ, 13 April 1951.

The existence of theologically segregated crowds revealed that the ecumenical nature of the Branham campaigns was not without problems. The non-doctrinal policy was criticized by some as a compromising of the faith. Moreover, despite the plea for nonpartisan cooperation, many ministers were obsessed with sectarian zeal. They often attempted to identify Branham with their own doctrinal causes. Sectarian spirit made "the placing of new converts somewhat difficult," Jack Moore lamented, "so like Paul's seamen of old 'we cast anchor and wished for the day,' and the Lord seemed to lead us thus."[77] Even with such problems, however, the ecumenical character of the campaigns facilitated immensely Branham's success.

Another contributing factor of Branham's success was his most dominant personality trait: humility. Branham readily remembered his humble origins, and often apologized for his lack of education and cultural qualifications. Acknowledging that he was a seer to whom God revealed visions, Branham cautioned, "that doesn't make me any more than the drunkard who was converted ten minutes ago somewhere. He is a Christian the same as I am."[78] This simple humility captivated audiences and gained the respect of Pentecostal leaders. Len Jones, editor of the Australian Pentecostal journal *Evidence,* described Branham as "one of the meekest and humblest men you could ever meet."[79] Oral Roberts elaborated that Branham was "a genuine humble prophet of God" who possessed "a type of humility you responded to."[80]

Branham admitted that he was a very poor speaker.[81] Often he appeared timid before the crowds and preached with a quiet and halting voice. His sermons were replete with grammatical errors. W. J. Hollenweger, who served as an interpreter for some of Branham's overseas crusades, correctly judged that Branham's sermons were "not merely simple, but often naive as well."[82] Nevertheless, Branham captivated his

----

[77]Jack Moore, "Statement of Policy," *TVH* 1 (April 1948): 6. See also Lindsay, "Appraisal," 5.

[78]William Branham, "The Unpardonable Sin," sermon delivered and recorded in Jeffersonville IN, 24 October 1954. See also Lindsay, *Branham,* 12-13.

[79]Len J. Jones, "I Attend Another Branham Meeting," *HOF* 26 (February 1959): 17.

[80]Statement by Oral Roberts, telephone interview, Tulsa OK, 3 April 1984.

[81]William Branham, "Elijah and Elisha," sermon delivered and recorded in Phoenix AZ, 4 March 1954.

[82]Walter J. Hollenweger, *The Pentecostals,* trans. R. A. Wilson (London: S. C. M. Press, 1972) 355.

crowds with the simple sermons of biblical healings, and stories of his life and ministry. In contrast to the platform gyrations of many healing revivalists, Branham's humility facilitated a "quiet mastery" of his audiences.[83] Joseph D. Mattsson-Boze, editor of the *Herald of Faith* and close friend of Branham, said, "sometimes I was scared because of the deep sense of holiness that penetrated the meetings."[84] According to Harrell,

> Branham's sermons were indeed simple. . . . And yet, the power of a Branham service—and of Branham's stage presence—remains a legend unparalleled in the history of the Christian charismatic movement.[85]

The major reason for Branham's success was the magnetism of his healing gift. His pulpit method of relating personal experiences was geared to justifying his "supernatural" ministry. These colorful and dynamic stories consequently created a fervid expectancy for healing in the audiences.

Branham related several favorite miraculous events. The first was the story of the "maniac" from Portland, Oregon. In a 1947 meeting Branham was accosted during a service by a man who shouted, "I'll break every bone in that little frail body of yours."[86] With the crowd in suspense, Branham rebuked the demon out of the man. "The great congregation was awed by the scene," Lindsay wrote, "in which God so signally vindicated His servant."[87]

Several healings were constantly recalled by Branham as vindication of his chosenness. Before going to Finland in 1950, Branham told of a vision that indicated the resurrection of a young boy. When such an experience was claimed during the Finland revival, Branham exclaimed, "Thus Saith the Lord! There is the boy!"[88] Other significant miracles that Branham often claimed were the healings of King George VI of En-

---

[83]Harrell, *All Things Are Possible,* 38.

[84]Joseph D. Mattsson-Boze, "William Branham: In Memoriam," *HOF* 34 (February 1966): 3.

[85]Harrell, *All Things Are Possible,* 162.

[86]Branham, *Footprints,* 185-86.

[87]Lindsay, *Branham,* 25.

[88]William Branham, "The Whole Will of God," sermon delivered and recorded in Toledo OH, 19 July 1951. See also Jack Moore, "Resurrection in Finland," *TVH* 3 (June 1950): 8.

gland,[89] and a Canadian boy named Donny Morton whose story was published in *Reader's Digest*.[90]

The most prized healing, and "one of the more famous healings in the healing revival's history," was received by William D. Upshaw in 1951.[91] Upshaw, a cripple for fifty-nine of his sixty-six years, had been a member of Congress from Georgia, and the 1932 Prohibition Party nominee for President of the United States. After he was healed in a Branham service, Upshaw sent a letter describing his experience to each member of Congress. The testimony of Upshaw, one commentator wrote, "is perhaps the most effective healing testimony this generation has seen."[92] For Branham, the healing was a vindication of his commission to pray for kings and statesmen.[93]

* * * * *

In the late 1940s the cultural and religious context of Pentecostalism was ripe for the reemergence of healing revivalism. Such a "spiritual explosion" was initiated in the ministry of William Branham. Thrust into a ministry of healing by an experience he described as his angelic commission, Branham was the pacesetter of the early revival. He toured the

---

[89]"Interview with William Branham," *TVH* 7 (May 1954): 22. In the interview Branham related that a friend had received a letter asking Branham to pray for the king. After fulfilling the request, Branham received a thank-you letter from the king that indicated that he was well. On another occasion, Branham embellished this story. He said that the king sent him a cablegram asking for prayer. Indeed, the king acknowledged that part of Branham's commission was to pray for monarchs. See William Branham, "At Thy Word," sermon delivered and recorded in Los Angeles CA, 6 May 1951.

[90]Alma Edwards Smith, "The Miracle of Donny Morton," *Reader's Digest* 61 (November 1952): 29-35. According to the article, physicians diagnosed a condition of deteriorating brain tissue and gave the boy only six months to live. Morton's father spent all the money he had and took his son on a 2800-mile bus trip to secure the services of Branham who was in California. The deliverance evangelist prayed that with "faith in God's power and help from the medical world" the boy would live. The child did survive four operations but died within the year. According to Smith, the miracle was the provision of funds for the operations by a woman who read of Morton's pilgrimage in a newspaper article. Whenever Branham related the story, he remembered the healing of Donny Morton and the article by *Reader's Digest*. The boy's death was never mentioned. See William Branham, "His Unfailing Words of Promise," *TSW* 15:3 (n.d.): 21.

[91]Harrell, *All Things Are Possible*, 35.

[92]Anna Jeanne Moore, "Convention Diary," 3. See also "Healing of Former Congressman Upshaw Stirs Nation; Los Angeles Times Reports Miracle," *TVH* 4 (July 1951): 17.

[93]Branham, "The Whole Will of God," recorded.

country and attracted throngs to successful Pentecostal "union" meetings. Several elements contributed to Branham's success; effective organization from Gordon Lindsay and Jack Moore, the ministerial support of Bosworth, the yearning for miracles by the Pentecostal masses, and Branham's humble character all facilitated campaign triumphs.

Branham often emphasized his soul-winning achievements. Nevertheless, the humble evangelist's magnetism and fame were rooted in his unique healing exploits. Utilizing his two sign-gifts, Branham built a reputation as a "man sent from God." He was the first American to triumphantly tour Europe with a ministry of deliverance. Foreigners even traveled to the United States in order to seek healing from him.[94] No disease was seemingly beyond his reach. The angelic commission had granted Branham "an infallible prescription for cancer," one supporter exclaimed.[95]

Despite a brief retirement on account of nervous exhaustion, and the influx of other deliverance evangelists, Branham maintained a successful ministry up until 1955. Along with Oral Roberts, Branham was the most revered leader of the revival. As the pacesetter, the evangelist had reignited a significant movement in religious America that remains on the scene today.

---

[94]Bosworth reported that an invalid from Bolivia, South America, flew to a meeting in Flint, Michigan. See F. F. Bosworth, "Looking at the Unseen," *TVH* 2 (January 1950): 5. A perusal of the tapes from Branham's campaigns confirms that the emphasis was clearly physical deliverance. Of course, the topic of salvation was not excluded. Yet, it was not dominant. A European Pentecostal leader was annoyed by Branham's "disturbingly vague" altar call during a campaign in Zurich. See Hollenweger, *Pentecostals,* 355.

[95]William Branham, *Do You Fear Cancer?* (n.p., n.d.) 1.

CHAPTER FOUR

BRANHAM THE HEALER

Frederick Dale Bruner asserts that, alongside the gift of tongues, "there is an emphasis on healing in many Pentecostal circles which makes it almost a second Pentecostal distinctive."[1] This attitude was especially prevalent during the peak years of the healing revival. Dependent upon the "faith cure" movement of the nineteenth-century Holiness tradition, Pentecostals continued to develop a theology of divine healing. William Branham was no exception. As the pacesetter of the revival, Branham taught a theology of healing and utilized a methodology of healing that were undoubtedly significant to the tradition of divine healing in America.

1.

Branham's belief in healing for the twentieth-century Christian was rooted in his biblical literalism. The practices of apostolic Christianity, Branham contended, were being restored among full gospel Pentecostal believers. Furthermore, the gospel was defined as "the power and demonstration of the Holy Spirit put in action."[2] God had always appeared with accompanying signs and wonders. Eighty percent of Christ's ministry was healing. Consequently, Branham preached that "the faith delivered to the saints by

---

[1]Frederick Dale Bruner, *A Theology of the Holy Spirit: The Pentecostal Experience and the New Testament Witness* (Grand Rapids MI: William B. Eerdmans, 1970) 141.

[2]William Branham, "The Uncertain Sound," sermon delivered and recorded in Jeffersonville IN, 31 July 1955.

Christ was one of signs and wonders" (Jude 3).[3] Signs and wonders were still necessary today, according to Branham. In his exegesis of John 4:48—"Unless you see signs and wonders you will not believe"—the evangelist noted that a man asked Jesus to pray for healing. Instead, Jesus responded with a prophecy that "you must see signs first before you'll believe."[4] Applying this prophecy to today, Branham concluded that persons must ask for the supernatural since God is by nature supernatural.[5]

Several biblical passages were especially important for Branham's defense of divine healing. One example was Jesus' promise in John 14:12, "Verily, verily, I say unto you, He that believeth on me, the works that I do he shall do also and greater works than these shall he do, because I go unto my Father." Branham interpreted the phrase "greater works" as an indication that "more" works would be done among contemporary Christians. Indeed, Branham declared that more works were performed by God in one of his services than was recorded in the entire New Testament.[6]

Many of Branham's favorite passages had become popular in the theology of divine healing that was developed during the "faith cure" movement of the nineteenth century. The first was Mark 16:17-18.[7] The passage reveals that certain signs such as healing "shall follow them that believe." Branham emphasized that this last commission of Jesus to his apostles reiterated the command to heal found in the first commission of Matthew 10:1-2. In contrast to the scholarly debate over the authority of the long ending of Mark 16, Branham proclaimed that the chapter was the "identification of a Scripture Christian."[8]

---

[3]Idem, "Contending for the Faith," sermon delivered and recorded in Chicago IL, 23 January 1955. See also William Branham, "Faith without Works Is Dead," sermon delivered and recorded in Cleveland OH, 22 August 1950.

[4]Idem, "Works That I Do Bear Witness of Me," sermon delivered and recorded in Phoenix AZ, 13 April 1951.

[5]Idem, "Acts of the Holy Spirit," sermon delivered and recorded in Jeffersonville IN, 19 December 1954.

[6]Julius Stadsklev, ed., *A Prophet Brings His Message: Sermons by Rev. William Branham* (Tucson: Julius Stadsklev, 1972) 79.

[7]Ethan O. Allen, the father of healing revivalism in America, was healed by the prayer of faith at a meeting of Methodist class leaders in 1846. The class leaders justified their prayer by referring to Mark 16:17-18. See Paul G. Chappel, "The Divine Healing Movement in America" (Ph.D. diss., Drew University, 1982) 88.

[8]William Branham, "Perfect Faith," *TSW* 6:11 (n.d.): 13. See also William Branham, "Ministry Explained," sermon delivered and recorded in Minneapolis MN, 11 July 1949. Branham conveyed an inconsistent biblical literalism in his exposition of Mark 16:17-18.

A second passage, also given prominence among nineteenth-century healing advocates, was Hebrews 13:8, "Jesus Christ the same yesterday, and today, and forever."[9] The same Jesus who healed on earth in the first century must heal today in the form of the Holy Spirit. However God acted in a past situation, Branham contended, the same action must occur again for God to be eternally consistent and perfect. God was never inconsistent; and he had always desired physical deliverance to be manifest.[10]

The key scriptural justification for any theology of divine healing was a belief in the atonement of Christ as the basis for supernatural healing.[11] The death of Jesus purchased healing for both body and soul, according to Branham. Isaiah 53:4-5—especially the words, "he was wounded for our transgressions, with His stripes we are healed"—was the most important biblical reference. Branham, by advocating a "dual atonement" idea, offered his audiences a double comfort. First, one could be healed because of Christ's finished work at Calvary. Second, since it was easier to say "thy sins be forgiven" rather than "take up thy bed and walk," a person's healing indicated that his sins were indeed forgiven.[12]

One of the central questions in Branham's theology of healing was the relationship of sin, sickness, and the demonic. The deliverance evangelist had a very literal conception of the demonic. The Devil and his demons were real persons. Branham claimed that he had talked face-to-face with demons. Moreover, he offered a description of a demon in the story of his first exorcism. After relating how he commanded Satan to leave a young woman, Branham asserted, "The screen door began opening and shutting by itself. . . . leave her Satan. In Jesus' Name come out of her! When I said that, it looked like a great big bat . . . rose up from behind her, with long hair hanging down out of its wings and off of its feet. . . .

He asserted that snake handling was not required to prove one's faith. See William Branham, *Conduct, Order, Doctrine of the Church*, 2 vols. (Jeffersonville IN: Spoken Word Publications, 1973-1974) 2:1174.

[9]Chappel, "Divine," 279.

[10]William Branham, "God Testifies of His Gifts," sermon delivered and recorded in Hammond IN, 13 July 1952. See also William Branham, "God's Word Shall Not Pass Away," *HOF* 24 (January 1957): 5.

[11]The Holiness advocate, Robert Kelso-Carter, popularized the idea of the atonement's provision for healing. See Chappel, "Divine," 179-80.

[12]William Branham, "God in His People," sermon delivered and recorded in Little Rock AR, 27 February 1950. See also Nils Bloch-Hoell, *The Pentecostal Movement: Its Origin, Development, and Distinctive Character* (New York: Humanities Press, 1964) 149. Branham was citing Mark 2:9. Other scriptural justifications for healing were Num. 21:9 and Ps. 103:3.

A devil went out of her."[13] Traditional Pentecostals generally regard sickness as a significant result of the Fall. With the first sin, disease entered the world. Some healing revivalists, including Branham, made a total and direct connection between sin, sickness, and demonic power.[14]

Branham believed that Satan was the author of all sickness. Diseases—for example, cancer, epilepsy, cataracts, and tuberculosis—were simply the physical forms of spiritual beings called demons.[15] According to Branham, what doctors referred to as "a cancer, God calls it a devil."[16] Moreover, sin and sickness were directly related. "God sometimes permits Satan to put sickness on you as a whip," Branham suggested, "to bring you back to the House of God when you disobey him."[17] God also permitted sickness and natural disasters, however, in order to test a person's faith. Enduring the test of suffering was a mark of the true Christian.[18]

If a sick person did not receive healing in a Branham service, the problem was either some unconfessed sin or the presence of a demon. Either phenomenon, Branham believed, prohibited faith. To complicate matters, the sin might have been committed by an ancestor of previous generations. Consequently, demon-possessed persons had to receive an exorcism before healing could occur. The exorcism itself did not heal, Branham declared, but it cleared the path for healing to eventuate.[19] Accordingly, a major element of Branham's gift of healing included the practice of exorcism. He initiated the belief that the authority to perform the rite was rooted in his commission: "Come out of them in the Name of Jesus Christ. I say as God's servant by a message from an angel, who

---

[13]William Branham, *Footprints on the Sands of Time: The Autobiography of William Marrion Branham* (Jeffersonville IN: Spoken Word Publications, 1975) 123. See also William Branham, "Early Spiritual Experiences," sermon delivered and recorded in Hammond IN, 14 July 1952.

[14]Bloch-Hoell, *Pentecostal Movement,* 148.

[15]William Branham, *Demonology* (Jeffersonville IN: Spoken Word Publications, 1976) 86-87. Branham also identified insanity and temper tantrums as demons. See William Branham, *Conduct,* 1:475, 489.

[16]Idem, *Demonology,* 32.

[17]Ibid., 23. Branham noted other instances in which the demonic was the root of sin. For example, religious persons who scorned divine healing or who made a habit of complaining, "if I could only quit lying, if I could only quit lusting" were demon-possessed. See Ibid., 86-87, 90.

[18]William Branham, "Possessing the Enemy's Gates," *TSW* 11:6 (n.d.): 6.

[19]Idem, *Demonology,* 14-15, 18. See also Branham, *Conduct,* 1:104.

anointed and has proven to the people that Jesus is here . . . come out
of them in the Name of Jesus Christ."[20]

The healing revivalist had an ominous warning for all skeptics who
ridiculed the message of divine healing. Espousing his characteristic biblical literalism, Branham asserted that exorcised, demonic spirits immediately looked for new habitats. Accordingly, he told skeptics that they
had better leave the meeting site before the healing portion of the service. If they did not, Branham avowed, he would not be responsible for
what evil fate befell them.[21] A warning was even given to all the faithful
who observed the exorcisms—keep your heads bowed. Exorcised demons headed for the eyes, the gateway to the soul. "Epilepsy is the one
thing that gets away from me," Branham concluded, "twenty-eight people in the audience got it in one night."[22]

According to Branham, demonic spirits were at the root of sin and
sickness. If a person desired healing, the sin had to be confessed and the
demon exorcised. When these took place, faith became operative. If faith
was sufficient, physical deliverance was achieved.

For Branham or any deliverance evangelist, the crux of a theology of
healing was the necessity of faith. Branham boldly announced to his audiences that the "only thing that keeps you from being healed is a lack of
faith."[23] He claimed that he did not possess any supernatural power that
effected healings. Rather, God in Christ was the healer who granted
healing when proper faith was manifest. If a person desired healing,
Branham preached, he must believe and confess that Christ died for his
healing. God was then "obligated" to heal because his Word promised the
believer healing. Branham concluded, "God is as good as his Word. If not,
he isn't God."[24]

Expostulating upon the nature of faith, Branham frequently quoted
Hebrews 11:1, "Now faith is the substance of things hoped for, the evi-

---

[20]Idem, "The Tower of Babel," *TSW* 2:7 (n.d.): 26.

[21]Idem, "Children in the Wilderness," sermon delivered and recorded in Phoenix AZ,
23 November 1947. See Luke 11:24-26 for the source of Branham's warning.

[22]Idem, "Jesus Christ the Same Yesterday, and Today, and Forever," sermon delivered and recorded in Chicago IL, 9 August 1952. See also Gordon Lindsay, *Divine Healing in the Branham Meetings* (Jeffersonville IN: Branham Healing Campaigns, n.d.) 18.

[23]William Branham, "Africa Trip and Faith," sermon delivered and recorded in Zion
IL, 25 July 1952.

[24]Idem, "I Am the Resurrection and the Life," sermon delivered and recorded in Chicago IL, 8 August 1952. See also "Hundreds Testify to Being Cured in Branham Tour,"
TVH 4 (February 1952): 10.

dence of things not seen." Faith was a sixth sense, according to Branham. Whereas God gave the natural man five senses to function in the earthly realm, he granted the spiritual man two additional senses—faith and unbelief. Since God is Spirit, Branham argued, persons desiring healing must contact him "by spirit through faith believing."[25]

Faith was real; and it provided sure evidence of the things the natural senses would not declare, according to Branham. He vividly illustrated this conviction with tangible analogies during his preaching. Branham declared, "How many believe that shirt is white? That shows you can see. Now, if your faith says you are going to be healed, and is just as real to you as your sight which says that shirt is white, you are healed. Faith declares it. It is perfect."[26] Faith could make all things possible.

Branham's concept of faith was rooted in his belief in spiritual revelation. A person had to demonstrate faith in order to receive healing; however, faith was solely obtained by divine revelation. Branham suggested that "faith is God by the Spirit revealing to you something he is going to do. . . . Faith is believing what God reveals to you."[27]

Branham suggested that the biblical story of Cain and Abel vividly demonstrated the relationship between faith and revelation. God revealed to Abel that the Son of God was a lamb slain before the foundation of the world. When Abel demonstrated faith in the revelation by offering a lamb sacrifice, God accepted him.[28]

Since faith was based on the solid rock of spiritual revelation, a person possessed the power to believe that he would receive healing under any circumstance. Even if every scientist in the world deemed an event impossible, Branham opined that the Christian must have faith in the revelation. The revelation for Noah to build an ark required a miracle of faith, for example, since it was the first time that God had ever sent rain upon the earth.[29] Branham further declared that reason was not compatible with

---

[25]William Branham, "Faith," sermon delivered and recorded in Jeffersonville IN, 24 February 1952. See also William Branham, "Explaining the Ministry and Healing," sermon delivered and recorded in Louisville KY, January 1950. Branham, often fascinated with numerology, suggested that the seven senses manifested the perfection of God.

[26]Julius Stadsklev, *William Branham: A Prophet Visits South Africa* (Minneapolis: Julius Stadsklev, 1952) 55.

[27]William Branham, "Exodus—The Pillar of Fire," sermon delivered and recorded in Chicago IL, 6 October 1955.

[28]Ibid.

[29]William Branham, "Seven Great Junctions," *HOF* 30 (May 1962): 9.

faith. "If you understand It, then that makes faith annulled," Branham proclaimed, "You can't understand It, but believe it anyhow."[30]

The major problem for deliverance evangelists was the glaring fact that many people who desired healing did not receive it. Branham remained convinced that a lack of faith was the crux of the failure. He simply admonished his audiences to persevere in their faith. Moreover, he complained that the masses always expected immediate healings. Rather, healings were sometimes gradual, and often did not become visible anywhere from an hour to two years later. Yet gradual healing did not contradict the promise that healing was guaranteed by faith. Abraham and Sarah, Branham often noted, had to wait with unwavering faith for twenty-five years before God fulfilled the promise of giving them a son.[31]

Another difficult problem for the healing revivalists was the complaint that many healings were temporary. One Canadian minister who assisted Branham in a 1947 meeting later reported that many of his parishioners received "apparent healings." Their Christian faith was severely tested, however, when numerous reports bore witness that the healings had not lasted.[32]

Branham's candid response to temporary healings was that the healings could very well be lost. Healing lasted only as long as unwavering faith endured. The biblical precedent for such a phenomenon, Branham believed, was found in Matthew 14:28-31. Peter's faith enabled him to walk on water, but his surrender to doubt made him sink.[33]

The primary reason that people lost their healing was a misunderstanding of the side effects, according to Branham. He "scientifically" explained that the death of demonic life resulted in a shrinkage of tissues. Consequently, the sick person experienced relief. After about three days, however, swelling occurred. Instead of thinking their healing was lost, the recipients should view this "scientific" process as the surest sign that they were healed. If faith faltered at this time, however, the healing disappeared. Branham reasoned, "Just as sure as faith took it out, unbelief brings it right back again. As faith kills it, unbelief resurrects it."[34]

---

[30]Idem, "Lean Not unto Thy Own Understanding," *TSW* 19:3 (April 1984): 18. See also Branham, "The Uncertain Sound," recorded.

[31]William Branham, "Beginning and Ending of Gentile Dispensation," sermon delivered and recorded in Jeffersonville IN, 9 January 1955.

[32]Carl Dyck, *William Branham: The Man and His Message* (Saskatoon SK Canada: Western Tract Mission, 1984) 13.

[33]"An Interview with William Branham," *TVH* 4 (October 1951): 23.

[34]Branham, *Demonology*, 35. See also Branham, "God Testifies," recorded.

Persons did not have to be a Christian to be healed, according to Branham, but had to become a Christian to remain healed. Moreover, the Christian seeking healing could not evince any doubt. Branham warned individuals not to request healing unless they were willing to promise God a lifelong commitment of service. Healing followed by a loss of faith, Branham announced, eventuated in a person becoming sicker than before the recovery had occurred.[35]

Branham was concerned with those cases in which healing was never achieved nor sustained. Nevertheless, he never doubted his foreordained mission to give the world an unprecedented gift of deliverance. All of the problems were simply the result of a lack of faith on the part of the person desiring healing. This theological safeguard, for Branham and others, was necessary to preserve the belief that Christ's atonement promised healing. Just as some sinners did not exercise faith for salvation of the soul, some persons afflicted with disease did not evince enough faith to claim the salvation of their body.

Any theology of divine healing would not be complete without some explanation of the role of medicine vis à vis the role of faith. In the earliest days of Pentecostalism, medicine was suspect. The recourse to medical treatment manifested a lack of trust in God and was viewed as something contrary to a belief in divine healing. Prudencio Damboriena suggests that current Pentecostals accept the possible use of medicine; nevertheless, believers should seek divine healing first.[36] In essence, Branham's attitude toward medicine was more akin to the earliest Pentecostals.

On occasion Branham praised the work of medical science. Utilizing medical treatment for his family, he asserted that physicians were servants of God. Their power and knowledge were limited, however. Branham suggested that medicine merely kept the body clean while God performed the healing. "There's not one speck of medicine ever did cure any sickness," according to Branham.[37]

The deliverance evangelist argued that the Christian should put his faith in God's ability to heal, regardless of what any doctor might diagnose. Branham bluntly exlaimed, "You may have been through every doctor's office and clinic in the country, but even now whatsoever you ask of God, He will

---

[35]Idem, "The Angel of God," sermon delivered and recorded in Phoenix AZ, 4 March 1948. See also Branham, "Ministry Explained," recorded.

[36]Prudencio Damboriena, *Tongues as of Fire: Pentecostalism in Contemporary Christianity* (Washington: Corpus Books, 1969) 128-29.

[37]Branham, *Demonology*, 33, 92. See also Stadsklev, *William Branham*, 60. Branham used all doctors, including optometrists and dentists.

give it to you."[38] Even if a physician declared that a patient was without hope, Branham considered that diagnosis irrelevant in light of God's promise of healing.[39] Branham bristled at the suggestion that divine healing was fanaticism. He noted that medicine was never defined as fanaticism when a person died from incorrect medical treatment. Indeed, the evangelist retorted that his father died from a dose of medicine.[40]

Branham believed that recourse to medical treatment usually indicated a lack of faith in divine healing. In essence, faith in divine healing was superior to a Christianity that employed medical assistance. Branham related a story about the healing of his wife's tumor that vividly revealed his condescending attitude toward medicine. Branham and his wife decided to delay recourse to surgery while healing was sought through prayer. When the tumor had grown to the size of a grapefruit, however, the decision was made to operate. Branham recalled his extreme disappointment, admitting that "our faith is not sufficient."[41]

Branham regarded his own gift of healing as a major witness to the superiority of divine healing over medical treatment. Through his gift, Branham acknowledged, sicknesses were defeated that physicians had failed even to diagnose.[42] On the one hand, Branham's attitude toward medicine was primarily a condescending acknowledgment of its necessity for persons of insufficient faith. He also evinced, however, an inconsistency of thought and practice. Ironically, Branham insisted that recipients of healing have their healings confirmed by signed doctor's statements.[43] Although divine healing was regarded as superior to medicine, the latter was a useful tool when it confirmed the effectiveness of his ministry.

Undoubtedly, Branham developed some of his theology of healing under the tutelage of the famous deliverance evangelist, F. F. Bosworth.[44]

---

[38]William Branham, "The Supernatural Gospel, Installment II," *TVH* 8 (March 1956): 11.

[39]Idem, "It Becometh Us to Fulfill All Righteousness," *TSW* 15:4 (n.d.): 15.

[40]Idem, "Gifts and Callings Are without Repentance," sermon delivered and recorded in Chicago IL, 4 October 1955.

[41]Idem, "Testimony," *TSW* 17:5 (n.d.): 20. Branham added that a miraculous cure finally took place and no surgery was needed.

[42]Idem, "Experiences # 1," sermon delivered and recorded in Phoenix AZ, 7 December 1947.

[43]Idem, "Calling Jesus on the Scene," *TSW* 17:9 (n.d.): 17.

[44]For example, Bosworth used Heb. 11:1 to say that faith was a sixth sense. Persons seeking healing should believe they have received it, regardless of the contrary evidence of the senses. See F. F. Bosworth, "The Faith That Takes," *TVH* 1 (June 1948): 11-12.

Whatever the source, Branham's views were important. As pacesetter of the revival, he promulgated a theology of healing that influenced significantly the contours of the deliverance movement.

2.

In addition to a theology of healing, Branham had a multifaceted methodology of healing. He was guided by the instructions that he received in the angelic commission. Moreover, other ideas were developed in order to make a Branham service conducive to the achievement of healing; the organization of his revival campaign revolved around the creation of an atmosphere. Branham emphasized early in his career that preaching was not his primary role. Instead, God foreordained him to pray for the sick. Branham attempted, consequently, to avoid personal interviews and to utilize his days in preparatory prayer for the night services. If it were possible, three days of prayer and fasting were undertaken prior to a campaign.

Branham's participation in a revival team facilitated his desire to limit his ministry to healing. Although the members of Branham's team varied from time to time, F. F. Bosworth, W. J. Ern Baxter, and Gordon Lindsay were the most prominent co-workers. Baxter and Bosworth each led morning or afternoon services. These meetings were intended to raise the level of faith among the crowds before Branham spoke at night. Baxter usually fulfilled a preaching role, emphasizing Bible teaching and evangelism. Bosworth offered special instructions for the sick and emphasized the necessity of faith. He often asked God to confirm his messages with two or three faith-inspiring miracles such as the healing of totally deaf ears. Lindsay, the coordinator of the campaigns, often handled the altar call. [45]

In addition to the preparation provided by these co-workers, Lindsay authored a small booklet, *Divine Healing in the Branham Meetings*. This tract offered instructions for persons who sought healing. Different from Branham, Lindsay noted, earlier deliverance evangelists had given a full week of instruction on healing and the necessity of faith. Seldom did they

---

[45]"Rev. and Mrs. F. F. Bosworth Work with Branham Party," *TVH* 1 (May 1948): 1, 5. See also "Branham Meetings in Germany and Switzerland," *Voice* 3 (September 1955): 3-11. See also Gordon Lindsay, *The Gordon Lindsay Story* (Dallas: The Voice of Healing Publishing Co., n.d.) 169. Before joining the Branham team, Bosworth was over seventy years old and had essentially retired from the ministry. "However, after he had been in the Branham meetings," Lindsay wrote, "he received a fresh anointing from the Lord and a renewed vision." See Gordon Lindsay, "The Story of the Great Restoration Revival, Installment II," *WWR* 11 (April 1958): 18.

pray for the sick the first night of their campaigns. Since the demand for Branham's services was so extensive, however, one of his campaigns seldom lasted more than a few days in each city. Consequently, Lindsay's booklet offered some biblical background so that people would not approach the Branham meetings ignorant of their responsibilities of faith in the healing process.[46]

Branham meetings were also geared toward creating the most effective atmosphere for possible healing. The theme of every Branham campaign was "Jesus Christ, the same yesterday, and today, and forever." The keynote song was "Only believe, only believe, all things are possible, only believe." This theme and song provided a positive reinforcement for the audiences to exercise their faith to its fullest potential.[47]

The use of a prayer line was the primary medium for Branham to have contact with the sick. This method had biblical precedent, according to Branham. When Jesus exercised his healing powers, he employed a prayer line in which people walked by him and received healing.[48] Accordingly, Branham instructed people to file into one of two prayer lines. Invalids on crutches and other persons who were able to walk formed the "fast line." Patients in wheelchairs or on stretchers comprised the "slow line." Branham was never satisfied by the confusion of ministering to two lines. After 1949, when the gift of discernment was added to Branham's healing repertoire, the concept of a fast line was disbanded.[49]

Branham considered the prayer line to be the best method for administering the gift of healing to specific individuals. He added one peculiar twist to the mechanics of the line, however. People were instructed

---

[46]Lindsay, *Divine Healing*, 1-3. See also Gordon Lindsay, "An Appraisal of the Branham Campaigns," *TVH* 1 (April 1948):5. Lindsay asserted that Branham prayed victoriously for the sick on the very first night of a campaign. Nevertheless, the sick were admonished to attend all the services. Frequent attendance increased one's level of faith and helped the chances of being healed.

[47]Stadsklev, *William Branham*, 133.

[48]Branham, "Jesus Christ the Same," recorded. Prayer over persons who passed through a healing line was a method employed by healing evangelists, like Charles Cullis and John Alexander Dowie, in the nineteenth-century evangelical healing movement. Early Pentecostal evangelists like Aimee Semple McPherson continued the practice. See Lately Thomas, *Storming Heaven: The Lives and Turmoil of Minnie Kennedy and Aimee Semple McPherson* (New York: William Morrow and Company, Inc., 1970) 20-22. See also Chappel, "Divine," 149-50, 309.

[49]Joel Brinkley, "Many at Easter Vigil in Jeffersonville Hope for Return of Prophet," *The Courier-Journal* (Louisville KY) 12 April 1982, A1:5-6. See also Branham, "God in His People," recorded.

to line up on his right side since that was the side where the angel stood. Under this arrangement, Branham believed, the sick had the additional benefit of passing by the angel.[50]

The primary purpose of the prayer line, F. F. Bosworth contended, was to function as an objective lesson for the people who remained in their seats. Branham insisted that the healing demonstrations indicated God's presence at the meeting. When those seated in the audience witnessed a healing on stage, additional healings could instantaneously occur as the level of faith was raised. This phenomenon justified Branham's method of praying for a limited number of persons each night.[51]

The nature of a Branham meeting was not without its problems. The tension of selecting who would be permitted in the prayer line was especially acute. When Branham first began to conduct healing services, all persons who desired healing were allowed to join in the prayer line. Yet this method was too taxing upon Branham's strength. Moreover, too much confusion and congestion resulted. A decision was made to limit the number of persons in the prayer line; and the idea of prayer cards was conceived. The only persons allowed in the prayer line were those who had obtained prayer cards. One hundred cards were divided among the ministers who sponsored a campaign.

Inequities soon appeared in this method also. Many ministers gave the cards only to their own parishioners. Branham lamented that sometimes only persons from one congregation comprised the prayer line for four or five consecutive nights. Moreover, the crowds swamped Branham team members in an effort to receive one of the lower numbered cards. Even after Branham began varying the numbers that he called in each service, the use of prayer cards was always inadequate. Since the evangelist prayed for such a small number each night, obtaining a card still did not guarantee that a person would receive Branham's personal attention.[52]

---

[50]Stadsklev, *A Prophet,* 84. Pearry Green contended that Branham's right shoulder was lower than his left because the anointing was always on the right where the angel stood. See Pearry Green, *The Acts of the Prophet* (Tucson: Tucson Tabernacle Books, n.d.) 123.

[51]Bosworth, quoted in Gordon Lindsay, *William Branham: A Man Sent from God* (Jeffersonville IN: William Branham, 1950) 178. See also Stadsklev, *William Branham,* 93.

[52]Branham, "God in His People," recorded. See also Branham, "Explaining the Ministry," recorded. See also Stadsklev, *William Branham,* 93. Critics have often charged that deliverance evangelists carefully screened the healing candidates. Consequently, persons with difficult diseases were avoided by the healer. See Damboriena, *Tongues,* 134.

Like the prayer line, Branham believed, the use of prayer cards facilitated the increase of faith levels necessary for healing. Each person was instructed to write the nature of his illness on the card. As he passed through the prayer line, a Branham team member collected the card. When the person had been healed, Gordon Lindsay or another campaign manager told the audience the nature of the illness that was listed; then Branham's diagnosis was confirmed.[53] The obvious implication of this practice was that the audible confirmations, in addition to vindicating Branham, further heightened the audience's faith for additional healings.

Branham did not limit his healing ministry to those persons that attended a campaign. Like Pentecostal deliverance evangelists before him, Branham provided anointed handkerchiefs to the masses who could not attend campaigns. A handkerchief (or ribbon), "prayed over and anointed" by Branham, was sent to anyone, free of charge, who requested it.[54] The sick person was instructed to pin the handkerchief to his clothes at the spot of the disease and pray for healing. Branham espoused that God honored the prayer just as much as he answered the prayers of those who attended the meetings.[55]

The biblical precedent for anointed handkerchiefs came from Paul, according to deliverance evangelists. Handkerchiefs that Paul anointed were carried to the sick, and diseases were cured (Acts 19:12). Paul derived the idea of anointed handkerchiefs, Branham conjectured, from the story of Elisha and the Shunnamite woman (2 Kings 4:8-37). The healing revivalist related how Elisha laid his staff upon the face of the woman's dead child in an attempt to effect a resurrection. Elisha knew that God was present in his ministry, and whatever the prophet touched was divinely blessed. In the same way Paul knew that God was present in his ministry, and whatever he touched was blessed.[56]

Branham never explicitly stated that his handkerchiefs were blessed because he had touched them. In his later years, however, he implied that the handkerchiefs were effective on account of his followers' faith in him. The evangelist prayed over some handkerchiefs: "Now, we know

---

[53]William Branham, "Obey the Voice of the Angel," sermon delivered and recorded in Minneapolis MN, 13 July 1949.

[54]"Untitled Article," *TVH* 1 (February 1949): 3. See also Bloch-Hoell, *Pentecostal Movement*, 151.

[55]Branham, *Footprints*, 15.

[56]Idem, "Resurrection of Lazarus," sermon delivered and recorded in Erie PA, 30 July 1951.

that we're not Saint Paul, but we know that it wasn't Saint Paul, it was the people's faith in him being Your servant. Lord these people wouldn't drive hundreds of miles [to hear Branham in Jeffersonville on a regular basis] if they didn't believe."[57]

Despite all the precautions, many persons left Branham campaigns disappointed. The Branham team's conviction that all could receive deliverance, whether in the prayer line or seated in the crowd, often did not bear fruit. Critics charged that wheelchair patients were conspicuously avoided.[58] Moreover, the success ratio of the anointed handkerchiefs was impossible to estimate. Nevertheless, the drawing power of Branham's healing ministry sustained his popularity throughout the peak revival years of the 1950s.

3.

The Branham team was concerned with organizational techniques in order to facilitate the proper atmosphere for healing. The role of the angel, and the use of the two sign-gifts, however, were more essential ingredients in Branham's healing methodology. Throughout the peak years of success, Branham manifested an extreme dependence upon the angel's presence. In his description of Branham's ministry, F. F. Bosworth revealed that

> Branham does not begin to pray for the healing of the afflicted in body in the healing line each night, until God anoints him for the operation of the gift, and until he is conscious of the presence of the Angel with him on the platform. Without this consciousness, he seems to be perfectly helpless.
>
> ....
>
> When he is conscious of the angel's presence, he seems to break through the veil of the flesh into the world of the spirit, to be struck through and through with a sense of the unseen.[59]

A biblical justification for the existence of angels dominated Branham's earliest campaign messages. The evangelist disagreed with the suggestion that the arrival of the Holy Spirit in the early church obviated the need for angels. He responded that a ministry of angels was still present after the Holy Spirit had come at Pentecost. He noted, for ex-

---

[57]William Branham, "Proving His Word," *TSW* 9:6 (n.d.): 46.

[58]Hollenweger affirmed, "by contrast to what he [Branham] claimed, only a small percentage of those who sought healing were in fact healed." See Walter J. Hollenweger, *The Pentecostals*, trans. R. A. Wilson (London: S. C. M. Press, 1972) 355.

[59]Bosworth, quoted in Lindsay, *Branham*, 169, 173.

ample, that a Spirit-filled Peter was visited in jail by an angel (Acts 12:7). Furthermore, the appearance of angels in the Pentecostal return to gospel primitivism was to be expected. Branham concluded:

Before any great event, God always forewarns us. In the Ante-deluvian Dispensation, He sent Noah. Before the close of the next dispensation, He sent Jesus. We are at the end of another 2000 years. Every 2000 years something tremendous happens. . . . Notice, when God makes these announcements, He usually sends angels to do the announcing. [60]

One element of curiosity aroused by Branham's supernatural experience was the identity of the angel. When asked to name the angel, Branham retorted, "You're so scared you don't know what to say. He does the talking. You listen."[61] On different occasions, however, Branham conjectured that the angel might have been simply a minor angel, or the angel at the pool of Bethesda (John 5:1-18).[62]

Most important to Branham's "angelology" was the assertion that his angel performed all the healings. To justify this claim, he cited the biblical story of the healing at the pool of Bethesda. The first sick person to enter the pool was healed, Branham noted, because an angel had provided the water with healing virtue (John 5:4).[63]

In light of the angel's role in the healing process, Branham described his own function. He declared: "When the children of Israel were down in Egypt crying for a deliverer, God sent his angel to Moses. Moses had nothing to do with it. . . . It was God's angel that did the work, performed the miracles. Moses was a mouthpiece for the angel of God; and that is all I am today. . . . Just a mouthpiece for the angel."[64] Branham elaborated that under the anointing his words were not his own. He was simply speaking the words of the angel.[65] In essence, Branham functioned in a "prophetic" role by delivering divine messages. Indeed, in a 1951 sermon Branham made a rare acknowledgment of his "prophetic" identity. He exclaimed:

---

[60]William Branham, "The Supernatural Gospel," *TVH* 8 (February 1956): 6.

[61]Ibid.

[62]William Branham, "Believest Thou This?" *TVH* 1 (August 1948): 1. See also Branham, "For Him," recorded.

[63]Idem, "Only One True Living Church," sermon delivered and recorded in Erie PA, 27 July 1951.

[64]Idem, "How the Gift Came to Me," *TVH* 1 (April 1948): 8.

[65]Idem, "Expectations," sermon delivered and recorded in New York NY, 5 April 1950.

Now, I'm just your brother by the grace of God. But when the Angel of the Lord moves down, it becomes then a Voice of God to you. Maybe if I offended you by saying that, forgive me, but I felt that might be resented. But I am God's Voice to you. See, I say that again, that time was under inspiration. See? . . . Now, see, I can say nothing in myself. But what He shows me, I say it, and you believe it and watch what happens.[66]

On a few occasions, witnesses affirmed that they had actually seen the angel standing beside the deliverance evangelist. The description given always matched the portrait that Branham painted in the story of his commission.[67] The majority of witnesses, however, experienced the angel's presence as a heavenly light. F. F. Bosworth, reporting on a meeting of the 1951 South African campaign, wrote that the angel appeared throughout the crowd. A supernatural light rested over the head of each person whose faith had reached the level necessary for healing. While under the anointing, Branham recognized the light. Immediately thereafter, he pronounced healing upon the persons that the angel had singled out.[68]

Branham most often referred to the angelic light as the biblical pillar of fire. Utilizing his favorite biblical idea of "Jesus Christ, the same yesterday, and today, and forever," the evangelist averred that Jesus Christ had always appeared in the form of a light/pillar of fire. He appeared to Moses, led the Hebrews in the wilderness and blinded Paul on the Damascus Road in the form of a light. In the twentieth century, Branham announced, Christ has appeared as the same pillar of fire in the Branham campaigns.[69]

In the later years of his ministry, Branham rarely spoke of his manlike angel. Continuous references, however, were made to the halo photograph from the 1950 Houston debate. The halo was a modern manifestation of the pillar of fire, according to Branham.[70] Perhaps references to the angel were rare as the subject became increasingly controver-

---

[66]Idem, *Footprints*, 214.

[67]Stadsklev, *William Branham*, 88, 109. Billy Paul Branham testified that he saw the angel in Vandalia IL, in 1949. See Billy Paul Branham, "I Am a Witness," eulogy delivered and recorded in Phoenix AZ, 10 December 1966.

[68]F. F. Bosworth, "The Miracle-Packed Revival in South Africa," *HOF* 32 (May 1964): 3. Most revival participants never saw the light.

[69]Branham, *Footprints*, 97.

[70]Idem, *An Exposition of the Book of Hebrews* (Jeffersonville IN: Spoken Word Publications, 1972) 35, 170.

sial.[71] More likely, however, Branham viewed the photograph as tangible evidence of his supernatural oriented ministry.

The healing revivalist interchangeably referred to his supernatural bodyguard as an angel, or Jesus Christ in the form of the pillar of fire. On one occasion, he even identified the "Circle of Light" as the Holy Spirit.[72] Regardless of the confusing references and manifold modes of manifestation, Branham firmly believed that God was with him during the healing process.

The presence of the angel enabled Branham to perform his role in the healing process. The primary feature of that role was the utilization of two signs—the detection of disease by a vibration of the left hand, and the discernment of the secrets of a person's heart.

The first to be manifested after the angelic commission was the vibration of the left hand. Branham captivated crowds across the country with this unique and amazing phenomenon. He was "the self-styled healer," according to *Time* magazine.[73]

The operation of the gift occurred after the angel anointed Branham. The deliverance evangelist grasped the right hand of the individual with his left hand. Immediately, Branham's hand experienced various vibrations and swelling. "Every disease had a peculiar pulsation of its own," Gordon Lindsay wrote, "and because of this, Brother Branham is able to diagnose the different types of disease."[74] F. F. Bosworth elaborated further:

> When the afflicting spirit comes into contact with the gift it sets up such a physical commotion that it becomes visible on Brother Branham's hand, and so real that it will stop his wristwatch instantly. This feels to Brother Branham like taking hold of a live wire with too much electric current in it. When the oppressing spirit is cast out in Jesus' Name, you can see Brother Branham's red and swollen hand return to its normal condition. If the affliction is not a germ disease, then God always reveals the affliction to Brother Branham by the Spirit.[75]

---

[71]Statement by Robert Moore, former follower of Branham, telephone interview, Phoenix AZ, 9 September 1984.

[72]William Branham, "Convinced Then Concerned," *TSW* 3:3 (n.d.): 30.

[73]"Self-styled Healer in Vandalia, Ill.," *Time* 50 (14 July 1947):20.

[74]Gordon Lindsay, "The Ministry of Angels and the Appearance of the Angel to William Branham," *TVH* 1 (May 1948): 12.

[75]Bosworth, quoted in Lindsay, *Branham*, 171.

In defense of his gift, Branham emphasized that his hand possessed no power to heal. He reiterated that the only healer was Jesus Christ. The purpose of the sign was to raise faith in the observers so that deliverance could occur. Moreover, Branham confirmed Bosworth's analysis that the sign worked only with "germ diseases," and not with ailments such as crippled body parts.[76]

Gordon Lindsay, having witnessed many demonstrations of the sign, was "impressed by the remarkable accuracy of the diagnosis."[77] Though Bosworth described the sign as "perfectly miraculous," Branham admitted otherwise.[78] After the second sign of discernment appeared, Branham still continued to use the vibrating hand to detect diseases. He readily acknowledged that the latter method was not perfect, however. Diagnoses were often guesses; for example, the vibrations for "female trouble" and cancer were especially difficult to distinguish. As Branham's ministry progressed, the use of the first sign became increasingly rare. An almost exclusive dependence upon the gift of discernment developed.[79] According to the angelic commission, if the first sign failed to raise totally the people's faith, a second sign would be provided.

The appearance of the second sign came in 1949 after Branham's brief retirement from healing revivalism. In dramatic style Branham described the sign's emergence at a campaign in Saskatchewan, Canada:

> I looked at that woman, and she was standing there, her regular size, and seen her get real little and start going back. Now you'll hear that spoke right here. And I seen a little bitty girl standing way down where she went, down to a little bitty girl about twelve years old. And I seen her sitting by a desk. I said, "Something's happened, friend. I see a little girl, that woman left me."
>
> I said, "I see a little—a little girl. She's sitting in a room, she . . . a schoolroom. She's hitting her pencil, no it's a pen. Oh," I said, "I—I see it fly. It struck her in the eye."
>
> And the woman begin to screaming. It left off. She said, "Brother Branham, that was me. I'm blind in my right eye." She said, "the pen struck."

---

[76]William Branham, "The Angel and Three Pulls," sermon delivered and recorded in Phoenix AZ, 14 April 1951.

[77]Lindsay, "The Ministry of Angels," 12.

[78]Bosworth, quoted in Lindsay, *Branham*, 170.

[79]Branham, *Footprints*, 188. For the use of the vibrating hand near the end of Branham's ministry, see William Branham, "His Unfailing Words of Promise," *TSW* 15:3 (n.d.):24.

After Branham revealed other events of the woman's past, she was healed. Subsequently, Branham utilized this new gift throughout the rest of his life.[80]

The essence of the sign was the discernment of the secrets of the heart. The gift had no limitations, Branham believed. He constantly asserted that he had no previous knowledge of the persons in the prayer line. They were complete strangers to him. Yet, Branham told these strangers their names and addresses. He often revealed to the sick, Bosworth reported, "how many times they had been operated upon, even describing the surgeons and quoting their very words."[81] The decisive element of the sign was the revealing of a person's past unconfessed sins. Branham warned the audience that he was not responsible for the revelation of embarrassing past deeds. Nevertheless, the evangelist usually pushed away the microphone so the healing candidate was not unmercifully exposed before the crowd. When a person acknowledged and promised to forsake his sin, Bosworth noted, healing often eventuated before Branham had time to pray the intercessory prayer of faith.[82]

Branham's second sign, supporters believed, was the operation of two spiritual gifts—the word of knowledge and the discerning of spirits. Branham exclaimed, however, that his gift was distinct from the spiritual gifts to which all Christians had access. He identified his sign with the gift of discernment practiced by Jesus. During his commission, Branham later revealed, the angel had reminded him about Jesus' use of discernment upon Nathaniel. According to Branham, Jesus discerned the thoughts of Nathaniel and knew his character before the two had ever met (John 1:48).[83] Branham elaborated that Jesus used the gift of discernment to reveal the sins of the immoral and often-married Samaritan woman (John 4:7-30). Branham's gift of discernment, the healing revivalist concluded, was another manifestation of Hebrews 13:8, "Jesus Christ, the same yesterday, and today, and forever."[84] Indeed, the second sign was "pro-

---

[80]Branham, *Footprints*, 188-90.

[81]"Branham Meetings in Germany and Switzerland," *Voice* 3 (September 1955): 4.

[82]Bosworth, quoted in Lindsay, *Branham*, 171. See also William Branham, "The Two Signs Explained," sermon delivered and recorded in Dallas TX, 28 October 1949.

[83]William Branham, "Get the People to Believe," sermon delivered and recorded in Hammond IN, 17 July 1952.

[84]"An Interview with William Branham," 8. See also William Branham, "Three Witnesses," sermon delivered and recorded in Erie PA, 28 July 1951.

phetic." "You can be sure He knows what you are thinking about and He can reveal those thoughts through His servant," Branham proclaimed.[85]

The deliverance evangelist made a further unique distinction between his revelatory second sign, and spiritual gifts available to all Christians. In a 1951 sermon he cited Romans 11:29, "Gifts and callings are without repentance," and his concomitant exposition that "prophetic gifts is [sic] ordained before the foundation of the world to come forward." Branham contended that his unique "prophetic" gift was possessed by just one person in a generation. Commenting on the possibility that another minister could equally utilize the second sign, Branham bluntly affirmed, "That'll never be until I die."[86]

The implementation of the second sign was greeted with amazement and adulation by the crowds. Moreover, Branham's colleagues in the healing revival were greatly impressed. Unlike the first sign, Branham maintained that the second sign never failed. Gordon Lindsay affirmed that the gift was "practically infallible."[87] The Pentecostal historian, W. J. Hollenweger, who served as an interpreter for some of Branham's overseas meetings, stated that "he was not aware of any case in which he [Branham] was mistaken in the often detailed statements he made."[88] Even the cautious Donald Gee admitted "in many cases this was remarkably accurate."[89] F. F. Bosworth and Len Jones, the Australian Pentecostal leader, were the most adulatory in asserting the 100% accuracy of Branham's gift. Bosworth said that such a miraculous phenomenon had not been witnessed to the same extent for nineteen centuries. Moreover, the gift made Branham "a channel for more than the mere gift of healing; he is also a Seer as were the Old Testament Prophets."[90] Jones placed Branham in a class by himself. "This man will never be appreciated until after he is gone," Jones suggested, "and then maybe he will be spoken of with hushed breath."[91] Undoubtedly, the use of the second sign furthered immensely the growing Branham legend.

---

[85]Stadsklev, A Prophet, 79.

[86]Branham, "Three Witnesses," recorded. See also Robert Moore, Quotations of William M. Branham (n.p., n.d.) 202.

[87]Gordon Lindsay, "William Branham as I Knew Him," TVH 18 (February 1966): 11.

[88]Hollenweger, Pentecostals, 354.

[89]Donald Gee, Wind and Flame, rev. ed. (Croydon England: Heath Press, Ltd., 1967) 242.

[90]Bosworth, quoted in Lindsay, Branham, 172.

[91]Len J. Jones, "I Attend Another Branham Meeting," HOF 26 (February 1959): 17.

Branham was acknowledged as a seer because the contents of the discernment were given to him by divinely inspired vision. Branham advocated that God gave him the visionary experiences of his childhood and young adult life in order to prepare for their use in the healing ministry. In a subtle acknowledgment that other deliverance evangelists were surpassing his own popularity, Branham told an audience in 1956 that a sophisticated America responded better to an "educated" minister like Oral Roberts. In contrast, Branham had only a seventh-grade education. The uneducated African natives were more willing to believe in the supernatural, according to Branham. He concluded that God had negated his educational shortcomings with the provision of visionary experiences. His dependence upon visions, Branham asserted, was divinely foreordained.[92]

Branham described the mechanics of a vision in vivid terms. He declared:

> You're conscious that your [sic] standing here, and yet you're 40 years back in somebody's life watching what they are doing. The only thing that I say is just what I'm looking at; and then when I come to myself I realize that I said something, but many times I don't know what I said. The way I get it is these boys; them sitting down here with tape recorders; they play it back over for me. That's how I pick it up. So it isn't myself at all.[93]

In this description, Branham strangely omitted his dependence upon the angel. Nevertheless, discernment by way of vision was infallible. Branham was simply a mouthpiece acting out the "foreordained" events that God had revealed to him.[94] Consequently the evangelist had an indomitable faith in visions. He often told sick persons to pray that God would grant him a vision concerning them.[95] He further contended that the Holy Spirit would give visions to sick persons who were totally unaware of his

---

[92]William Branham, "Visions and Prophecy," *TSW* 2:9 (n.d.): 6. Ironically, Branham never made another campaign tour of Africa.

[93]Ibid., 4.

[94]William Branham, "Testimony and Inside Life," sermon delivered and recorded in Cleveland OH, 23 August 1950. Branham asserted that his visionary discernment was another manifestation of Heb. 13:8. He primarily cited John 5:19, "the Son can do nothing of himself, but what he seeth the Father do," as proof that Jesus healed solely by vision. See Branham, "Jesus Christ the Same," recorded.

[95]Lindsay, *Branham*, 197.

ministry. These usually included instructions on how to find a William Branham if healing was desired.[96]

The role of mysticism in Branham's life was not simply limited to providing revelation that ignited faith for healing. Visions sometimes revealed the imminent death of an individual. One woman "dropped dead" in a meeting after hearing a vision of death, according to Branham.[97] Gordon Lindsay asserted that Branham evinced an extrasensory perception in mundane matters. On one occasion, Branham arrived in a city and checked into the correct motel without previous knowledge of where lodging reservations had been made. His explanation was simply, "I just seemed to know."[98]

As Branham's ministry struggled and became more radical in the late 1950s and early 1960s, he added the interpretation of dreams to the mystic repertoire. The interpretations were also considered infallible since they were seen by vision. Moreover, after hearing a person's dream, Branham filled in the gaps that the dreamer had forgotten. Citing the example of Nebuchadnezzar, he responded with a sense of justification: "If you can't tell me what I dreamed, then how would I know you got the interpretation of it?"[99]

The "prophetic" nature of Branham's second sign was especially evident in his function as a divine spokesman. As God's messenger, he pronounced infallible visions and dreams. These declarations were usually accompanied by the Old Testament prophetic formula, "Thus Saith the Lord." On one occasion, Branham told a woman that her faith had effected the healing of her sick infant. Branham exclaimed, "Thus Saith the Lord, your baby shall live and not die."[100]

The deliverance evangelist refrained from calling himself a prophet. Nevertheless, he argued: "The only person that has the right to say 'Thus Saith the Lord' is a vindicated prophet . . . [Isaiah and Jeremiah] were

[96]Branham, "Expectations," recorded.

[97]Idem, "The Authority of God's Word," sermon delivered and recorded in Wood River IL, 17 February 1954.

[98]Lindsay, *Branham*, 139.

[99]William Branham, "Sirs, Is This the Time?," *TSW* 2:11 (Rpt., 1983): 8. Branham encouraged his followers to dream in fulfillment of Joel's prophecy (2:28-32). They might not have the subconscious ability to experience visions; nevertheless, they could experience a dream that is a vision if interpreted. See William Branham, *The Revelation of the Seven Seals* (Tucson: Spoken Word Publications, 1967) 347.

[100]Idem, "It Shall Be Even as It Was Told Me," sermon delivered and recorded in Cleveland OH, 18 August 1950.

prophets, foreordained and borned [sic] in the world to be prophets and they forsaw the thing by vision and then said 'Thus Saith the Lord' for the Lord had already said it."[101] Without a doubt, Branham regarded his use of "Thus Saith the Lord" as "prophetic." Indeed, in his later radical years, he readily acknowledged that the use of "Thus Saith the Lord" was a "prophecy."[102]

This unique role of the evangelist as prophet was the final, and ultimately the most significant, aspect of Branham's healing methodology. In his negative assessment of faith healing, Theodore Graebner asserted that when faith healers use the term faith, "it amounts to the belief that God is able to perform a miraculous cure through this particular healer. A mental attitude of trust in the healer's power, confidence in his gift to heal disease by prayer, is the 'faith' demanded of the patient."[103] Branham was a perfect illustration of Graebner's contention. Moreover, Branham's primary and unique thrust was that belief in him as a prophet was the key to healing.

Branham repudiated the suggestion that he possessed any healing power. The presence of Jesus Christ in the angel was the healing agent. The vibration of the left hand and the visionary discernment were simply vehicles to raise the faith of the people. According to the commission, Branham's responsibility was to pray for the sick. Consequently, Branham often asked the sick whether they believed in Jesus Christ. When an affirmative answer was given, Branham pronounced the person well.[104]

Branham's primary thrust, however, was that belief in him and his message was the key to healing. He was instructed, according to the angelic commission, "IF YOU WILL BE SINCERE, AND CAN GET THE PEOPLE TO BELIEVE YOU, NOTHING SHALL STAND BEFORE YOUR PRAYER, NOT EVEN CANCER."[105] For healing to occur, the person had to affirm that God had given Branham a special gift of healing. Specifically, faith had to be exhibited that the angelic commission was real and the use of the two signs was ordained by God. Branham constantly reiterated this requirement:

---

[101]Idem, "Expectations," recorded.

[102]Idem, "Possessing," 20.

[103]Theodore Graebner, *Faith Healing: A Study of Its Methods and an Appraisal of Its Claims* (St. Louis: Concordia Publishing House, n.d.) 19.

[104]William Branham, "God's Way That's Been Made for Us," sermon delivered and recorded in Jeffersonville IN, 10 January 1950. See also Branham, "The Authority," recorded.

[105]Lindsay, *Branham*, 77.

Moses was a prophet sent of God. He had two signs to show he had God's message. When he performed those two signs the people believed him. . . . If I can perform the signs that God's [*sic*] promised me to do then you all ought to believe with all your heart. [106]

I want you to believe me with all your heart. . . . that is the only way I can help you . . . Believe they [Father, Son, Holy Spirit] have sent me for this purpose. Now you could be a renown [*sic*] Christian and fail to believe what I've told you to be the truth and you would never be able to reap a bit of benefit from it. [107]

I ask you in the name of the Lord Jesus to believe that [the angelic commission to pray for the sick] and you shall be made well. [108]

If the sick affirmed Branham's testimony, they were in a position to believe that he could intercede with God for their healing. The deliverance evangelist often queried:

If you'll accept it and accept my word and believe that I have told you what God has said in my heart, you'll get well. [109] Do you believe if I will ask Jesus for you to get well. . . . you know you will. [110]

Ultimately, the gift of healing was a divine vindication of Branham's "prophetic" identity. He demanded an affirmative assent to his identity as God's "servant/prophet." To the family members of Betty Daugherty, the first recipient of Branham's gift, the question was posed, "Do you believe I am God's servant? . . . Then do as I tell you doubting nothing."[111] For the duration of his ministry, Branham bluntly questioned candidates in the prayer lines:

Sir, do you believe me? Do you accept me as God's servant? Do you believe that I am his prophet that was sent here for your purpose that you might be healed, and will you obey what I tell you to do? . . . You have arthritis . . . jump up like this on the platform like this. You're healed my brother. [112]

---

[106]Branham, "Expectations," recorded.

[107]Idem, "Obey," recorded.

[108]Moore, *Quotations*, A7.

[109]William Branham, "Believe Ye That I Am Able to Do This?," sermon delivered and recorded in Cleveland OH, 20 August 1950.

[110]Idem, "I Was Not Disobedient to the Heavenly Vision," sermon delivered and recorded in Zion IL, 18 July 1949.

[111]Lindsay, *Branham*, 85.

[112]Branham, "Expectations," recorded.

Gentleman sitting right there, you with the brown shirt on, you have a back trouble don't you? Is that right? Do you believe me as God's prophet? Would you obey me as God's prophet? Would you obey what I told you to do? Stand on your feet and be healed then. Jesus Christ makes you well. Amen. God bless you.[113]

What about you lady sitting there, do you believe with all your heart? Do you believe God sent me as his servant? Do you believe I'm his prophet sitting here? . . . If I tell you something will you believe it? Jesus Christ just healed you of that tumor. Go home and pass it in the name of the Lord Jesus Christ.[114]

Without believing that Branham was a prophet commissioned to bring the gift of healing to the world, a person could not claim the promise of physical wholeness. In essence, faith was defined as belief in Jesus Christ as Savior and healer, and as belief in Branham as the prophet who mediated the healing.

Until the twilight of his ministry, Branham consistently denied that he was a prophet. When informed that he claimed the identity of a prophet while under the anointing, Branham responded:

You've heard me never as far as speaking I'd say, "God made me His prophet." I've heard people say on tape they picked it up when the inspiration was on, but that was him speaking, not me, see. Better for him to tell you that than for me to tell you that. See? More you can believe him, you got a right to doubt me . . . don't even cut me into it. It's Jesus Christ, the Son of God. Just look to him. Some people say, "Oh, if I could just go make it up on the platform and He'd pray for me" . . . that don't have much to do with it. It's not up to me, it's up to him.[115]

Branham's sincerity and humility made him emphasize the centrality of Jesus Christ in the healing process. Branham's role was secondary; but the evidence demonstrates that it was still necessary. Faith was insufficient without belief in Christ *and* Branham. Furthermore, Branham's humble disclaimer regarding his role in the healing process subtly acknowledged a "prophetic" identity. To speak God's words under the anointing was the central element of Branham's conception of a prophet with "Thus Saith the Lord." Moreover, to claim the identity of a prophet

---

[113]Idem, "Believe Ye," recorded.

[114]Idem, "The Second Miracle," sermon delivered and recorded in Toledo OH, 21 July 1951.

[115]Idem, "Gifts," recorded.

only under the anointing was greater proof for his followers. Unmistakably, they believed, the confirmation was coming from God.[116]

Branham's acknowledgment of a "prophetic" consciousness was also manifested indirectly. Often he challenged persons to brand him as a false prophet. In one instance, he boldly informed an audience that sixty to eighty percent of them would be healed. If not, they could disregard him as a false prophet.[117] Moreover, Branham often compared the works of God's Spirit in his ministry to the presence of the Spirit in the Old Testament prophets. Relating the story of the resurrection in Finland, Branham commented, "It was not me, your brother, but the Spirit of God. The same Spirit that was upon Elisha . . . is the same Spirit that is moving the world today. It sees, foretells. You who have been in meetings know this to be true."[118]

The most unique method of indirectly claiming the identity of a prophet was Branham's bodeful warnings about respecting the message of God's servants. Branham often related morbid stories about people having accidents, contracting diseases, or dying after they had criticized divine healing or other aspects of the Pentecostal experience. A garage owner, for example, once told Branham to keep his "fanatical religion" at home. Immediately thereafter, the owner's feet and ankles were crushed by a truck backing out of the garage.[119] On another occasion, a woman scornfully declared that "if my cow got that kind of religion Billy's got, I'd kill the cow."[120] According to Branham, she died within two hours after making the blasphemous statement. Indeed, none were spared God's wrath. A minister who criticized Branham's use of the vibrating hand—the deliverance evangelist averred—immediately found his hand paralyzed and "spotted like leprosy."[121]

Branham contended that such fateful circumstances were a result of disrespect for the gospel, rather than any criticism toward him.[122] Nevertheless, the implication was that such events occurred because God's anointed spokesman had been ridiculed or disobeyed. Describing

[116]Statement by Robert Moore.

[117]Branham, "Expectations," recorded.

[118]Stadsklev, *A Prophet*, 77.

[119]Lindsay, *Branham*, 184.

[120]Branham, *Footprints*, 127.

[121]Idem, "Faith in the Son of God," sermon delivered and recorded in Hammond IN, 15 July 1952.

[122]Idem, *Footprints*, 71.

a critic who classified him with sorcery, Branham retorted "that whoever speaks against the Holy Spirit can't be forgiven in this world or world to come."[123] One of Branham's supporters, Julius Stadsklev, wrote that "while Brother Branham is under the anointing, it is very important that one does exactly as he requests. His words are not his own words, but the words of the Holy Spirit."[124] Stadsklev confirmed the dire consequences of disobeying Branham. A woman who was healed of cancer promised Branham that she would be baptized. After missing her church's next baptismal service, the woman died the following week, according to Stadsklev.

Branham, the anointed healer and Spirit's mouthpiece, demonstrated by implication his "prophetic" consciousness. As the "prophetic" identity became more pronounced in the 1960s, Branham preached a sermon about respecting God's messengers. He emphasized that God was treated with disrespect when the biblical prophets were criticized. In this context, Branham recalled the fateful consequences of those who had ridiculed or rejected him.[125] Indeed, a theme still emphasized among Branham's "Message" believers today is "don't criticize God's anointed."[126]

The maturation of a "prophetic" consciousness was undoubtedly facilitated by the blandishments of Branham's colleagues and supporters. Branham was constantly hailed as a prophet for his ministry of healing. Gordon Lindsay and Jack Moore regarded Branham as a prophet. F. F. Bosworth emphasized that the healing revivalist was a seer like the Old Testament prophets.[127] Joseph Mattsson-Boze declared, "This man is indeed God's vessel and God's prophet for our time."[128] Even the book written about the 1951 South African campaign was entitled *William Branham: A Prophet Visits South Africa*. The praise afforded Branham especially extended to the masses. Congressman Upshaw, after being healed, proclaimed Branham to be "God's Humble Bible Prophet."[129]

---

[123]Idem, "Faith in the Son of God," recorded.

[124]Stadsklev, *William Branham*, 101.

[125]William Branham, "Respects," *TSW* 13:4 (n.d.): 30-31.

[126]Billy Paul Branham, "Personal Testimony," sermon delivered and recorded in Harding AR, 23 June 1984.

[127]Lindsay, *Branham*, 11, 102, 172.

[128]Joseph D. Mattsson-Boze, "Branham-Baxter Campaign in Chicago," *HOF* 18 (October 1953): 5.

[129]William D. Upshaw, *I Am Standing on the Promises* (n.p., n.d.) 3.

Moreover, the members of the Branham Tabernacle exclaimed in unison: "We the people at Jeffersonville believe that William Branham is a prophet sent of God."[130]

The obvious conclusion is that Branham's healing ministry was motivated by his "prophetic" identity during the healing process. Indirectly, he challenged critics to brand him as a false prophet; he implied that their ridicule against God's servant and His message would bring tragedy. Moreover, Branham could have hardly eschewed the confirmations of the "prophetic" identity showered upon him by his peers.

* * * * *

Branham's theology of healing was compatible with a ministry of deliverance. His extensive biblicism demanded an emphasis on the supernatural. Specifically, his theology was based upon a hermeneutic that made physical healing the focus of the ministry of Jesus Christ. A dual atonement—salvation for the soul and healing for the body—was offered to every believer. "Jesus Christ, the same yesterday, and today, and forever," (Heb. 13:8) became the justification for a miraculous perspective to contemporary Christianity. God desired, according to Branham, physical deliverance for all.

Like any deliverance evangelist, Branham emphasized the interdependence of sin, sickness, and the demonic. He represented the extreme view that Satan was the author of all sickness. Consequently, a way of escape was needed; and faith was that way.

Faith was the key to any deliverance evangelist's theology of healing. Any disease could be conquered by the sixth sense of faith. God was obligated, Branham argued, to grant deliverance when faith was present. Branham never clearly defined the amount of faith necessary for healing. Sufficient faith was simply a dogmatic and unwavering conviction that God was going to provide healing. Of course, such an unrealistic and nebulous assertion facilitated the theological safeguard that unsuccessful healing signaled a lack of faith. Indeed, Branham emphasized divine healing so adamantly that recourse to medical treatment usually indicated a lack of faith.

Like his theology of healing, Branham's methodology of ministering deliverance was immersed in the supernatural. The existence of a personal angel, the manifestation of the two signs, the dependence upon revelatory dreams and visions all bespoke a miracle-oriented ministry.

---

[130]Lindsay, *Branham*, 81.

The unique perspective of Branham's ministry of healing was found in his "prophetic" identity. Branham considered himself a prophet who had been chosen by God to bring a message of healing to the masses. Such a supernatural ministry would prepare the people for Christ's second coming.

Branham believed that his gift of visionary discernment was a modern manifestation of Jesus' healing method, fulfilling Hebrews 13:8, "Jesus Christ the same yesterday, and today, and forever." Branham contended that his gift was foreordained by God. Moreover, he alone was given the gift in his generation.

The "prophetic" identity was especially clear when Branham functioned as a visionary seer. The visions were infallible, he declared, since they were of divine origin. Espousing a mechanical theory of inspiration, Branham said that he was a mouthpiece for the angel. He was simply acting out the drama seen in the vision; so Branham pronounced healings with a declaration reserved only for prophets—"Thus Saith the Lord."

Branham argued that, under the anointing, he was God's voice to the people. Like Moses, he spoke only the words of the angel. Healing was possible for the afflicted since God was speaking through his prophet. In essence, Branham defined his "prophetic" identity in terms of being a seer. God revealed the thoughts of the people to his prophet; and he subsequently spoke infallibly God's words to the audience. Such a process raised faith, and deliverance occurred. Undergirded by this "prophetic" understanding of his role in the healing process, Branham made the sick answer affirmatively the question, "Do you believe me to be God's prophet?" For healing to occur they had to believe Branham's angelic commission was true. Faith had to be confessed in Christ the healer, and in Branham the prophet who mediated that deliverance.

Branham's ministry of deliverance was often ridiculed by secular newspapers and skeptics of healing revivalism. Critics variously accused him of mental telepathy, fortune-telling, and spiritualism. In addition, the gift of discernment was associated with an occult angel.[131] Branham constantly rebuked these accusations and scornfully retorted, "if they called Jesus, the master of seers, Beelzebub, a spiritualist, how much more will they call minor seers."[132]

---

[131]Statement by Charles Farah, professor of Systematic Theology, Oral Roberts University, personal interview, Tulsa OK, 5 April 1984. See also Branham, *Demonology*, 15. Gordon Lindsay defined spiritualism as a Satanic phenomenon which "pretends to reveal hidden things in a person's life." See "An Interview with William Branham," 8.

[132]Branham, "Only One," recorded. For a negative critique of the validity of healings, see Damboriena, *Tongues*, 137-38.

Some devotees of healing revivalism also pondered a possible link between Branham's ministry and spiritualism.[133] What troubled most observers was the strange fact that Branham's physical strength weakened rapidly when the anointing came upon him. He lamented, "one vision or one case of healing takes more out of me than eight hours of preaching. It just tears the life out of you."[134] This weakening phenomenon was the main reason that Branham ministered to a very limited number during a service. Indeed, Branham often had to be carried off the platform by his son at the conclusion of a few healings. Sometimes it would take two or three hours for him to regain his consciousness.[135]

Branham admitted that he did not have a full explanation of the weakening phenomenon. In one instance he declared that the presence of the angel on the platform almost paralyzed him and resulted in his loss of strength.[136] Moreover, Branham cited biblical precedents in his defense. The most important passage was the story of the woman who touched the hem of Jesus' garment for healing. Branham interpreted Jesus' response to the woman's actions, "Somebody hath touched me, for I perceive that virtue is gone out of me," (Luke 8:46) as an indication that Jesus was weakened during the healing process.[137]

Despite this biblical justification, Branham was troubled about the inability to sustain his strength while under the anointing. He was annoyed that the masses clamored for him to minister healing to more persons as Oral Roberts did. Branham constantly prayed for more endurance. Yet, he also questioned whether he was being completely obedient to the angelic commission. By allowing the visions to dominate the healing services, he had hindered the central thrust of his commission—to pray for the sick. Therefore, Branham decided in 1954 to deemphasize the use of visions.[138]

At the same time that Branham was berating himself for not simply praying for the sick, he evinced a desire to preach more. Branham bemoaned the fact that, even if he offered a "mass prayer" for the crowds, they "don't feel they've been prayed for if not given discernment to find

---

[133]Statement by Howard Ervin, professor of Old Testament, Oral Roberts University, personal interview, 5 April 1984.

[134]Branham, "Resurrection of Lazarus," recorded.

[135]Idem, "Expectations," recorded.

[136]Idem, Footprints, 74.

[137]Idem, "Then Jesus Came," HOF 29 (December 1961): 5.

[138]Idem, "Get the People," recorded. See also Moore, Quotations, 15.

things."[139] Branham reasoned: "I believe if maybe I could preach . . if I could get the people to see that they got to absolutely come clean before God, then I believe I'd have the authority by Jesus Christ to break the power of any demon there is . . . There's something I'm studying on. I want you to pray for me."[140] By raising the faith of the audiences through preaching, Branham believed that simple prayer for the sick would effect successful healings, and his physically exhausting visions could be avoided.

Instead of diminishing, however, the visions became more grandiose with Branham's increasing emphasis on preaching and teaching. Despite the contention that more preaching would facilitate additional healings, the seeds had been planted for preaching to become the primary medium for Branham's controversial, "prophetic," doctrinal revelations. Having just returned from overseas in 1954, Branham declared:

> I'll lay aside the healing services, being first, for awhile, and preach the gospel. . . . The first thing I had to do with the divine gift was win the hearts of the people. If I haven't got their hearts they wouldn't listen. Now God has confirmed it and their hearts believe me. They've seen the things that's been said come to pass word by word. . . . Now what you say they'll believe it.[141]

Branham believed that he had been foreordained with a "prophetic message" of healing. His "prophetic" identity did not have to be overtly claimed, since God authoritatively confirmed it during the anointed healing process. When God's confirmation was reiterated by the blandishments of Branham's supporters, the context was ripe for the deliverance evangelist to increase the boundaries of his "prophetic" role. In the midst of campaign failure in late 1955, the shift to a more radical "prophetic" ministry became pronounced. Physical deliverance remained a concern with Branham; however, the emphasis of the ministry clearly shifted to new doctrinal revelations. Branham had found a way to recapture the days of glory by cultivating a greater, more unique ministry.

---

[139]Branham, "Faith," recorded.

[140]Ibid.

[141]Moore, *Quotations*, 15.

CHAPTER FIVE

THE DECLINE OF THE HEALING REVIVAL, 1955-1965

In 1952—one of the peak years of the revival—Gordon Lindsay featured forty-nine "associate evangelists" in *The Voice of Healing*. By 1956, however, the size of the group declined; and by 1960 less than a dozen were being promoted regularly.[1] By 1958, the deliverance evangelists realized that the glory days of the healing revival were over. Those ministers who were able to sustain independent ministries did so by adapting their methods to a broader charismatic revivalism that gave greater emphasis to all the gifts of the Holy Spirit.[2]

The primary reason for the revival's decline was the growing opposition of Pentecostal churches. Initially, the churches encouraged the reemergence of deliverance ministries, and used them to bolster their own local work. Denominational hierarchies also gave visible support. Up until 1953, *The Pentecostal Evangel*—the official organ of the Assemblies of God—published accounts of some of the healing campaigns. From the outset, however, Assemblies of God leaders cautioned that the deliverance evangelists were overemphasizing divine healing vis à vis other

---

[1]William W. Menzies, *Anointed to Serve: The Story of the Assemblies of God* (Springfield MO: Gospel Publishing House, 1971) 332-33.

[2]David E. Harrell, Jr., *All Things Are Possible: The Healing and Charismatic Revivals in Modern America* (Bloomington: Indiana University Press, 1975) 8.

biblical doctrines.[3]

The most integral element of tension between the independent evangelists and the Pentecostal churches was money. Local church ministers were threatened by the financial needs of the evangelists. High-pressure fund-raising methods, however, were primarily a recourse to desperation, not greed. The financial demands of a successful ministry were immense. Nevertheless, some revivalists were fraudulent as they exploited the masses for personal monetary gains. Therefore, the local pastors disliked the wealth of the evangelists. Ultimately, the loss of the churches' financial support doomed the continued success of the revival.[4]

Other factors also contributed to the decline of the revival. Denominational pride and doctrinal conflicts—especially over Oneness and trinitarian views of the Godhead—destroyed the ecumenical spirit of the early years. The missionary ventures of the revivalists adversely affected denominational missions. Financial jealousy among some deliverance evangelists also crippled the revival's reputation.

As the revivalists were threatened by the loss of support, they countered with unbelievable claims of the miraculous. New entrants onto the scene attempted to produce greater miracles than their more established predecessors. Respected leaders like Gordon Lindsay and Donald Gee detested the fanaticism that was evidenced in the proliferation of "counterfeits" and "gimmicks."[5]

Increasingly disturbed by the "commercialism, lack of credibility, and the lack of ethics" displayed in the revival, the Assemblies of God repudiated the movement.[6] With the censuring of Jack Coe—its most powerful independent evangelist—in 1953, the Assemblies clearly demonstrated opposition. Cooperation between churches and the revivalists became rare. Indeed, disciplinary sanctions were threatened by the denominations if churches supported some of the radical evangelists. The revivalists defended their ministries and labeled the Pentecostal denominations as backslidden. Lindsay and Gee worked diligently to effect reconciliation between the warring forces. Many of the evangelists like A. A. Allen, however, continued to lambaste the Pentecostals for their op-

---

[3]Occasional testimonies of healings that occurred in Branham's meetings were reported. The last one published was on 12 July 1953. See "Tumor," *TPE* 2044 (12 July 1953): 7.

[4]Harrell, *All Things Are Possible*, 107.

[5]Ibid., 115. See also Menzies, *Anointed to Serve*, 333.

[6]Harrell, *All Things Are Possible*, 108.

position. The breach proved irreconcilable. Many devotees of the revival undoubtedly agreed that the church had experienced "the greatest revival of history." Nevertheless, the consensus by 1958 was that the revival was over.[7]

The influential Branham was not spared from the decline of the revival. Near the end of 1955 he held some meetings in California that signaled a faltering ministry. Attendance was down, and a $15,000 deficit was incurred. Concurrently, Branham's mail gradually dropped from 1000 to seventy-five letters a day. His lack of sophistication and organizational skills finally took effect.[8] Coupled with the increasing tendency to preach controversial doctrine, Branham did not successfully make the transition from a healing-oriented revivalism to a broader charismatic revivalism.

1.

Throughout the healing revival, Branham had always been unconcerned with business matters. He often missed scheduled meetings. Lindsay recalled that Branham's business acumen was "almost childish in some ways."[9] Branham, however, defended his inability to follow a strict itinerary; if a meeting was missed, he argued, Jesus "wasn't willing for it to happen."[10]

The revivalist was also careless in financial matters. To his credit, Branham decried the excessive concern for money in the revival and exclaimed that he would never beg for campaign contributions.[11] He even claimed that he turned down a gift of one and a half million dollars.[12] Branham's lack of concern for money was so prominent that many observers felt that some of his managers misappropriated his funds for their own wealth.[13]

---

[7]William Branham, *Easter Revival, April 17-21, 1957* (Jeffersonville IN: Spoken Word Publications, n.d.) 8. Most of this introduction was taken from Harrell, *All Things Are Possible*, 105-116.

[8]Idem, "Visions and Prophecies," *TSW* 2:9 (n.d.): 12.

[9]Statement by Gordon Lindsay, interview with David E. Harrell, Jr., Dallas TX, 27 July 1972. Tape available at the Holy Spirit Research Center, Oral Roberts University, Tulsa OK.

[10]William Branham, "Gifts and Callings Are without Repentance," sermon delivered and recorded in Chicago IL, 4 October 1955.

[11]Idem, "The Inner Veil," *TSW* 2:14 (n.d.): 3.

[12]Idem, *Conduct, Order, Doctrine of the Church*, 2 vols. (Jeffersonville IN: Spoken Word Publications, 1973-1974) 1:200.

[13]Harrell, *All Things Are Possible*, 39.

During the peak of the revival, the lack of Branham's business so-sophistication did not hamper his success. The weaknesses became vividly apparent, however, as the revival fires waned. Financial difficulties became more acute in 1956 when the Internal Revenue Service filed a tax evasion suit against the evangelist. While his manager had paid taxes on $80,000 of personal income, Branham reported earnings of only $7,000. Branham was apparently ignorant of his responsibility for keeping an account of contributions to his ministry. During the period of negotiations with the government, Branham defended himself to his Jeffersonville congregation. He insisted that he had personally never collected an offering; moreover, the funds of the ministry were unsolicited gifts, and therefore untaxable. "Now the government owes me for all I've paid income tax for the past 20 years," Branham concluded.[14] Despite his objections, the evangelist agreed to an out-of-court settlement of a $40,000 penalty. For the rest of his life, this financial burden remained.[15]

When Branham experienced the financial disasters of the California meetings of November 1955, he resolved to return to Jeffersonville and retire from full-time healing evangelism. Such a drastic move was in accordance with his promise to God to minister healing as long as money was not emphasized. Amidst this crisis situation, however, Branham received his famous tent vision. According to Branham, the vision reaffirmed God's promise of a unique ministry.

In the vision, Branham found himself at a lake surrounded by hundreds of ministers catching small fish. His reaction to the scene was, "I am as good a fisher as they are, or even better than they are. I wanted to catch the large beautiful fish."[16] Immediately Branham's angel appeared and gave instructions on how to fish:

> Now, first pull easy and get the attention of the little fish. Then pull faster and pull the lure away from them, and the big fish will take after it. Remember, keep still and don't say any thing about this to anyone! For the third pull, set your line tight—you are ready for the catch.[17]

---

[14]William Branham, "Holy Spirit Explained," *TSW* 5:2 (n.d.): 20. Branham claimed he was being sued for $200,000.

[15]Statement by Pearry Green, interview with David E. Harrell, Jr., Tucson AZ, 27 December 1973. Tape made available by David E. Harrell, Jr., University of Alabama in Birmingham.

[16]Thomas R. Nickel, "The Angel of the Lord Visits William Branham!," *Voice* 4 (March 1956): 12.

[17]Ibid.

In his excitement to show off his fishing skills to the other ministers, Branham jerked the lure completely out of the water and only caught a very small fish. The angel reappeared, and explained Branham's disobedience. The first pull symbolized the first healing sign of the vibrating hand. The second pull signified the gift of visionary discernment. The angel chastised Branham for having attempted to explain the mechanics of the two signs. "Instead of keeping quiet about these things, you got on the platform and made a public show of these Divine gifts," the angel scolded, "look what you have caused: a lot of carnal impersonators."[18]

The vision did not reach a climax until Branham was taken into a "higher dimension." He found himself "standing in the air in the largest tent I have ever seen in my life." The tent was filled with a great revival crowd. In addition, inside the tent was a "square wooden room" that was surrounded by the angelic light. When Branham saw two sick persons enter the room, the angel responded, "I'll meet you in there . . . this is the third pull." Subsequently, the persons emerged from the room, healed but ignorant of how the deliverance occurred. The vision ended after the angel took Branham into the room to reveal the third pull. "What he said to me there," Branham promised, "I will have to keep a secret the rest of my life."[19]

Until he died, Branham yearned for the tent vision to materialize. He constantly reiterated that the "third pull" was imminent. Often he tried to facilitate the fulfillment of the vision. Once he announced that $100,000 had been borrowed toward the purchase of a tent. Yet no tent was ever bought. In October 1958, he actually sent five sick persons into a side room of the Branham Tabernacle in an effort to initiate the new ministry. When the attempt proved futile, Branham lamented that the "third pull" evidently would not occur before the great tent campaigns were begun.[20]

Like all deliverance evangelists, Branham was reassessing his ministry by 1958. Joseph Mattsson-Boze, editor of the *Herald of Faith*, reported that Branham had received 400 invitations from foreign lands and large churches in the major cities of the United States. Nevertheless,

---

[18]Ibid., 13.

[19]Ibid., 14.

[20]Robert Moore compiled an extensive list of quotes that demonstrated Branham's yearning for the fulfillment of the tent vision. See Robert Moore, *Quotations of William M. Branham* (n.p., n.d.) 18, 21-22, 26-27, 32, 36, 51-52, 146-47, 246-48, A9-A12, B7-B11.

Branham only accepted some smaller meetings because he was "not at liberty to move too freely yet."[21]

In 1959, Branham declared that he was abandoning the emphasis on the visionary discernment in order to return to praying for the sick. He declared that in a recent Chicago campaign, a woman was present that had appeared in the tent vision. This signaled the first phase of the new ministry, according to Branham. Thereafter, he asserted that he was better able to pull out of the visions and pray to "whole lines of people" like other evangelists.[22] Indeed, some campaigns of the early 1960s were so successful that supporters believed the glory days of the revival had returned.[23]

Despite some success, Branham realized that the glory days had not been permanently restored. Throughout the 1960s, he lamented the decline of his popularity. On one occasion he acknowledged that other evangelists like Billy Graham, Oral Roberts, Tommy Osborn, and Tommy Hicks had surpassed him in popularity. At the beginning of 1964, he complained that for the last five years, "I've been off the field, just going to churches and whatever I could."[24] Moreover, Branham's ministry operated in the late 1950s and early 1960s on a precarious financial basis. While he increasingly criticized Pentecostal organizations, he attempted to garner the churches' support. Only limited cooperation was achieved.[25]

---

[21]Joseph D. Mattsson-Boze, "Rev. William Branham's Schedules, 1957-1958," *HOF* 25 (February-March 1958): 10. *The Herald of Faith* was Branham's primary publicity organ of his later ministry. One manifestation of the revival's difficulties and Branham's decline of popularity was his conflict with A. A. Allen. At a 1957 Christian Fellowship Convention one of Allen's followers circulated an "Open Letter" that criticized Branham and included warnings of death. Branham had criticized Allen's contention that the evidence of Spirit baptism was the appearance of oil and blood on the hands. Lindsay defended Branham, saying that the evangelist had a positive ministry that did not include attacks on personalities. Moreover, persons should accept Scriptural correction from the revival's pacesetter. See "Christian Fellowship Convention Replies to 'Open Letter' to William Branham," *TVH* 10 (July 1957): 3. Lindsay did not identify Allen, but Branham's son confirmed that Allen was the other evangelist involved in the conflict. See Statement by Billy Paul Branham, son of William Branham, personal interview, Jeffersonville IN, 27 September 1984.

[22]William Branham, "New Ministry (William Branham)," sermon delivered and recorded in Los Angeles CA, 6 April 1959.

[23]Harrell, *All Things Are Possible,* 160.

[24]William Branham, "God's Word Calls for a Total Separation from Unbelief," *TSW* 3:20 (rpt., 1983): 22. See also William Branham, "The Spoken Word Is the Original Seed," *TSW* 3:1-2 (rpt., 1982): 44.

[25]Harrell, *All Things Are Possible,* 161.

Branham's most dependable support group was the Full Gospel Business Men's Fellowship International. Branham was a speaker at its meetings from the outset, having appeared at the second annual convention of 1954. Many of his meetings were underwritten by the fellowship, and naturally, he frequently praised its work. Sounding an outspoken theme of his later years, Branham commended the businessmen for not being bound to dead denominational religion. He often announced that the only organization to which he belonged was the Full Gospel Business Men's Fellowship International, because "it's not an organization. Its just an organism working among the people."[26]

President Demos Shakarian and Vice President Carl Williams of Phoenix deeply respected Branham. Moreover, in 1961, *Voice*—the fellowship's journal—exclaimed that "in Bible Days, there were men of God who were Prophets and Seers. But in all the Sacred Records, none of these had a greater ministry than that of William Branham."[27] As Branham became increasingly controversial in his doctrine, however, the businessmen began to use him less. His criticism of Pentecostal organizations and the abusive harangues against women were especially offensive. The evangelist's reception at fellowship meetings in the 1960s epitomized his inability to adapt to the broader charismatic revivalism. In essence, Branham was rejected by the neo-Pentecostals of the fellowship.[28]

Branham recognized this rejection, and told his disciples that only Carl Williams kept the door open for him when others had closed it on account of his doctrine.[29] The evangelist occasionally criticized the businessmen in his preaching at the Branham Tabernacle. He asserted that the wealth of these men and other Pentecostal organizations "has choked out the glory and Spirit of God."[30] He also ridiculed the fellowship's desire for another great revival as a prelude to Christ's imminent return. Ultimately, the businessmen did not understand or accept that his "mes-

---

[26]William Branham, "Doors in Door," *TSW* 17:3 (n.d.): 2. See also William Branham, "The Seed Shall Not Be Heir with the Shuck," *TSW* 18:5 (May 1983): 8. See also "Speaking of the Second Annual Convention," *Voice* 2 (July-August 1954): 5-6.

[27]"Concerning Photograph on Front Cover," *Voice* 9 (February 1961): 3.

[28]Statement by Howard Ervin, professor of Old Testament, Oral Roberts University, personal interview, Tulsa OK, 5 April 1984. Ervin suggested that Branham was still used by the fellowship on account of the attitude, "Don't touch God's anointed, even if he is wrong."

[29]Pearry Green, *The Acts of the Prophet* (Tucson: Tucson Tabernacle Books, n.d.) 26.

[30]Branham, "Spoken Word," 22.

sage" was the eschatological forerunner of Christ's return.[31] Despite such criticism, Branham became more and more dependent upon the fellowship for support in his last years.

2.

In the midst of the declining revival, Branham coped with—and, ironically, furthered—his dwindling popularity by lending his influence to a small group of disciples. As they hoped for the fulfillment of the tent vision, and its mysterious promise of an unparalleled ministry, he assured his unique status among them by asserting "prophetic" revelations. The conscious avoidance of doctrinal conflicts of the early revival years was superseded by dogmatic doctrinal convictions. The willingness to espouse new "prophetic" revelations made Branham increasingly controversial in full gospel circles. Gordon Lindsay, Jack Moore, and Joseph Mattsson-Boze defended him in spite of his teachings. Many observers believed that Branham was being misled by "intellectually dishonest coworkers for whose doctrinal positions he was not responsible."[32]

The evangelist's desire for uniqueness was surely encouraged by a coterie of devoted disciples. Nevertheless, Branham asserted that his doctrinal positions were given to him by divine revelation. The controversial teachings included a wide range of issues. Branham's strict morality, particularly for women, became more rigid, and thus more unpopular with neo-Pentescostals who were not raised in the "Christ against culture" tradition of classical Pentecostalism. On the other hand, the evangelist condoned divorce, which upset classical Pentecostals. He condemned denominationalism as the mark of the beast and espoused a "Jesus only" position regarding the Godhead and baptism. Moreover, Branham's increasing emphasis on predestination and eternal security was disliked by Pentecostals of Arminian heritage. Other "revelations" included the denial of an eternal hell, and the doctrine of the serpent's seed. According to Branham, Eve and the Serpent had sexual intercourse and Cain was born. Consequently, every woman potentially carries the literal seed of the Devil. The race of Satan continues to the present day, most clearly revealed in those who reject the supernatural nature of the gospel.

The most controversial "revelation" dealt with the major concern of Branham's preaching—eschatology. During the 1960s, Branham con-

---

[31]William Branham, "Recognizing Your Day and Its Message," *TSW* 5:1 (rpt., 1984): 40.

[32]Harrell, *All Things Are Possible,* 163.

stantly spoke about the forerunner of Christ's second coming. The "message" of this eschatological prophet would be the catalyst for the rapture of his followers—the Bride of Christ. Undoubtedly, Branham came to regard himself as this prophet.[33]

Several events of the 1960s contributed to the development of this unique "prophetic" identity. In 1960, Branham preached a series of sermons at Jeffersonville on the seven church ages that dispensationalists find in the Book of Revelation. Branham felt that the election of John F. Kennedy as President of the United States meant that Catholicism would soon attempt to take over the world. Such a belief prompted the evangelist to warn his church about the "lateness of the hour."[34] The sermons manifested a heavy dependence upon C. I. Scofield's dispensationalism. After the sermons were preached, Branham proclaimed, God sent the familiar heavenly light to confirm their "revealed" truth.[35]

Branham described each age and suggested that the angel of each age was an earthly messenger. The most important "revelation" was the description of the messenger to the last age before the rapture. This Laodicean messenger was unknown, but his characteristics were all strikingly compatible to Branham's personality. Although the evangelist did not claim to be the messenger, his supporters drew such a conclusion.[36]

The most significant experience of the 1960s was Branham's opening of the seven seals of Revelation 6-8. As early as 1953, Branham asserted that the opening of the seals would be "revealed in the last days."[37] Moreover, during the preaching of the church ages, Branham stated that

---

[33]These doctrines are discussed in the next chapter. In his analysis of the relationship of Christian faith to culture, H. Richard Niebuhr categorized five responses. The category of "Christ against Culture" places Christ and culture in an either-or situation. Exclusive loyalty was given to Christ while accommodation to culture was rejected. See H. Richard Niebuhr, *Christ and Culture* (New York: Harper & Row, Publishers, 1951) 45-82.

[34]Robert Moore, *1977, Circa 1976* (n.p., 1976) 49.

[35]William Branham, *The Pergamean Church Age*, vol. 5 of *The Revelation of Jesus Christ* (Jeffersonville IN: Spoken Word Publications, n.d.) 278. See also William Branham, "If God Be with Us Then Where Is All the Miracles?," *TSW* 15:1 (n.d.): 36. See 37 n. 56, for an explanation of dispensationalism.

[36]William Branham, *Is This the Time?* (Jeffersonville IN: Spoken Word Publications, n.d.) 11-21. Green said that this was the first time that Branham asserted his identity. See statement by Pearry Green. Currently hanging on a wall adjacent to the podium in the Branham Tabernacle is a diagram, drawn by a church member and dated December 1960, that lists Branham as the Laodicean messenger.

[37]Moore, *Quotations*, A3.

the mysteries of the seals were about to be revealed. He implied that his ministry would play an integral role in the revelation.[38]

On 30 December 1962, Branham told his Jeffersonville congregation of a mysterious vision that he had received. In the vision, Branham saw himself standing on the side of a mountain when a terrible blast occurred. Troubled because he did not know the meaning of the vision, Branham wondered if the "third pull" was imminent. In addition, Branham informed his supporters that he felt a divine compulsion to move to Tucson, Arizona.[39]

In January 1963, Branham was in Sabino Canyon, located in the Catalina mountains of Arizona. There he sought solitude to determine the meaning of the mysterious vision. Suddenly, Branham claimed, a sword appeared in his hand. A voice informed him, "That is the King's sword," and just as suddenly the sword disappeared. Branham described the incident: "If it would have said, 'A King's sword,' it might have been that I would have understood it, but it said, 'The King's sword.' . . . I thought, There's only One The King; that's God. And His sword is this—sharper than a two-edged sword. 'Ye abide in me and my Words' . . . see."[40] Branham later asserted that the incident of the King's Sword was God's method of preparing him for the reception of God's Word in the opening of the seven seals.[41]

Nevertheless, it was not until 28 February 1963 that Branham finally claimed to understand God's reason for sending him to Arizona. On that date Branham had an experience which fulfilled the vision of the terrific blast. While hunting in the Arizona mountains, he heard an explosion. Immediately, Branham contended, he was caught up in a large cloud that was, in reality, a heavenly constellation of seven angels. The angels commanded: "Return back east from where you came and by revelation and vision, God will open the seven seals that have been sealed since John the Revelator wrote them in the Book of Revelation."[42] God had sent him

---

[38]William Branham, *Revelation, Chapter Five*, vol. 15 of *The Revelation of Jesus Christ* (Jeffersonville IN: Spoken Word Publications, n.d.) 758, 773.

[39]Idem, "Sirs, Is This the Time?," *TSW* 2:11 (rpt., 1983): 13. Branham frequently had visions and his disciples had dreams that showed him living in the west.

[40]Idem, *The Revelation of the Seven Seals* (Tucson: Spoken Word Publications, 1967) 68-69.

[41]Idem, "One in a Million," *TSW* 18:1 (n.d.): 4.

[42]Green, *Prophet*, 103-104. See also Branham, *Seals*, 556-70, 576-78.

to Arizona, Branham later concluded, to receive the "message" of the end-time mysteries of God. [43]

Like the halo photograph of 1951, Branham appealed to scientific proof for the reality of the angelic constellation. On the cover of the April issue of *Science* magazine was a photograph of a large cloud that was visible over Flagstaff, Arizona, and near the location of Branham's experience. The cloud's "unusually great height and unusually low altitude plus its remarkable shape" prompted a scientist to suggest "that it was a cloud of previously unrecorded type." In May, the popular *Life* magazine reported on the mysterious cloud. [44] Scientists eventually attributed the unusual cloud formation to a rocket blast from Vandenburg Air Force Base. Still, Branham believed that the pillar of fire had been manifested in a unique way. [45]

In March 1963, Branham returned to Jeffersonville for a series of special services to preach the seals. His supporters listened anxiously for the unveiling of the final mysteries of God. Indeed, the question was raised whether the rapture would come immediately after the seals were opened. Despite an injunction to "keep on living,"[46] Branham's disciples treasured the sermons. Pearry Green later called them "the most outstanding and enlightening series of sermons ever known in the Church."[47]

In reality, the opening of the seals "revealed" very little new doctrine. Branham's exposition was essentially a laborious restatement of the dispensationalism espoused in the sermons on the seven church ages. When he preached on the climactic seventh seal, of which the Book of Revelation gives no description, Branham simply suggested that the mystery was related to the ambiguous "third pull."[48]

After preaching on the seals, Branham seemed even more convinced that his "message" was the eschatological prelude that would produce

---

[43]William Branham, "What House Will You Build Me," *TSW* 19:6 (June 1984): 3.

[44]James E. McDonald, "Stratospheric Cloud over Northern Arizona," *Science* 140 (19 April 1963): 292. See also William Branham, "Standing in the Gap," *TSW* 6:7 (n.d.): 21-22. See also William Branham, "Is Your Life Worthy of the Gospel?," *TSW* 5:5 (n.d.): 2. "Odd Sights at Heights," *Life* 54 (17 May 1963): 112.

[45]Letter received by Robert Moore from Louis J. Batten, Director, The University of Arizona, Institute of Atmospheric Physics, 5 June 1980.

[46]Branham, *Seals*, 515-16.

[47]Green, *Prophet*, 104.

[48]Branham, *Seals*, 40.

"rapturing faith" in the Bride of Christ.[49] He regarded these sermons as giving "the complete revelation of Jesus Christ, altogether new to us, but perfectly, exactly with the Scriptures."[50] Though Branham had merely restated earlier doctrinal themes, he began to assert that all of his "message" originated in the "seals' sermons."[51]

The importance of the revelation of the seals to Branham's "prophetic" identity cannot be overestimated. The evangelist announced that the final mysteries of God had not been revealed to the previous church age messengers like Martin Luther and John Wesley, since they were only reformers. Only a prophet could receive the revelation of the seals, Branham asserted; and that prophet was the messenger of the Laodicean church age. Branham never identified himself as that messenger, but obviously he was the recipient of the opening of the seals.[52]

Branham's increasing emphasis on "prophetic" revelations was readily accepted by a small group of disciples. Undoubtedly, their reverence for Branham encouraged and abetted his obsession with the "message" of the Laodicean prophet. Even in the 1950s, Branham's closest disciples were encouraging his desire for a unique ministry. Such reverential support especially became apparent after the 1955 tent vision. One of the evangelist's staff aides, Leo Mercier, wrote articles for the *Herald of Faith* that called Branham "God's prophet to this generation." Mercier also reported a dream that he had experienced that confirmed the truth of Branham's tent vision.[53]

Adulation of Branham's "prophetic" identity intensified in the 1960s. The evangelist was consistently described as the prophet to this generation.[54] Supporters from around the country moved their residences to Jeffersonville to be near Branham. Others consistently traveled to Jef-

---

[49]Statement by Robert Moore, former follower of Branham, telephone interview, Phoenix AZ, 9 September 1984.

[50]William Branham, "Feast of the Trumpets," *TSW* 3:16 (rpt., 1982): 8.

[51]Idem, "Trying to Do God a Service without It Being God's Will," *TSW* 7:2 (n.d.): 10-11. Branham's followers explain that some of the doctrines were revealed before this time but that the opening of the seals confirmed their truth. See statement by Robert Moore.

[52]Idem, *Seals*, 111, 145-46, 237.

[53]Leo Mercier, "The Mount of God; Concerning Rev. William Branham," *HOF* 24 (March 1957): 3, 22-23. See also Leo Mercier, "God's Tremendous Works through His Servant Rev. William Branham," *HOF* 24 (October 1957): 16.

[54]Branham, *Conduct*, 2:515.

fersonville from long distances on the Sundays that Branham was going to preach.[55]

A few followers even ascribed divinity to Branham; baptism in the name of William Branham was advocated. In a 1961 sermon, Branham quickly denounced such beliefs as heresy, and threatened to retire from the ministry if the situation was not rectified. Yet the belief persisted. Branham continued to refute the error, but he rationalized that the ascription of divinity "only identified the Message true." Branham concluded, "Did not they come and try to tell John, the—that forerun the first coming of Christ, "Aren't you the Messiah?"[56]

Not surprisingly, many of Branham's disciples followed their leader to Arizona after the revelation of the seals. Leo Mercier set up a colony to wait for the rapture. Some supporters who did not make the exodus were disturbed that they might miss the rapture if they did not change their residences. Branham assured his supporters that a move to Arizona was not necessary. He even lamented the fact that a cult was potentially being formed. Branham affirmed, however, that he had to remain in Arizona for a divine purpose that he could not disclose.[57]

Branham's exclusivistic attitude was more pronounced than ever in the last year of his life. A growing sense of isolation was present. He complained that in the three years he had lived in Tucson, he had never preached there. According to Branham, the churches were threatened with excommunication by their denominations if he was allowed to preach.[58]

In December 1964, Branham pronounced one of his most radical predictions ever. He warned that judgment would strike the west coast, and Los Angeles would sink into the Pacific Ocean.[59] Until his death in December 1965, Branham reiterated this warning and added embellishments with each succeeding reference. He ultimately warned:

> The world is falling apart. Fifteen hundred-mile chunk of it, three or four hundred miles wide, will sink—or maybe forty miles down into that great

---

[55]Idem, *Seals*, 526. See also William Branham, "The Stature of a Perfect Man," *TSW* 2:18 (rpt., 1984): 10. Branham asserted that ninety-eight percent of his congregation came from outside Jeffersonville. Eighty percent were from 100 miles away, and thirty-three percent traveled over 500 miles.

[56]Idem, *Conduct*, 2:976.

[57]Idem, *Seals*, 973-75.

[58]Idem, "Lean Not Unto Thy Own Understanding," *TSW* 19:3 (April 1984): 17.

[59]Idem, "Who Do You Say This Is?," *TSW* 6:9 (n.d.): 10.

fault out yonder one of these days, and waves will shoot plumb out to the state of Kentucky.[60]

Branham informed his audience that if they believed him to be God's prophet, they had better believe the "message" regarding this eschatological earthquake. Some California disciples—including ninety-five percent of one church—took Branham's words to heart and moved to Tucson.[61]

The last revival that Branham ever held was during Thanksgiving week, 1965, at Jack Moore's church in Shreveport, Louisiana. Moore, though not a "Message" believer, had remained Branham's friend, and tolerated his controversial teachings. Ironically, Branham's sermons included his boldest suggestions ever regarding his identity as *the* end-time prophet. He exclaimed, "As John the Baptist was sent to forerun the first coming of the Lord Jesus, you are sent to forerun the second."[62] Indeed, Branham's 1933 baptismal experience was now considered the most important event of the last dispensation: "Notice, the Word came to the prophet in this dispensation of grace, in the water (uh-huh). I thought you'd catch it (uh-huh). In the water! Now you see where the Bride started, the Evening light Message? In the water."[63]

3.

On 18 December 1965, Branham was critically injured in an automobile accident caused by a drunken driver. He was traveling in Texas en route to Jeffersonville for Christmas. Comatose for several days, he died on Christmas Eve. Funeral services were held at the Branham Tabernacle on 29 December with many prominent healing revivalists present.[64]

Branham's disciples were shocked by his death. Speculation about his resurrection developed in the aftermath of the tragedy. The Pentecostal world was also stunned by Branham's death. Tacit acknowledgment of

---

[60]Idem, *Footprints on the Sands of Time: The Autobiography of William Marrion Branham* (Jeffersonville IN: Spoken Word Publications, 1975) 540.

[61]"Memorial Service #1," eulogy delivered and recorded in Phoenix AZ, 25 January 1966. See also William Branham, "Choosing a Bride," *TSW* 2:28 (rpt., May 1983): 34.

[62]Branham, "Trying," 56.

[63]Idem, "On the Wings of a Snow-White Dove," *TSW* 7:5 (n.d.): 18.

[64]Harrell, *All Things Are Possible*, 164. See also "Evangelist Branham Dies of Injuries," *The Courier-Journal* (Louisville KY), 26 December 1965, A33:1. Lindsay, Mattsson-Boze, Tommy Osborn, and other lesser-known evangelists attended the funeral.

his controversial reputation was made in published eulogies. The evangelist's positive contributions were emphasized, however. Joseph Mattsson-Boze affirmed that, despite deep doctrinal cleavages, "the warm spirit of friendship between us never ceased."[65] Moreover, one journal described Branham's funeral as a "coronation day" for "a great soldier who fell in battle."[66]

Though saddened by Branham's death, some leaders in the Pentecostal world were not surprised. Gordon Lindsay's eulogy stated that Branham's death was the will of God. "God may see that a man's special ministry has reached its fruition and it is time to take him home," Lindsay wrote.[67] Privately, however, Lindsay accepted the interpetation of Kenneth Hagin, a rising, young evangelist of Tulsa, Oklahoma. Hagin claimed to have prophesied the exact time of Branham's death two years before it happened. According to Hagin, God revealed that Branham was teaching false doctrine. Branham had erred by attempting to function as an authoritative teacher when he had no anointing to do so. Since Branham disobeyed his calling and created doctrinal confusion, Hagin believed, God had to remove the father of the healing revival from the scene.[68]

* * * * *

In the late 1950s, the glory days of healing revivalism were over. Fraud, chicanery, the proliferation of "counterfeit" evangelists, and especially opposition and loss of support from the Pentecostal denominations all contributed to the revival's decline. In the process, the ministries of many revivalists, including that of William Branham, severely retarded. Branham's lack of sophistication and organizational skills finally began to take their toll amidst the waning crusade crowds. Coupled with an increased tendency to preach controversial doctrine as "prophetic" revelations, Branham did not successfully adapt from the primary emphasis on healing to the emerging, broader charismatic revivalism.

---

[65]Joseph D. Mattsson-Boze, "William Branham: In Memoriam," *HOF* 34 (February 1966): 3. The expectation of Branham's resurrection by his disciples will be discussed in chapter 7.

[66]"Coronation Day," *TVD* 1 (January 1966): 2.

[67]Gordon Lindsay, "William Branham as I Knew Him," *TVH* 18 (February 1966): 11.

[68]Kenneth Hagin, *Understanding the Anointing* (Tulsa: Rhema Bible Church, 1983) 60-61. In this book, Hagin did not mention Branham by name. In a letter to the author, however, Hagin confirmed that Branham was the subject of his prophecy. See letter received from Kenneth Hagin, 8 August 1984. For Lindsay's agreement with Hagin, see letter received from Donna Hobbs, employee, Christ For the Nations, Inc., 6 June 1984.

The evangelist's desire for a unique ministry persisted, however. He was rejuvenated by a belief in the tent vision and its mysterious "third pull," and he was encouraged by a devoted group of disciples who accepted without question his "prophetic" doctrinal revelations. Consequently, Branham came to understand his "uniqueness" in an ultimate sense—he was the prophet whose eschatological "message" would precede the second coming of Christ.

CHAPTER SIX

FROM HEALER
TO PROPHET

When healing revivalism was transformed into a broader charismatic revivalism in the late 1950s, Branham did not readily adapt. Though he still engaged in healing campaigns, the thrust of his ministry shifted from healing to "prophetic" doctrinal revelations. Branham felt the call to restore the "Word." In essence, the restoration of gospel primitivism had been left to the prophet. Several themes dominated this eschatological "message." These included condemnations of culture, especially modern women, and denominationalism. Doctrinal issues that helped make Branham increasingly unpopular were a denial of an eternal hell, predestination, eternal security, and the serpent's seed. The most controversial idea, however, dealt with the identity of an eschatological messenger who would prepare the Bride of Christ for the rapture.

1.

When Branham shifted his emphasis to "prophetic," doctrinal revelations, he asserted that his teaching was confined to the Branham Tabernacle, and that persons who disagreed with his views were still his Christian brothers and sisters. In campaign meetings, the conscious avoidance of doctrinal conflict was still practiced. Yet tapes of Branham's sermons became readily accessible; and the controversial teachings proved unpopular with most Pentecostal ministers. Many ministers began to shun cooperation with the evangelist.[1]

---

[1]William Branham, *Conduct, Order, Doctrine of the Church*, 2 vols. (Jeffersonville IN: Spoken Word Publications, 1973-1974) 2:205.

Branham asserted that Pentecostal leaders admonished him to confine his ministry to prayer for the sick. He responded that God gave him a healing ministry in order to get the attention of all the people. He often quoted a favorite saying of F. F. Bosworth:

> You, always, to catch the fish, you don't show them the hook, you show them the bait. And the fish grabs the bait and gets the hook.[2]

Since the masses had been attracted by miracles of healing, Branham argued, they were prepared for the truth of his doctrinal preaching. The time had come to move beyond a "minor thing" like divine healing and toward the supernatural revelation of the doctrinal "message."[3] To those who suggested that his gift of discernment was given by God, but that the doctrinal teachings were erroneous, Branham responded: "Whoever heard of such tommyrot? . . . It's either all of God or none of God."[4] Indeed, the evangelist saw the decline of his popularity like that of Jesus, as a vindication of his cause. He contended that Jesus was popular as a bearer of deliverance. The crowds deserted the Messiah, however, after he began to expound on "the Truth of the Word."[5]

Throughout the 1960s, as Branham felt more isolated, his sermons outside the Tabernacle became more controversial. In an effort to appeal to campaign audiences, he still could minimize doctrinal differences. Persons did not have to agree with his teachings to be Spirit-filled Christians. This humble attitude was part of the "prophet's" rhetoric, however. Under the inspiration, Branham—paradoxically—was so bold that only those who accepted the eschatological "message" were part of the rapture-bound Bride.[6]

2.

The element of Branham's later ministry that clearly revealed his incompatibility with the transition from healing revivalism to a broader charismatic revivalism was the increasing condemnation of modern culture. Throughout his ministry, Branham had always illustrated the "Christ against

---

[2]Idem, *Jehovah-Jireh* (Jeffersonville IN: Spoken Word Publications, n.d.) 7.

[3]Idem, *The Pergamean Church Age*, vol. 5 of *The Revelation of Jesus Christ* (Jeffersonville IN: Spoken Word Publications, n.d.) 250.

[4]Idem, *Adoption* (Jeffersonville IN: Spoken Word Publications, n.d.) 56.

[5]Idem, "The Unfailing Realities of the Living God," *TSW* 16:1 (n.d.): 34.

[6]Idem, "Invisible Union of the Bride of Christ," *TSW* 2:15 (rpt., 1982): 3-4.

Culture" approach that was characteristic of classical Pentecostalism.[7] He denounced such worldly amusements as cards, dancing, cigarettes, and alcohol. He condemned television, rock and roll music, and the paganism of Christmas and Easter.[8] By the 1960s, his denunciations of modern culture were increasingly caustic. He identified himself as a true champion of the poor. His most dominant themes, however, were denunciations of the immorality of modern women and the evils of education.

Branham especially identified with the lower-class roots of the Pentecostal tradition. He was proud to affirm "I'm a poor man."[9] The evangelist often claimed that he could have been a millionaire from the revenue of his ministry. He spoke of refusing a Cadillac for a gift because "I want to be like the people that comes [sic] to be prayed for."[10] When he finally accepted a Cadillac from a Full Gospel Business Men's Fellowship International leader, out of embarrassment he kept the car in his garage for two years.[11]

In the latter years of his ministry, Branham increasingly chastised other evangelists and Pentecostalism as a whole for selling out to a gospel of prosperity. Prosperity was not an automatic result of receiving the baptism of the Holy Spirit, Branham argued. Moreover, the worldly emphasis on big salaries, fancy choir robes, and expensive church structures was inconsistent with a belief in the imminent coming of Christ. Indeed, Branham encouraged his followers to believe that God was on the side of the poor and common folk. The wealthy had shut their eyes to the supernatural presence of God.[12]

The crux of Branham's condemnations of culture was reserved for the immorality of modern women. Branham had always preached a strict

---

[7]For an illustration of rigid moralism in the full gospel tradition, see John Thomas Nichol, *Pentecostalism* (New York: Harper & Row, Publishers, 1966) 119.

[8]William Branham, *Footprints on the Sands of Time: The Autobiography of William Marrion Branham* (Jeffersonville IN: Spoken Word Publications, 1975) 26. See also William Branham, "Witnesses," sermon delivered and recorded in Jeffersonville IN, 5 April 1953.

[9]Idem, "Faith in the Son of God," sermon delivered and recorded in Hammond IN, 15 July 1952.

[10]Ibid.

[11]Statement by Pearry Green, interview with David E. Harrell, Jr., Tucson AZ, 27 December 1973. Tape made available by David E. Harrell, Jr., University of Alabama in Birmingham.

[12]Branham, *Conduct*, 1:77. See also William Branham, "A True Sign That's Overlooked," *TSW* 6:2 (n.d.): 11. See also William Branham, "What Is the Holy Ghost?," *TSW* 4:2 (n.d.): 26.

moral code. He criticized women for their indulgences in a variety of worldly ways. Smoking cigarettes was "the lowest thing she can do."[13] A woman with short hair was breaking the commandments of God. Branham affirmed the Old Testament law that said a man had a right to divorce his wife for "bobbing off her hair."[14] Dishonoring her head was a blatant sign of disobedience to the husband, the head of the household. Moreover, Branham ridiculed women's desire to artificially beautify themselves with make-up. "The only woman in the Bible who ever painted her face to meet a man was Jezebel and God sent her to the dogs," Branham warned.[15]

Women were especially criticized for their disrespectful appearance in public. Branham hated the sight of shorts—the clothes of men—on a woman. He exclaimed that scantily clad women were guilty of committing adultery because their appearance motivated men to lust. Only the woman was guilty, however. "Watch her go down the street with her clothes all stripped down, don't care who the man is," Branham contended, "if he's a healthy normal man, when he looks at the woman, he's bound to have something to pass over him."[16] Branham's disdain for modern freedoms of women was graphically epitomized in his denunciation of women who went to public swimming pools: "They go right into that pool, and many of them with diseases, syphilitic [sic], gonorrhea, and everything else, right in there. And just spitting it through your mouth . . . and that's sanitary, of course?"[17]

A woman's place was in the kitchen, according to Branham. Unlike many Pentecostals, Branham's belief in the subordination of women prohibited him from accepting women as ministers. He cited 1 Timothy 2:14, "And Adam was not deceived, but the woman being deceived was in the transgression," to suggest that a woman's sin prohibited her from ruling a church. Branham stated that "everytime that a—a funeral goes down

---

[13]Branham, *Footprints*, 26.

[14]William Branham, *The Spoken Word*, 2:24-28 (Jeffersonville IN: Spoken Word Publications, 1972) 53.

[15]Idem, "I Am the Resurrection and the Life," sermon delivered and recorded in Chicago IL, 8 August 1952.

[16]Idem, "Why Are We Not a Denomination?," *TSW* 11:7 (n.d.): 28. See also Branham, *The Spoken Word*, 53.

[17]Idem, "The Ever-Present Water from the Rock," *TSW* 14:6 (n.d.): 7.

the street, a woman caused it. . . . Everything that's wrong, a woman caused it. And then put her head of the church . . . shame on her."[18]

Branham's extremist views on women became more apparent after he began emphasizing his infamous doctrine of the serpent's seed in 1958. Eve gave birth to Cain through sexual intercourse with the serpent; consequently, every woman potentially carried the literal seed of the devil. Therefore, Branham argued that women were not qualified to be preachers. Indeed, Branham reminded women that they were not even a "created product of God." Rather, she was merely a by-product of man. [19]

The denunciations of women naturally led to the criticism that the evangelist was a woman hater. He responded that he hated only the immorality of modern women. Moreover, Branham qualified his fervid denunciations by affirming that obedience to his rigid moral code was not a requirement for salvation. Rather, issues of hair and dress were elements of church order. [20]

Branham's pronouncements were often contradictory, however. Once he informed women who wore shorts not to call themselves Christian. [21] In another instance he "wondered" if women were spirit-filled since they "did not follow God's word to the letter."[22] Although Branham never consigned a Christian woman of "worldly ways" to hell, the implication of his denunciation was clear. No woman who disobeyed his "Thus Saith the Lord" moral code was following the "message" that was needed to be a part of the rapture-bound Bride of Christ.

The rigid moral code of the evangelist became very unpopular, especially among the new wave of neo-Pentecostals. On the other hand, he offended strict Pentecostals with a "prophetic" revelation that allowed divorce. On 21 February 1965, Branham presented his "supernatural revelation." He announced that the question of divorce could be answered, since the seals had been opened and the final mysteries of God revealed.

The sermon that Branham preached elaborated upon many facets of his misogynistic attitude. He clarified his belief that a woman was a by-

---

[18]Idem, "Why Are," 30. Branham also cited 1 Cor. 14:32-34. For a discussion of women preachers in Pentecostalism, see Vinson Synan, *The Holiness-Pentecostal Movement in the United States* (Grand Rapids MI: William B. Eerdmans, 1971) 188.

[19]William Branham, "Serpent's Seed," *TSW* 2:4 (rpt., 1983): 27.

[20]Idem, *Conduct*, 1:130.

[21]Idem, "Is Your Life Worthy of the Gospel?," *TSW* 5:5 (n.d.): 17.

[22]Idem, "What the Holy Ghost Was Given For," *TSW* 4:3 (n.d.): 29.

product of man. Every other living animal or thing, Branham argued, was a part of God's original creation. This secondary status meant that women were the most easily deceived and deceitful living beings on earth. [23]

Branham believed that God's original plan was to populate the world "through the dust of the earth" as occurred in the creation of Adam. Eve's sexual intercourse with the serpent, however, altered the divine plan, and the inferior method of procreation through sexual intercourse resulted. Consequently, Branham blamed women for sexual promiscuity and described "an immoral woman" as "a human garbage can, a sex exposal [sic]."[24]

Since women introduced men to sex, polygamy became rampant after the fall, according to Branham. The conditions of polygamy were that a man could have many wives but not vice versa. When Jesus spoke on divorce, therefore, he said that a woman could not remarry under any circumstances. Branham noted that Jesus did not extend this prohibition of remarriage to men. The evangelist "revealed" that a man could divorce and remarry a virgin. [25]

For those "Message" believers who had remarried other divorcees, Branham had a comforting "revelation." God had allowed Moses and Paul to condone divorce under certain circumstances for their people. Now, God allowed Branham to command his disciples: "to suffer . . . on the way as you are, and do it no more! Go with your wives and live in peace, for the hour is late."[26]

Despite his objections, Branham conveyed a misogynistic attitude toward women. This attitude was comprehensive, covering physical appearance, sexual drive, and marital relationships. Indeed, Branham's strictures about women have greatly influenced "Message" believers. Robert Moore, a lay leader wrote upon leaving the movement:

Let me speak further about women, since that is the "number one temptation" and major subject of conversation for men in the Message. It is commonly alleged that only by constantly hearing tapes [of sermons] can one hope to resist the allure of sensuous females, and that once out from behind that shield one will be committing adultery forthwith. . . . I sometimes think the extreme repression of all sexual feeling that this Message demands is partly responsible for our aching temptations (which we

---

[23]Idem, "Marriage and Divorce," *TSW* 3:13 (rpt., May 1984): 13, 16-17.

[24]Ibid., 25, 30.

[25]Ibid., 30, 34.

[26]Ibid., 44.

piously relieve by forever dwelling on the topic in our discussions and "denouncing" the evil of womankind—as Freud long ago observed).[27]

A final element of Branham's rejection of modern culture was his negative attitude toward education. He often apologized to his audiences for his poor grammar and lack of education. At the same time he was highly critical of the belief that education, especially theological education, was necessary for a Christian.[28] He constantly referred to seminaries as cemeteries and a person with a "D.D." as a "dead dog."[29] Branham viewed the possession of theological education as the haughty license to explain away the supernatural aspects of Christianity. He reiterated, "I'm not trying to support my ignorance but the biggest hindrance the gospel of Jesus has ever had is modern day education."[30]

As the Pentecostal movement matured and began to attract a more educated constituency, Branham's negative critique of education became more hostile. The common people, characterized by their lack of education, were the sincerest followers of Christ. Branham suggested that Jesus "went to the up-and up's, the educated and the intellectuals, could he find anybody? No, sir. They called Him, Beelzebulb, the devil."[31] Furthermore, Branham preached that God very seldom called an educated man to do an important ministry. The most effective servants of Christ were those not hindered by intellectual conceptions.[32]

The most extreme renunciation of education became apparent after Branham began publicly espousing the doctrine of the serpent's seed. He declared that civilization, the educational system, and scientific development all began with the building of a city by Cain, the son of Eve and the serpent. Cain's descendents were masquerading today as the educated and the scientists, according to Branham.[33] He concluded:

> What did Satan pregnate Eve with? To disbelieve the Word for intellectuals, intellects and it ruined the whole creation. That is exactly what she had done in the world today, the church. She has pregnated herself with Bible schools and colleges. . . . They know all their creeds . . . but know

---

[27]Robert Moore, *1977, circa 1976* (n.p., 1976) 61.

[28]Branham, *Conduct,* 1:77.

[29]Idem, "I Am," recorded.

[30]Idem, *Conduct,* 1:77.

[31]Idem, "Unfailing," 27.

[32]Idem, *The Spoken Word,* 129.

[33]Idem, "The Rapture," *TSW* 5:14 (n.d.): 11.

nothing about God. They'd know when the Word is vindicated. . . . When God spoke back there and lotted out His Word to each generation as it came along.[34]

As Branham's "prophetic" identity peaked, he scorned education as Satan's tool for obscuring the "simplicity of the Message and the messenger."[35]

Branham's attitude toward culture was a very extremist perspective of "Christ against Culture." The evangelist criticized the gospel of wealth that he felt had compromised the faith of full gospel Christians. His heaviest strictures were reserved for modern women and education. Modern women were essentially immoral sexual machines who were to blame for adultery, divorce, and death. They were tools of the Devil. Likewise, education was Satan's snare for intellectual Christians who rejected the supernatural. Indeed, the central sins of modern culture, immoral women and education, were a result of the serpent's seed.

3.

Another contributor to the controversy that surrounded Branham's later ministry was his belief in denominationalism as the mark of the beast. During the peak years of the revival, Branham's enthusiasm for ecumenical campaigns, and the conscious avoidance of doctrinal conflict were the dominant traits of his public attitude toward denominationalism. He constantly preached the theme of unity of the Spirit to all full gospel Christians.[36] On the rare occasions that the evangelist was critical of a denominational tenet, he was apologetic and pleaded for the listeners not to be offended.[37]

Branham stated that he did not belong to any organization or denomination. This stance did not mean, however, that he was theoretically against the concept of organization. He explained that since people had different tastes, God gave his children the liberty to worship in different organizations. Separation from denominationalism was not necessary, according to Branham.[38]

Nevertheless, the evangelist was concerned that denominational loyalties were potential roadblocks to salvation and spiritual unity. He

---

[34]Idem, "Invisible," 24.

[35]Idem, "Recognizing Your Day and Its Message," *TSW* 5:1 (rpt., 1984): 19.

[36]Idem, *The Spoken Word*, 11.

[37]Idem, *Demonology* (Jeffersonville IN: Spoken Word Publications, 1976) 53.

[38]Ibid.

warned his listeners that they were not saved simply because of their membership in a particular denomination. He complained that when he asked a person the question, "Are you a Christian?" the response was always, "I belong to the Baptist church."[39] Moreover, the evangelist proclaimed:

> If you believe me to be God's prophet, you listen to this. And I say it with inspiration . . . that there will not be one organization represented (or what I mean, the whole organization) into the Kingdom of God, but God will pull out of every one of them the cream of the crop, and fill it up with the Spirit, and take it up into glory.[40]

Having abolished the importance of denominational loyalties, Branham emphasized that God judged a person by his faith.[41]

As the ecumenical spirit of the healing revival weakened in the middle 1950s, Branham asked the various Pentecostal groups to continue striving for a harmony of spirit. Nevertheless, many revival participants felt that Branham was becoming more dogmatic. On some occasions, Branham "forgot" his assertion that denominations were acceptable religious structures. As early as 1951, he criticized Pentecostals for organizing around the gift of tongues as the initial evidence of the Spirit baptism.[42] In 1955, Branham preached a sermon entitled "Why I Think Pentecost Failed." Just as Luther organized around the doctrine of justification, and Wesley organized around the doctrine of sanctification, the Pentecostals were making a creed out of the initial evidence of tongues. When organization around a doctrine resulted, Branham suggested, the movement of the Spirit was squelched, and the church died.[43]

Moreover, Branham's fierce anti-denominationalism was already being preached in the mid-1950s at the Branham Tabernacle. In May

---

[39]Branham, *Conduct,* 1:159.

[40]William Branham, *Israel and the Church* (Jeffersonville IN: Spoken Word Publications, n.d.) 121.

[41]"An Interview with William Branham," *TVH* 4 (October 1951): 8.

[42]David E. Harrell, Jr., *All Things Are Possible: The Healing and Charismatic Revivals in Modern America* (Bloomington: Indiana University Press, 1975) 96. See also William Branham, "Words That I Do Bear Witness of Me," sermon delivered and recorded in Phoenix AZ, 13 April 1951.

[43]William Branham, "Where I Think Pentecost Failed," sermon delivered and recorded in San Fernando CA, 11 November 1955. Other revivalists criticized Pentecostals for organizing and losing their spiritual life. See David Nunn and W. V. Grant, *The Coming World-Wide Revival* (Dallas: W. V. Grant, n.d.) 8.

1954, Branham preached a sermon on the "Mark of the Beast." In his introductory remarks, the evangelist contended that the sermon was "not directed toward any individual or any other religion." He admitted that his teachings might be wrong, but added that "this is divinely revealed by the Holy Spirit, the same Angel that directs me to see visions."[44]

Much of Branham's "revelation" was reminiscent of Scofield's dispensationalism and the anti-Catholic rhetoric of classical Pentecostalism. According to Revelation 17:5, Roman Catholicism was "Babylon the Great, the Mother of Harlots." Under Constantine, Rome was the first church that ever organized and became "the mother church of organizations." Branham was more specific, however. He charged that the "harlots" were the denominations of Protestantism. In essence, Catholicism was the "beast," and Protestantism was the "image of the beast."[45]

Like many Pentecostals, Branham vehemently denounced the possibility of the union of Protestantism in a universal church.[46] Already in 1954, Branham was warning his Jeffersonville congregation that the establishment of a "confederation of Churches" had begun. All denominations, Branham believed, would unite under the Pope and form the "image of the beast." Consequently, membership in this confederation was "the mark of the beast."[47]

In his later years, Branham became more outspoken in his anti-denominationalism, and his vociferations extended to audiences outside Jeffersonville. His extensive exposition of the seven church ages was a tirade against Catholicism. He traced the "fall" of the Church, depicting the progression of evil in Catholicism.[48] During the 1960s, Branham's distrust of Catholicism became a paranoia. He contended that Kennedy's

---

[44]William Branham, "The Mark of the Beast," sermon delivered and recorded in Jeffersonville IN, 12 May 1954.

[45]Ibid. Scofield identified Rome in his exposition of Rev. 17. See C. I. Scofield, ed., *The Scofield Reference Bible* (New York: Oxford University Press, 1945) 1346n. For a discussion of the anti-Catholic perspective of Pentecostalism, see Walter J. Hollenweger, "The Pentecostal Movement and the World Council of Churches," *Ecumenical Review* (July 1966): 310-20.

[46]Hollenweger, "World," 310-20. In 1963, the Assemblies of God resolved that "we believe that the combination of many denominations into a World Super Church will probably culminate in the Scarlet Woman of Religious Babylon of Revelation." See William W. Menzies, *Anointed to Serve: The Story of the Assemblies of God* (Springfield MO: Gospel Publishing House, 1971) 221.

[47]Branham, *Footprints*, 245.

[48]Idem, *Pergamean*, 272-73.

presidential victory was "set up" through illegal tampering of the voting machines. More important, Branham believed that Rome owned all the world's gold. After the United States went bankrupt, Branham predicted, Rome would intercede, pay the debts, and rule America.[49]

Branham's radical years also revealed an increased vehemence toward Protestant bodies. All denominations were "synagogues of Satan" (Rev. 2:9)[50] and any person who adhered to their man-made doctrines and creeds was a "prostitute religionist" who committed spiritual adultery.[51] Indeed, Branham "indicted" denominational ministers who accepted creeds or beliefs like trinitarianism for "crucifying afresh" Jesus Christ.[52]

As Branham more openly identified denominationalism as the mark of the beast, he frequently addressed the issue of separating from these infidel organizations. On a few occasions, he assured his audiences that such a radical step was not necessary. He urged them to remain in their churches, but to reject false, denominational doctrine.[53]

The heart of Branham's "message," however, was the call for the elect Bride to "come out" of denominationalism. Since denominationalism was extra-biblical dogma, the purpose of the eschatological, Laodicean messenger was to announce "the Message of the hour"—"Come out of her, my people that you may not be partakers of her plagues" (Rev. 18:4). Accordingly, Branham exhorted his listeners: "Come out of Babylon! Come out of the organizations! . . . the Holy Spirit will only vindicate the Word. It can't vindicate dogmas, there is no life in them."[54]

Discussing the status of those persons who refused to "come out," Branham admitted that there were Christians within the denominations. He quickly added, however, that "they're unbelievers in the Word, or wouldn't be in there."[55] Continued allegiance to a denomination would guarantee identification with the World Council of Churches—the mark of the beast. Subsequently, these Christians would miss the rapture, and

---

[49]Idem, "The Stature of a Perfect Man," *TSW* 2:18 (rpt., 1984): 57-58.

[50]Idem, *The Philadelphian Church Age*, vol. 8 of *The Revelation of Jesus Christ* (Jeffersonville IN: Spoken Word Publications, n.d.) 410.

[51]Idem, "Holy Spirit Explained," *TSW* 5:2 (n.d.): 30.

[52]Idem, "The Indictment," *TSW* 3:19 (rpt., 1983): 21.

[53]Idem, *Conduct*, 2:968. See also William Branham, "Lean Not Unto Thy Own Understanding," *TSW* 19:3 (April 1984): 17.

[54]Idem, "Why I Am Against Organized Religion," *TSW* 12:1 (n.d.): 39.

[55]Ibid., 26.

go through the tribulation imposed upon the world by the Antichrist. The obvious implication was that to be a part of the Bride and experience the pre-tribulation rapture, a person had to repudiate all denominational loyalties. Indeed, current Branham disciples accept this tenet.[56]

One scholar has suggested that Branham's anti-denominationalism contained a note of vindictiveness against his Pentecostal peers, since they were rejecting his forays into "prophetic" teachings. Whatever the motivation, Branham's repudiation of organized religion was particularly repugnant to Pentecostals. To call Catholicism the beast was not unusual, but to label Protestantism—Pentecostalism included—as the image of the beast was a totally different matter.[57]

4.

The controversial nature of Branham's later years is especially seen in his development of a theology that emphasized a few select doctrines. Though not always consistent with each other, these doctrines conveyed a distinctive theology that proved unpopular with many adherents of the full gospel tradition. In addition to his primary emphasis of eschatology, Branham's most important doctrinal concerns were a denial of an eternal hell, Oneness Pentecostalism, predestination, eternal security, and the serpent's seed.

During the peak years of the healing revival, Branham preached a doctrine of eternal punishment in hell. If there was no eternal punishment for the unsaved, Branham surmised, one could not postulate a belief in eternal life in heaven.[58] By 1957, however, Branham was proclaiming that hell was not eternal. He elaborated:

> If you see a man that's cheating, stealing, lying, just remember, his part's waiting in hell for him. . . . He'll be tormented there. Not forever, he can't be tormented forever, forever don't mean all . . . for all times. Eternity's forever, Eternity . . . has no beginning or end. But forever is a space of time.[59]

The duration of a sinner's punishment in hell might be "a hundred million years," according to Branham, but the torment will eventually end and

---

[56]William Branham, "The Seed of Discrepancy," *TSW* 12:15 (n.d.): 14-15. See also Statement by Billy Paul Branham, son of William Branham, personal interview, Jeffersonville IN, 27 September 1984.

[57]Robert Price, "Branham's Legacy," unpublished paper, 2.

[58]Branham, *Demonology*, 48.

[59]Idem, *An Exposition of the Book of Hebrews* (Jeffersonville IN: Spoken Word Publications, 1972) 158.

the wicked will be annihilated. Eternal life was reserved only for God and his children.[60]

Branham continued to refute the idea of an eternal hell for the remainder of his ministry. After reiterating the unorthodox doctrine in a 1960 sermon, he amazingly suggested that the Holy Spirit had just revealed it to him. Presented as a new "revelation," Branham's belief assumed a significant role as one of the mysteries that God was revealing in the "end-time."[61]

The doctrine that was particularly offensive to trinitarian Pentecostals was Branham's espousal of the "Jesus only" views regarding the Godhead and baptism. David Harrell noted that, early in his healing ministry, Branham equivocated in his assertions regarding these issues. The evangelist reportedly assured the trinitarians that he agreed with them, but he felt obligated to "Jesus only" adherents for their support at the outset of the revival.[62]

In his early campaigns, Branham did manifest an acceptance of the term "trinity." He often referred to the Holy Spirit as "the third person of the trinity."[63] Moreover, he told a "union" meeting of trinitarian and "Jesus only" Pentecostals that their doctrinal differences about the Godhead were not important.[64]

To his congregation at Jeffersonville, however, Branham was already defending the basic "Jesus only" position in the early 1950s. He asserted that for the past twenty years he had taught baptism in the name of Jesus. Whatever the case, Branham baptized his son, Billy Paul, in 1950, and used the formula of baptism "in the Name of the Lord Jesus Christ."[65] Moreover, doctrinal teaching from 1953-1954 rehearsed the "Jesus only" idea that the "Father," "Son," and "Holy Spirit," of Matthew 28:19 were

---

[60]Ibid. See also Branham, *Conduct*, 1:247. The belief in the annihilation of the wicked was not new to Pentecostalism. Charles Parham advocated the doctrine. See Robert Mapes Anderson, *Vision of the Disinherited: The Making of American Pentecostalism* (New York: Oxford University Press, 1979) 89.

[61]Branham, *Pergamean*, 233.

[62]Harrell, *All Things Are Possible*, 163.

[63]William Branham, "Resurrection of Lazarus," sermon delivered and recorded in Erie PA, 30 July 1951.

[64]Idem, "Works That I Do," recorded.

[65]Idem, *Footprints*, 217. Branham claimed that he was baptized by his Baptist minister "in the Name of the Lord Jesus." This could not have been the "Jesus only" baptism that he later preached. Branham had not yet heard of the Pentecostal group when he was baptized. See Branham, *Is This the Time?*, 52.

simply titles of manifestations for the one God whose name was Jesus. Trinitarianism, Branham contended, was tritheism. The evangelist also required his parishioners to be rebaptized in Jesus' name in imitation of the example of the Apostle Paul. [66]

In his later ministry, Branham openly advocated the "Jesus only" position, and trinitarians increasingly rejected him. Branham argued that he was not an adherent of the Oneness doctrine, however. The evangelist criticized the emphasis on rebaptism as a belief in baptismal regeneration. [67] Moreover, he distinguished between Oneness baptism in the name of "Jesus" and baptism in the name of "the Lord Jesus Christ." There were many people called Jesus, Branham objected, but there was only one Lord Jesus Christ. [68] Perhaps by utilizing this casuistry, Branham attempted to disassociate himself from the "Jesus only" adherents in an effort to be more acceptable to trinitarian crowds. [69]

Branham intensified his criticism of trinitarianism in the 1960s. Resorting to his "prophetic" authority, Branham exclaimed:

Trinitarianism is of the Devil. I say that Thus Saith The Lord! . . . And as far as three Gods, that's from hell. [70]

Thus Saith The Lord, the baptism using the title of Father, Son, and Holy Ghost is false. Thus Saith The Lord, I command every one of you here, on tape that hasn't been baptized in the Name of Jesus Christ, be baptized in the Name of Jesus Christ. [71]

Branham occasionally affirmed that persons baptized with a trinitarian baptism were Christian and possessed the Holy Spirit. [72] At other times, however, he emphasized the necessity of rebaptism in determining one's possession of the Holy Spirit. He caustically criticized trinitarians:

Any man that calls himself spiritual or a prophet acknowledges that every word of this is true [Bible]. How can he be a trinitarian? How can he bap-

---

[66]Idem, *Conduct*, 1:42, 178-86. Branham was referring to Acts 19:1-7.

[67]Idem, *The Revelation of Jesus Christ*, vol. 1 of *The Revelation of Jesus Christ* (Jeffersonville IN: Spoken Word Publications, n.d.) 46.

[68]Idem, *The Spoken Word*, 28.

[69]Statement by Robert Moore, former follower of Branham, telephone interview, Phoenix AZ, 9 September 1984.

[70]William Branham, *Revelation Chapter Four, Part III*, vol. 13 of *The Revelation of Jesus Christ* (Jeffersonville IN: Spoken Word Publications, n.d.) 676.

[71]Idem, "True Sign," 29.

[72]Idem, *Adoption*, 62. See also Branham, *The Spoken Word*, 31.

tize in the Name of the Father, Son, and Holy Ghost and say that he's anointed with the Spirit? How can he teach people that error and still be anointed with the Spirit? It cannot be done. It's an impossibility.[73]

Branham's inconsistency regarding the necessity of rebaptism in the name of the Lord Jesus Christ is another example of his desire to appeal to the various Pentecostal subgroups. By the end of his ministry, however, the implication was clear that fidelity to the eschatological "message" necessitated the acceptance of the "oneness" of the Godhead and baptism in the name of the Lord Jesus Christ.

Pentecostals, heirs of the Arminian heritage of the nineteenth-century Holiness movement, were also critical of Branham's belief in predestination. Influenced by the Calvinistic perspective of his Baptist background, Branham began to press a rigid concept of predestination in his latter radical years.

In the campaigns of the healing revival, the soteriology of Branham was usually a blend of Arminianism and Calvinism. This perspective had long been a characteristic of revivalists. Branham asserted that redemption was possible because of the power of "the blood of God."[74] Salvation came solely through grace. Consequently, a person could do absolutely nothing to merit salvation. God had to call the individual before one could accept and receive salvation. The initiative of God was necessary since humanity was totally depraved. Branham preached, "You was [sic] condemned before your first breath. . . . For you were judged by the sexual desire of your father and mother."[75] On the other hand, the revivalist appealed to the free moral agency of persons in the process of salvation throughout his ministry. He even suggested that a person could guarantee his salvation by fulfilling God's requirement of faith. "If you believe and repent of your sins," Branham admonished, "God is under obligation to save you."[76]

When discussing the possibility of salvation, however, Branham's primary thrust was a belief in predestination. The evangelist attempted to avoid the use of the term predestination when conducting revival meetings. He felt the term was usually misunderstood by the laity. Con-

---

[73]Idem, "True Sign," 40.

[74]Idem, "Resurrection of Lazarus," recorded.

[75]Idem, *Hebrews*, 180.

[76]Gordon Lindsay, ed., *The William Branham Sermons: How God Called Me to Africa and Other Sermons* (Dallas: The Voice of Healing Publishing Co., n.d.) 59. See also William Branham, "Choosing a Bride," *TSW* 2:28 (rpt., May 1983): 6.

sequently, Branham opted for the term foreknowledge since "predestination is only the foreknowledge of God."[77] Branham explained his
position:

> But just individuals out of the church, who's predestinated to Eternal life,
> they'll come. That's all. But those who are not, cannot come; and God
> said so, said, "They were predestinated to condemnation." He is not
> willing that any should perish, but being God, He seen they would con-
> demn It . . . that's what the foreknowledge of God is, to see those
> things.[78]

Branham contended that the foreknowledge of God did not negate a
person's free choice regarding salvation. God simply knew before the
foundation of the world how an individual would choose. With this knowledge God then ordained that person to eternal life. The evangelist often
was inconsistent, however, in his assertion that God's foreknowledge was
compatible with the free moral agency of humanity. Telling a recently
saved individual about the gratitude that he owed God, Branham commented, "You should be the happiest person there is in the world. There
was [sic] millions that would do it if they could, but they can't. It's not for
them to have it."[79]

A corollary of Branham's belief in predestination was his emphasis on
eternal security. Drawing upon his Calvinistic roots, the evangelist suggested that predestination guaranteed eternal security. The soul of the
predestinated believer existed in the mind of God before the foundation
of the world. Since God was eternal, the immortal soul possessed eternal
life. "Part of God's life [is] in us," Branham remarked, "we could no more
perish than God could perish."[80]

Branham became more outspoken concerning predestination in the
late 1950s and 1960s. Moreover, the continued circulation of Branham's
taped sermons made Pentecostals more aware of the predestination
teaching. Consequently, Branham admitted in a 1961 sermon that he was

---

[77]Branham, *Conduct,* 1:494.

[78]Ibid., 165.

[79]Branham, "True Sign," 15. In defense of his belief in predestination, Branham cited
Eph. 1:4 and Rom. 8-9.

[80]Idem, "Redemption by the Blood," sermon delivered and recorded in Louisville KY,
29 March 1954.

criticized more for his teaching of predestination than any other facet of his ministry.[81]

A key element in Branham's rigid predestination concept of the 1960s was the emphasis on the Bride of Christ as God's seed. Like the literal seed of the serpent, the predestinated believer was an heir of the godly seed. The believer in the eschatological "message," Branham contended, "was born with a 'predestinated Germ.' "[82] His soul was "that gene that come from God."[83]

Branham's teachings on predestination were confusing and contradictory. The evangelist evidently did not realize the conflict between the relationship of God's foreknowledge and humanity's free choice, with his doctrine of the serpent's seed and the godly seed. In essence, the belief in two literal seeds as the sources of human ancestry negated any role of humanity's choice in the salvation process. Branham was actually asserting that simple genetics determined one's eternal destiny. A type of double predestination eventuated. The serpent's seed of Cain foreordained his descendents to damnation while the heirs of Seth's seed were bound for glory.

Perhaps the most disreputable belief espoused by Branham was his doctrine of the serpent's seed. The evangelist was heavily criticized for preaching his conviction that Cain was conceived from Eve's sexual intercourse with the serpent in the Garden of Eden. According to Pearry Green, "a minister well known all over the world" described the serpent's seed concept a "filthy doctrine" that "ruined his [Branham's] ministry."[84]

The first lengthy exposition of the serpent's seed doctrine was given in 1958. Branham evidently had accepted the tenet previous to this time, however. He told his audiences that he had had some "funny views" about the fall but he did not share them in the revivals.[85] Branham did hint at his belief when he analyzed the differences between Cain and Abel. Abel's sacrifice was acceptable to God since he received a spiritual revelation

---

[81]Idem, *The Seventy Weeks of Daniel* (Jeffersonville IN: Spoken Word Publications, 1970) 92.

[82]Idem, "Invisible," 34.

[83]Idem, "Leadership," *TSW* 7:7 (n.d.): 24.

[84]Pearry Green, *The Acts of the Prophet* (Tucson: Tucson Tabernacle Books, n.d.) 27.

[85]Robert Moore, *Quotations of William M. Branham* (n.p., n.d.) B4.

that "it was not apples that brought them out of the Garden of Eden. . . . it was blood"[86]

After 1958, however, Branham openly acknowledged his convictions about the serpent's seed. The serpent had sexual intercourse with Eve, and Cain was born. Such an audacious act was possible, the evangelist revealed, because the serpent was the "missing link" between the chimpanzee and the Man. This "prehistoric giant" was perhaps ten feet tall and looked just like a man. Only after the curse of the fall did the serpent become a reptile. Branham suggested that the serpent was able to have sexual relations with Eve because they both had literal seeds according to Genesis 3:15. Eve's exclamation "the serpent beguiled me," Branham concluded, was to be interpreted as an acknowledgment of physical defilement.[87]

Branham declared that "it's a law of God to ripen every seed, to make every seed produce itself. So it had to produce the serpent's seed."[88] Accordingly, Branham developed two genetic strains throughout history. Abel's godly seed was carried on through the progeny of Seth like Noah, Abraham, Isaac, Jacob, David, and Jesus Christ. Modern possessors of this godly seed were those Christians who accepted a supernatural gospel.[89]

A genealogy of Satan's ancestors was developed through the lineage of Cain. According to Branham, the descendants of Cain included the giants of Genesis 6, Ham, Ahab, and Judas Iscariot. They were intelligent, educated and were builders and scientists. In addition, they were overtly religious, but really possessed an anti-Christian spirit. Cain's modern descendants were most likely the theologians and scoffers of the Word. Branham compared the religious attitudes produced by the two genetic strains.

> In this last day . . . the spirit of the anti-Christ saying, "The days of miracles are past." The Spirit of Christ saying, "He is the same yesterday,

---

[86]William Branham, "I Will Restore unto You Saith the Lord," sermon delivered and recorded in Los Angeles CA, 9 August 1954. To his Jeffersonville congregation, Branham did assert that Cain "came from the line of Satan." No mention of a serpent's seed was made, however. See William Branham, "All We, Like Sheep, Have Gone Astray," sermon delivered and recorded in Jeffersonville IN, 3 April 1953.

[87]Idem, "Serpent's," 20-24.

[88]Idem, "The Future Home of the Heavenly Bridegroom and the Earthly Bride," *TSW* 3:5 (rpt., 1980): 47.

[89]Idem, "Serpent's," 27-28.

today, and forever." The spirit of anti-Christ says, "It doesn't make any difference if you are baptized in the Father, Son, and Holy Ghost."[90]

Branham concluded that the descendants of Cain were "a big religious bunch of illegitimate bastard children."[91]

To those who disagreed with the doctrine of the serpent's seed, Branham responded that the same God who gave him infallible visions inspired his teaching.[92] Consequently, the doctrine increased in importance since Branham regarded it as one of the eschatological mysteries of God. Indeed, current "Message" believers are more proud of the serpent's seed doctrine than any other. They believe it to be Branham's most original revelation.[93]

The belief in the serpent's seed had an indirect but significant effect upon Branham's Christology. The evangelist believed that the seduction of Eve by the serpent eventuated in procreation through sexual intercourse. Branham's vehement criticism of women and sexual relations consequently influenced his views on the nature of Christ.

The evangelist asserted that Jesus Christ possessed the "blood of God." God's blood was necessary because the blood of human beings was tainted by the sexual desire of women. Branham thus explained the virgin birth of Jesus:

> And God overshadowed the virgin and she brought forth a baby; not Jewish blood, not Gentile blood, but His Own Blood. God's created Blood, no sex at all in it at all [sic], no sexual desire. And this Blood Cell, created in the womb of this woman, brought forth the Son.[94]

For Branham, only the pure, unadulterated blood of God redeemed a sexually fallen humanity.

The evangelist further safeguarded the nature of Christ from the sexual sin of Eve and the serpent by disparaging the role of women in the

---

[90]Ibid.

[91]Ibid., 35.

[92]Ibid., 40.

[93]Letter received from Robert Moore, 10 October 1983. Perhaps Branham's views on the serpent's seed came from his Baptist roots. The views of Daniel Parker were well known among Calvinistic Baptists in Kentucky. Parker, the founder of the Two-Seed-in-the-Spirit-Predestinarian Baptists, popularized the theory that the "inlet of the serpent's seed into a natural existence in the world" came through "the conception of a woman." Branham's genealogy of the Devil's children also shows similarities to Parker's exposition. See Daniel Parker, *Views on the Two Seeds* (Vandalia IL: Daniel Parker, 1826) 5-9.

[94]Branham, *Hebrews*, 83. See also Branham, "What the Holy Ghost," 23.

birth process. God created the blood cell since only a father's blood was transmitted to a child. Branham declared that "not a speck of the mother's blood is in the baby." Moreover, a mother was simply an "incubator" that was "connected" to the baby only by a "navel cord."[95]

In addition to creating the blood cell, God created the egg in the Virgin Mary. Branham explained: "If the egg come from the woman, there has to be a sensation to bring the egg through the tube to the womb. See what you do with God? You make them in a sexual mess."[96] Branham was seemingly unaware that an ovum was released monthly, regardless of sexual activity. Therefore, he believed that if the egg involved in the birth of Jesus was Mary's, the Holy Spirit had been implicated with sexual intercourse. To allow a woman any role except that of an "incubator" was to negate Christ's victory over Eve's sexual fall.[97]

5.

The major doctrinal concern of Branham's later ministry was eschatology. Since its origin, Pentecostalism had emphasized the imminent second coming of Christ. The earliest Pentecostals interpreted their movement as a great "latter rain" outpouring of the Spirit that would immediately precede the return of Christ. Undergirding this millennial expectation was Scofield's system of dispensationalism.[98]

During the healing revival, Branham emphasized the imminent return of Christ. The appearance of the revival was a harbinger of the apocalypse. After the revival fires diminished, Branham persisted in his proclamations of the rapture's imminence. Branham told his audiences to

---

[95]Idem, *Conduct*, 1:240-41.

[96]Idem, "Oneness," *TSW* 10:2 (n.d.): 15.

[97]Harrell did not mention Branham's Christology as a point of conflict with his full gospel peers. Current anticult apologetics, however, condemn Branham for his Christological views. See Carl Dyck, *William Branham: The Man and His Message* (Saskatoon, Canada: Western Tract Mission, 1984) 27-32. Branham denied the eternal Sonship of Christ. See Branham, *Hebrews*, 177. He also advocated a type of adoptionistic and docetic Christology. Jesus was the Son of God at birth, but only became the Messiah when he was baptized. See William Branham, "Possessing the Enemy's Gates," *TSW* 11:6 (n.d.): 16. Branham's Jesus was platonic. He was God in his Spirit and "totally man" in his physical being. The anointed Spirit left Jesus in the Garden of Gethsemane, and the man died on the cross. Branham did not question the effect this partition had on the atonement. See Branham, *Adoption*, 40.

[98]Nils Bloch-Hoell, *The Pentecostal Movement: Its Origins, Development, and Distinctive Character* (New York: Humanities Press, 1964) 155. See also Menzies, *Anointed*, 328-29.

believe his words about the nearness of the rapture if they believed that he was God's prophet.[99] Indeed, Branham's emphasis on eschatological themes became the major obsession in the latter years of his ministry.

The evangelist had always adhered to many tenets of Scofield's dispensationalist system. One of the more intriguing elements for Branham was the breakdown of the dispensation of grace in the final era before the millennial reign of Christ—into seven church ages.[100] In 1954, he outlined the seven church ages at the Branham Tabernacle. His basic thrust was that the angels of the seven churches of Revelation 2-3 were earthly messengers. In each church age God sent one messenger with the divine message for that era. Branham emphasized the accepted, full gospel tenet that the Pentecostal movement had ushered in the last church age of Laodicea with the restoration of spiritual gifts. Nevertheless, Branham left the door open for another "move of God." Pentecostals had erred in developing an organization around tongues as the evidence of the Spirit baptism. The last message would not be hampered by denominational creeds, according to Branham.[101]

In 1960 Branham preached a whole series of sermons on the church ages, and he considered them a fresh revelation from God. The same basic material was presented, as in 1954, but with greater detail. Branham outlined the "fall" of the Catholic church and the gradual restoration of God's Word with Protestantism. He identified "by revelation" each age chronologically and named the respective messengers.[102]

The most important and most controversial element of Branham's "revelation" was a description of the prophet-messenger to the Laodi-

---

[99]Branham, *The Spoken Word,* 58.

[100]The dispensation of grace describes the era after Christ's crucifixion. The covenant of grace is available to Jews and Gentiles individually until the second coming of Christ.

[101]William Branham, "The Seven Church Ages," sermon delivered and recorded in Jeffersonville IN, 11 May 1954. For an explanation of the dispensationalism of Scofield, see 37 n. 56.

[102]Branham delineated the dates and messengers of the seven church ages as follows: 1) Ephesian, 53-170, Paul 2) Smyrnaean, 170-312, Irenaeus 3) Pergamos, 312-606, Martin of Tours 4) Thyatira, 606-1520, Colomba 5) Sardis, 1520-1750, Martin Luther 6) Philadelphia, 1750-1906, John Wesley 7) Laodicean, 1906-(1977, predicted)? See William Branham, "The Ephesus Church Age," sermon delivered and recorded in Jeffersonville IN, 5 December 1960. Branham primarily selected the messengers on the criterion that they reportedly believed in "signs and wonders." The most blatant error in Branham's outline was that he began the Thyatira Age in 606. Colomba, the messenger of the age, died in 597. In 1954, the only specific messengers that Branham identified were Luther and Wesley.

cean age. This messenger had the "message" that would close out the Gentile dispensation and usher in the rapture. Moreover, Branham re-iterated his prediction that the rapture would occur by 1977.[103]

The evangelist offered an extensive portrait of the Laodicean messenger. He "will be one like Elijah," Branham suggested.[104] The biblical proof for the return of Elijah's spirit lay in an exegesis of Malachi 4:5-6 that was prevalent among some Pentecostals. In these verses Malachi prophesied:

> Behold, I will send to you Elijah the prophet before the coming of the great and dreadful day of the Lord. And he shall turn the heart of the fathers to the children, and the heart of the children to their fathers, lest I come and smite the earth with a curse.[105]

Branham acknowledged that a portion of these verses was fulfilled in the life of John the Baptist. Luke 1:15-17 spoke of John coming in the spirit of Elijah to turn the hearts of the fathers to the children. John's preaching influenced the fathers—the Jews—to turn to the new Christian faith of the Gentiles, according to Branham.[106]

The evangelist believed, however, that the Malachi prophecy was not completely fulfilled. He noted that Malachi prophesied the appearance of an Elijah figure before the dreadful Day of the Lord. John the Baptist did not fulfill this function. Consequently, another prophet-messenger with the same spirit of Elijah would appear as the forerunner to Christ's second coming. This end-time messenger would complete the prophecy by turning the hearts of the children back to the New Testament fathers with the Pentecostal message of gospel primitivism.[107]

Based upon his compound interpretation of the Malachi prophecy, Branham "revealed" some of the characteristics of the Laodicean messenger. All the traits were compatible to the nature of Elijah and John the Baptist, the evangelist asserted. First, the messenger was a mighty prophet that obeyed the Word of God. Second, he despised denominationalism. Third, as Elijah hated Jezebel, and John hated Herodias, the

---

[103]William Branham, *Is This the Time?* (Jeffersonville IN: Spoken Word Publications, n.d.) 11-21.

[104]Ibid., 12.

[105]Lindsay exegeted the passage and said that God was raising up many men who were preaching with the spirit of Elijah in the last days. See Gordon Lindsay, "Will Elijah Come Again?," *TVH* 7 (June 1954): 6.

[106]Branham, *Is This the Time?*, 17.

[107]Ibid.

Laodicean messenger "hated fancy women." Fourth, God's man was a lover of the wilderness. Fifth, he was uneducated, and moody in temperament. In essence, his ministry would be so powerful and misunderstood that people would mistake him for the Messiah. All the characteristics that Branham described coincided with his own life. He did not claim to be the messenger, however, and even spoke as if this prophet was another on the horizon. [108]

The pivotal characteristic of the Laodicean prophet-messenger was the gift of visionary discernment. Branham's possession of this gift had always made him feel special. In 1958, while everyone was acknowledging the demise of the revival, Branham wrote an article re-emphasizing his commitment to prayer for the sick. He suggested that his loss of strength, which resulted from the visions, was largely responsible for the decline of the ministry. Concurrently, Branham boldly proclaimed that "before our very eyes was displayed one of the greatest miracles the ages have seen since the time of Christ. For the sign of the vision was the sign of the Messiah heralding the return of our Lord and Savior Jesus Christ."[109] As he had done in the healing campaigns, Branham cited biblical proofs for Jesus' use of discernment. He now asserted that Jesus "established his claims in the eyes of the Jews as being the Messiah because he filled the prophecy of Moses relative to God raising up the God-Prophet."[110] According to Branham, Christ appeared as Messiah to the Jews at the end of their dispensation. Therefore, the sign of the Messiah was being revealed by the Holy Spirit for the first time to the Gentiles, at the end of their age. Branham was not claiming to be the Messiah.[111] Nevertheless, he believed that God was utilizing the sign of the Messiah in his ministry in order to announce an imminent, second coming of Christ.

Branham also began in 1958 to connect the gift of discernment with Jesus Christ as the Son of man. Biblical justification was derived from Luke 17:30, "As it was in the days of Sodom, so shall it be in the days when the Son of man is being revealed."[112] The evangelist reasoned that the Laodicean age was immorally comparable to Sodom. Denominations had thrust Christ out of the Church (Rev. 3:20).

---

[108]Ibid., 15-19, 49.

[109]William Branham, "Rev. William Branham and the Future," *HOF* 25 (July 1958): 17.

[110]Ibid.

[111]Ibid., 18.

[112]Branham paraphrased Luke 17:29-30.

The Laodicean age also was receiving the same revelatory sign of the Son of man that Abraham did. In his exegesis of Genesis 18:20, Branham argued that two messengers went to Sodom and preached a message of repentance to sinners. A third messenger remained with Abraham who represented the Elect. Branham preached that the messenger was a stranger to Abraham, yet he knew Sarah's name. Then the stranger told Abraham that Sarah would soon have a child. Although the messenger could not see Sarah, he discerned her laughter regarding the news of a new baby. Branham exhorted that Christ as the Son of man had been revealed to Abraham and his seed, the Elect. Likewise, the Son of man now was revealing himself in the Laodicean age to the Elect, through the same sign of discernment.[113]

The frequency of exposition of Luke 17:30 steadily increased in Branham's later years. Some followers believed that Branham was actually the reappearance of the Son of man. The evangelist denied the identification, but it was obvious that he interpreted his ministry as a fulfillment of the verse. To his audiences, Branham queried, "What was the last sign before Sodom burned?—this very thing you're seeing tonight; God manifesting himself in human flesh, knowing the secret of the heart."[114]

Branham's relationship to Luke 17:30 became increasingly apparent as he identified the two messengers to Sodom in the Laodicean age. As early as December, 1958, the evangelist said "a Billy Graham and a Jack Schiller went down into Sodom" to preach the message of repentance.[115] By 1960, Branham was emphasizing that Graham had taken a revival to the "nominal" church, and Oral Roberts had done the same for the Pentecostals. The 1963 experience of opening the seals, however, occasioned the boldest implication yet regarding Luke 17:30. Branham declared:

> When was there ever a man—search down your history—that ever went forth to the church formal by the name ending with "H-A-M" before? Look here: "A-B-R-A-H-A-M." Now look, Abraham's name has *seven* letters, A-B-R-A-H-A-M, but not our Brother Billy Graham's has G-R-A-H-A-M—*six* not *seven* (the world). That is where he is ministering to—the church natural.

....

---

[113]William Branham, "Where Is He, King of the Jews," *TSW* 16:7 (n.d.): 30.

[114]Moore, *Quotations,* 202. See also Branham, *Conduct* 2:1021.

[115]Branham, "Where Is He," 30.

Watch now, there was one that came to the church spiritual—the Bride,
Abraham . . . He did the Messiahic [*sic*] sign.[116]

One only had to count the number of letters in Branham's name to learn
the identity of the messenger to the Bride.

The most critical development in Branham's use of Luke 17:30 was
its incorporation into the identity of the eschatological messenger of the
Laodicean age. Branham achieved this feat by revealing the interdependence of Luke 17:30 and Malachi 4:5-6. Especially in 1964 and 1965, the
evangelist began to emphasize that the Son of man was a prophet. Jesus
identified himself as a prophet to the Jews through visionary discernment. The modern manifestation of the Son of man to the Gentiles must
be in the ministry of a prophet with discernment, according to Branham.
Consequently, the appearance of the eschatological prophet of Malachi 4
was a fulfillment of Luke 17:30.[117]

Branham's obsession with Luke 17:30 and Malachi 4:5-6 dominated
the end of his ministry. Indeed, the story of his early life was reinterpreted in light of these pivotal verses and the opening of the seven seals.
To a 1964 audience in Tampa, Florida, Branham told the story of the angelic commission of 1946:

> I went back and told my pastor . . . he said, "Billy, what have you eat?
> Did you have a dream, was that a nightmare?" But to me, it was Malachi
> 4. He said, "How you going to do it?" It was Luke 17:30. It was also Revelation 10. . . . I didn't see it done right then. But I just held on.[118]

Branham never explicitly acknowledged that he was the eschatological prophet-messenger. When he first preached on Malachi 4 in his sermons on the seven church ages in 1960, the evangelist spoke as if he was
looking for someone else to fill this role. His supporters, however, justifiably interpreted Branham to be this unique prophet. All of the char-

---

[116]Idem, *The Revelation of the Seven Seals* (Tucson: Spoken Word Publications, 1967)
209-10.

[117]Idem, "Proving His Word," *TSW* 9:6 (n.d.): 41. See also William Branham, "The
Trial," *TSW* 12:2 (n.d.): 15.

[118]Branham also identified the angel of Rev. 10:7 as the Laodicean messenger. See
Branham, "The Trial," 14. Green argued that the first time Malachi 4 was applied to
Branham occurred before the 1946 angelic commission. Meda Broy helped care for
Branham's son before and after the death of his first wife. When rumors began about a
relationship between Broy and Branham, God comforted her with a revelation of the Malachi prophecy. Subsequently, Broy became Branham's second wife. See Green, *Prophet*,
60.

acteristics of the messenger that Branham had delineated were descriptive of the evangelist.

During the 1960s, Branham occasionally struggled with the beliefs of his followers regarding his identity. In a 1961 meeting of church leaders in Jeffersonville, he was asked, "Brother Branham, we know that you are a messenger sent from God to this church age. . . . Would you explain the difference in your relationship to God and that of Christ's?"[119] Branham responded, "Well, I know, brethren, that is true," and then he quoted the "forerunner message" that he received at the 1933 baptismal service. The evangelist immediately distinguished between having the "message" and being the messenger, however. He explained:

> I don't think I'd have anything to do with that messenger, see. That's right. I believe that I am maybe being sent for a part in His Church, to help build that Message up to a place to where it would when this forerunner comes, that he will come. But I believe, me being what I am . . . I believe that I have the Message of the day.[120]

Branham left an opening for his followers to call him the Laodicean messenger. He told them "even if I believed it, I wouldn't say it."[121] His audience immediately drew an analogy to the disclaimers of the first forerunner, John the Baptist:

> [A brother] says, "Even they came to John and said, ['Are you the Christ?' "—Ed.] Yeah, that's it, what I'm trying—to get to. [" 'Are you that Prophet?' "] He denied it, ["Didn't say either one, he says, 'I'm just one crying in the wilderness.' "] "The voice of one crying in the wilderness." He positionally placed himself.
>
> . . . .
>
> [A brother says, "When Christ came along then, following John, they come to Him and He said . . . believed and he taught to these that Elijah would come before the Messiah. He said, 'If you can receive it.' "—Ed.] That was him. That's right. That's right. And John kept saying, "I am nothing! I am nothing! I'm not worthy to loose His shoe.' "[122]

In another private meeting of ministers in 1962, Branham reiterated the confusing signals about his "prophetic" identity. He evinced a strong desire to be this prophet, but he was concerned that his work as an evan-

---

[119]Branham, *Conduct,* 2:571.

[120]Ibid., 572.

[121]Ibid., 573.

[122]Ibid., 573-74.

gelist conflicted with the role of a prophet. A prophet held no evangelistic meetings but hid in the wilderness until God gave him a message of "Thus Saith the Lord." Branham consoled himself, with the reminder that God had not called him to be an evangelist, but simply to do the work of one. [123]

After the experience of opening the seals in 1963, Branham seemed more sure of his identity. He noted that the "message" and the messenger were inseparable. "When a man comes with Thus Saith The Lord, he and the message is one." Branham declared, "The Word of God and the messenger of the age was the selfsame thing."[124] Even in the boldest sermons of 1965, however, Branham could demonstrate some conflicting reservations about his identity as the eschatological messenger. He could still say that his "message," if not the one prophesied in Luke 17 and Malachi 4, at least laid the foundations for the imminent appearance of the Laodicean messenger. [125]

Delineating Branham's thoughts about the identity of the Laodicean prophet-messenger reveals a plethora of conflicting and confusing assertions and disclaimers. Branham indisputably applied the biblical passages, Malachi 4:5-6 and Luke 17:30, to his own ministry. Coupled with reiterations about the 1933 baptismal experience, the opening of the seals, and his doctrinal pronouncements accompanied by "Thus Saith the Lord," Branham obviously regarded himself as the eschatological prophet-messenger that had a "message" for the predestinated rapture-bound Bride of Christ. The fact that Branham had doubts about his role was evident. The tension between being an evangelist or a wilderness prophet was frustrating for him. Branham constantly sought tangible evidence for a great and unique ministry. The full realization of the tent vision with its mysterious "third pull" was never completely fulfilled. Nevertheless, the adulation of Branham's disciples surely diminished the force of any doubts and confirmed Branham's desire to be the end-time prophet. Perhaps their indefatigable support of Branham's unique identity facilitated his reticence about the identity of the prophet-messenger. Indeed, in one of his last sermons, Branham repeated his analysis of the numerology of Billy Graham's and Abraham's name. The evangelist concluded with the story of how Jesus presented himself to the disciples on the road to Emmaus:

---

[123]Ibid., 758.

[124]William Branham, "Spiritual Food in Due Season," *TSW* 8:7 (n.d.): 11.

[125]Idem, "Marriage," 8.

He never come right out . . . and said, "Well, don't you know I'm your messiah for this age? . . . The real servant of God never identifies himself that way; the Scripture identifies who he is.

....

Am not I, tonight, trying to tell you, Word by Word (even to the position, the place, the names and numbers . .) that we're right at the end time?[126]

In addition to discussing the identity of the eschatological prophet-messenger, Branham was equally concerned with announcing his mission—the restoration of the "Word." Branham frequently utilized the Pentecostal theme that gospel primitivism was partially restored with Martin Luther's emphasis on justification and John Wesley's belief in sanctification. The Pentecostal recovery of the spiritual gifts was the final preparation for Christ's second coming. In his later ministry, Branham emphasized that Luther and Wesley were only reformers. Therefore, a prophet—the Laodicean messenger—must come to fully restore the "Word." The crux of his task, as Malachi 4 specified, was to turn the hearts of the predestinated children back to the faith of the "message" of the Bible. When the restoration of the "Word" was complete, the Bride of Christ was ready for the rapture. [127]

Branham believed that the infallible Bible was "God in word form."[128] The "Word" of God for this age was an admonition to return to the apostolic faith. Moreover, the "Word" of God, while in accordance with biblical truth, came afresh in each church age. The method of receiving this "Word" was not through private interpretation of the Bible. Rather, Branham asserted, the Bible was written and interpreted by the prophets. The modern believer must still adhere to the divinely inspired interpretation provided by a prophet. Branham quoted Amos 3:7, "Surely, the Lord God will do nothing, but he revealeth his secret unto his servants and prophets," as biblical justification for the prophet's role as the sole revealer of the "Word."[129] The genuine prophet had the divine authority to pronounce "Thus Saith the Lord," since he was true to the

---

[126]Idem, "Modern Events Are Made Clear by Prophecy," *TSW* 7:6 (n.d.): 41.

[127]Frederick Dale Bruner, *A Theology of the Holy Spirit: The Pentecostal Experience and the New Testament Witness* (Grand Rapids MI: William B. Eerdmans, 1970) 27-28. See also Branham, "Seven Church," recorded.

[128]Branham, "Modern," 9.

[129]Idem, "Trying to Do God a Service without It Being God's Will," *TSW* 7:2 (n.d.): 40-41.

"Word" and did not compromise with denominational teachings. Consequently, the "Word" of the prophet was the "Voice" of God to the age. [130]

Branham was even more specific about the relationship of the prophets to the revelation of the "Word." He asserted that God only had one major prophet in an age through which the "Word" was spoken. This theme naturally complemented the obsession with the identity of the Laodicean messenger. Using his favorite biblical comparison, Branham noted that Moses—and not an organization—had the "Word" in his day. Branham warned his listeners not to be like Dathan and Korah who rejected the "one-man Message" of the prophet Moses. [131]

Branham criticized any attempt to imitate God's chosen prophet. Throughout his ministry, he had complained about "carnal impersonators" who appeared on the scene of healing revivalism after he did. Other deliverance evangelists had tried to reproduce his two healing signs, the vibrating hand and visionary discernment. "The carnal impersonation only magnifies the right one," Branham retorted. [132] He emphasized that the "Word" was the criterion for identifying a carnal impersonator. The evangelist often cited as biblical precedent the impersonators of Moses, Jannes, and Jambres (II Tim. 3:8-9). Modern carnal impersonators—like those men of the Egyptian Pharaoh's court—performed miracles such as healing, but they "can't stay with the Word," Branham ridiculed. [133] In essence, Branham felt that he had been forsaken by other evangelists; and therefore he was a martyr for the attempt to fully restore the "Word" with his eschatological "message." [134]

After 1963, Branham proclaimed that the opening of the seals of Revelation had superseded the Pentecostal era, and ushered in the "Bride Age." To be a member of the Bride and participate in the rapture, one had to be baptized with the Holy Spirit. The evidence of the baptism was not tongues, as most Pentecostals contended, but "faith in the promised

---

[130]Idem, "The Voice of God in These Last Days," *TSW* 9:7 (n.d.): 6, 14. See also Branham, "True Sign," 16. Branham was inconsistent with the "Word" by calling Luther and Wesley reformers, rather than prophets.

[131]Idem, "Why It Had to Be Shepherds," *TSW* 6:15 (n.d.): 30. In a 1951 sermon Branham preached that "there never was in the age any two major prophets on the earth at one time. There were many minor prophets but there was one major prophet." See William Branham, "The Prophet Knows the Heart," sermon delivered and recorded in New York NY, 29 September 1951.

[132]Idem, "Testimony," *TSW* 17:5 (n.d.): 11.

[133]Idem, "The Anointed Ones at the End Time," *TSW* 5:3 (rpt., 1984): 33.

[134]Idem, "Present Stage of My Ministry," *TSW* 11:2 (n.d.): 25.

Word of the hour."[135] Pentecostals who believed in tongues as the evidence, or who advocated trinitarianism, disobeyed the "Word" and were not truly Spirit-filled. Branham's personal obedience to the "Word," moreover, was vindicated by his role in the Bride. Recalling his early life when people ridiculed him for his father's alcoholism, Branham proclaimed: "People didn't love me at all, nobody had any use for me. And now, by the help of God, I believe that I'm directing the Bride of Jesus Christ."[136]

While Branham criticized Catholicism for requiring priestly mediators between God and humanity, he had in effect done the same thing.[137] No one could approach God, nor interpret the "Word" except through the prophet. Indeed, the "Word" was the Bible and the "message" of the prophet. To accept this "Word" meant to accept the restorer.

The ultimate significance of Branham's emphasis on the "Word" is found in the mystery of the 1955 tent vision and promise of the "third pull." As Branham yearned for the fulfillment of the unparalleled tent campaign, he constantly conjectured about the meaning of the "third pull." He nebulously described several events to be the "third pull," such as the opening of the seals or the experience of the King's Sword.[138] Essentially, Branham gradually understood that the "third pull" was the ability "to speak the Word."[139] Whatever he spoke into existence would occur. The full manifestation of this final and climactic phase of Branham's ministry would be fully revealed in the little wooden room of the tent vision.

The equation of the "third pull" with the ability to "speak the Word" appeared in 1959. Three events had occurred in Branham's life that he

---

[135]Idem, "Trying," 34-35. See also Branham, *Conduct,* 2:524, 1003. Even during the peak years of the revival, Branham denied that tongues was the initial evidence of the Holy Spirit baptism. He said that every Christian would eventually speak in tongues but it was only an attribute of the Spirit. Before 1960, Branham preached that a Christian's life of love and holiness was the best way to discern the presence of the Spirit. See also Branham, *Hebrews,* 189. Branham was probably influenced by the views of F. F. Bosworth. In 1918, Bosworth, an early influential leader of the Assemblies of God, created a controversy over his denial of tongues as the initial evidence. Consequently, he left the denomination. Though tongues as the initial evidence unites the Pentecostal movement, Pentecostals have not unanimously insisted upon the doctrine. See Anderson, *Vision,* 4, 161-64.

[136]Branham, *Conduct,* 2:1041, 1053.

[137]Idem, "Ephesus," recorded.

[138]Idem, "Anointed Ones," 61. See also Green, *Prophet,* 143-60.

[139]Idem, *Conduct,* 1:412.

came to interpret as divine "vindications" of the truth of an imminent "third pull." The first event, which occurred in 1957, was the resurrection of a small fish that had been "laying dead for a half hour, on the water, with his entrails pulled out of his mouth."[140] Branham first reported the story as simply another evidence of the miraculous in his ministry. After two other experiences in 1959, however, he viewed the resurrection of the fish as the first vindication of the "third pull."

The event which was most significant to Branham's understanding of the "third pull" was an experience of *creatio ex nihilo*. Branham, an avid hunter, related that God spoke to him during a hunting trip:

And Something said to me, "Now this is the beginning of your new ministry. Now ask what you will, and it shall be given to you."[141]

Branham asked for the creation of three squirrels, which he promptly shot and killed. He then understood that this manifestation of the "third pull" was the key to understanding Mark 11:23, "Whatsoever you say, believe that what you say shall come to pass, and you can have what you say." The hunting incident was increasingly glorified in his later years. The "greater works" of John 14:12, which Branham had interpreted as "more" works during the healing revival, was literally defined as "greater." Branham noted that Jesus turned water into wine, and made bread and fish for the 5,000 from existing food. Just like God created *ex nihilo* in the beginning, Branham avowed, "in the woods there was nothing to make a squirrel."[142]

The first time the ability to "speak the Word" was performed on a human being occurred about two weeks after Branham's hunting trip. According to the evangelist, a Mrs. Hattie Wright was granted a wish from God after she confessed the truth of the *creatio ex nihilo* of the squirrels. When she requested the salvation of her sons, Branham spoke their conversion into existence. Instantaneously, two rowdy teenagers were converted.[143]

The appearance of these two manifestations of the ability to speak the "Word" into existence filled Branham with anticipation. Not until 1963,

---

[140]Idem, *Hebrews*, 77. "Vindication" is a very important word to current Branham followers. Vindication of the prophet requires 100% accuracy of prophetic pronouncements.

[141]Idem, *Footprints*, 313.

[142]Idem, "Shalom," *TSW* 13:5 (n.d.): 29.

[143]Idem, "Speak to This Mountain," sermon delivered and recorded in San Jose CA, 23 November 1959.

however, did he report the final two vindications of the new ministry. The fourth experience again occurred on a hunting expedition. In the midst of a raging Colorado blizzard, Branham asserted, God instructed him to rebuke and calm the storm with a command of "Thus Saith The Lord." Promptly, according to Branham, the storm was calmed.[144]

The climactic vindication of the "third pull" was the healing of Branham's wife of an ovarian tumor. Although she had received the tumor for criticizing her prophet-husband, God confirmed Branham's chosenness by commanding, "Just say the Word, and there will be no more tumor."[145] Branham concluded: "That is the fifth time. Five is the number of grace. A number of f-a-i-t-h, too. There is no doubt in my mind. I know what it does. Now be reverent, just keep quiet. The hour will soon arrive, when God is going to do some great things for us."[146]

For the remaining two years of his life, Branham did not report another manifestation of the "third pull." He explained that the gift would not fully and perfectly operate until the World Council of Churches initiated its persecution of the Elect.[147]

Branham never described the mechanics of the ability to "speak the Word" into existence. He had been instructed, according to the tent vision, to keep the details hidden from carnal impersonators. The evangelist did contend, however, that the operation of the gift required perfect faith on his part. Consequently, Branham's faith could intercede for the weaker faith of persons who needed healing.[148]

Branham never publicly specified the ultimate purposes of the "third pull" except to say that its perfect operation would bring "rapturing faith."[149] This ultimate purpose was much greater than physical healing, however. Branham evidently believed that he would "speak the Word" in the tent's little room to the predestinated Bride. Physical bodies would be changed into the glorified bodies that were needed for the rapture.[150] According to one source, this tremendous power would be unleashed because Branham's "spoken Word" would restore God's original name of

---

[144]Idem, "Testimony," 7-13.

[145]Ibid.

[146]Idem, *Footprints,* 494.

[147]Moore, *Quotations,* 241.

[148]William Branham, "Perfect Faith," *TSW* 6:11 (n.d.): 26, 34.

[149]Moore, *Quotations,* 241-42.

[150]Statement by Billy Paul Branham. See also Letter received from Robert Moore, 12 August 1984.

JHVH. Previously, the name had never been pronounced correctly. Branham's mouth, however, was specially formed to say it.[151] Indeed, the "third pull" was the ultimate restoration of the "Word."

* * * * *

As the pacesetter and preeminent visionary of the healing revivalism that flourished in Pentecostalism from the late 1940s through the late 1950s, William Branham was deeply respected for his legendary power. During the latter part of his ministry, however, the evangelist's reputation became tainted with controversy. Attempting to cope with the decline of the revival, and specifically his dwindling popularity in the late 1950s, Branham increasingly preached controversial doctrine. Consequently, he shifted his primary ministerial interests from healing to doctrinal preaching and "prophetic" revelations. Propagation of an eschatological "message" was the avenue to a greater and unique ministry.

The evangelist engaged in healing campaigns for the rest of his life. Nevertheless, the emphasis upon doctrinal "revelations" was even reflected in his healing methodology of the 1960s. The visionary discernment had become the last sign to be given in preparation for the rapture. The use of the formula, "Do you believe me to be God's prophet?," had also been transformed. To receive healing, the afflicted now had to affirm that Branham's teachings—for example, his exegesis of Luke 17:30—were true.[152] Indeed, the transformation of imperfect physical bodies to perfect glorified bodies in the operation of the "third pull" was the ultimate change in Branham's approach to deliverance in light of his eschatological "message."

Like the evaluation of Branham's ministry in the 1940s and 1950s, the unique perspective of his last years was found in a "prophetic" identity. During the revival, Branham considered himself a prophet who had been chosen by God to bring a message of healing to the masses. In his later ministry, Branham came to believe he was the eschatological prophet-messenger. As forerunner of Christ's second coming the purpose of his "message" was to prepare the Bride for the rapture.

Being God's "Voice," Branham's "message" was the "Word" to this eschatological age. Moreover, interpretation of the "Word" came only through the prophet. Since there was only one major prophet in an age, Branham considered ministerial colleagues who rejected his "message"

---

[151]Price, "Branham's Legacy," 3. Moore affirmed that Branham admitted this to one of the most loyal "Message" leaders. Statement by Robert Moore.

[152]Branham, "Proving," 52-53.

to be carnal impersonators. Indeed, he had broadened his earlier definition of a prophet as primarily a seer. In the 1960s a prophet was also "a revealer of the Word that's written in his own life."[153] For Branham, the "message" and the prophet-messenger were the same. The prophet of Malachi 4 had the Messianic sign of Luke 17:30, opened the seals of Revelation 2-3 and manifested Hebrews 13:8. Therefore, the prophet was the director of the Bride in the Bride Age.

Branham's "prophetic" pronouncement of "Thus Saith the Lord" upon his doctrinal "message" was criticized in the Pentecostal world. The moral rigorism became increasingly severe and thus unpopular. The "revelation" that condoned divorce offended some strict Pentecostals. Characterizing denominationalism as the mark of the beast and advocating the "Jesus only" positions on baptism and the Godhead damaged Branham's reputation, especially among trinitarians. The doctrine of the serpent's seed was repugnant to all. Moreover, the rigid predestinarian views were foreign to the Arminian heritage of the Pentecostal tradition. Most controversial, however, was Branham's "revelation" about the eschatological prophet-messenger. In essence, many adherents of the full gospel judged that Branham had "stepped out of his anointing." The result was a "bad teacher of heretical doctrine."[154]

Harrell has perceptively analyzed the failure of Branham's last years:

> To the modish charismatic movement of the 1960s, Branham was an outdated figure. He himself recognized he had no place there. He could not adapt to the new needs, nor compete with powerful organizations for funds. His lack of sophistication made him susceptible to those who wanted to use his reputation for their own financial or doctrinal benefit.[155]

Though Branham was surrounded by an obsequious group of disciples, he had constantly yearned for an unparalleled and unique ministry in the early years of the revival. Consequently, during the decline of his popularity Branham grasped upon the promises of the "infallible" tent vision. Seeking to recapture the glory days of the revival, he proclaimed divine revelations. Branham sometimes softened his teachings in order to appeal to campaign crowds. Once he told a former colleague that his followers were wrong in deifying his words.[156] Yet the indefatigable support of his disciples triumphed. Branham had achieved the ultimate ministry— as the eschatological prophet of the rapture-bound Bride of Christ.

---

[153]Idem, "Feast of the Trumpets," *TSW* 3:16 (rpt., 1982): 17.

[154]Statement by Charles Farah, professor of Systematic Theology, Oral Roberts University, personal interview, Tulsa OK, 5 April 1984.

[155]Harrell, *All Things Are Possible*, 165.

[156]Ibid., 163.

CHAPTER SEVEN

THE "PROPHET'S" LEGACY

The influence of William Branham did not end with his death. His ministry has made a significant impact upon the broader Pentecostal movement of this day. As the pacesetter of the revival, Branham was a primary source of inspiration in the development of other deliverance ministries. In a positive sense, the ultimate contribution of Branham was his influence among contemporary, full gospel evangelists.

Branham's legacy is best seen, however, from the perspective of his "prophetic" ministry. From Oral Roberts to such lesser known evangelists as H. Richard Hall, Branham is acknowledged as a prophet within the Pentecostal milieu. Though Branham's later years were marred by his controversial teachings, he is still considered a prophet on the basis of his ministry of deliverance, and his ability to function as a seer.

The enduring importance of Branham's "prophetic" identity is manifested in the desire by some in the Pentecostal tradition to claim his mantle. In an effort to enhance their ministries, a few independent evangelists like W. V. Grant, Jr. and Neal Frisby claimed to have inherited the mantle of leadership. The most significant influence of Branham's "prophetic" ministry, however, is the continued allegiance of his disciples in various feuding groups. This movement, known to its participants as the "Message," is devoted to Branham as the eschatological prophet of Malachi 4.[1] Some "Message" believers go beyond this sine qua non doctrine and see Branham as the greatest prophet ever. They claim that he was quasi-divine, possessing the fullness of Christ's Spirit. Finally, a

---

[1]Letter received from Robert Moore, 10 October 1983.

belief persists among a radical minority that Branham was God himself, the incarnation of Jesus Christ.

In addition to these attempts to sustain Branham's importance, the inheritance of his "prophetic" mantle is also a major controversy among "Message" disciples. Several "Elishas" have attempted to enhance their ministries by assuming the role of Branham's successor. Many believers also hope that Branham's son, Joseph, will claim the inheritance of his father's "prophetic" ministry. Indeed, this question of the inheritance of the "prophet's" mantle—among "Message" disciples and independent Pentecostal evangelists—vividly illustrates the enduring significance of Branham's place and "prophetic" office within segments of American Pentecostalism.

1.

During the early years of the healing revival, Branham's influence upon other evangelists was extensive. Gordon Lindsay wrote that one of the primary purposes of Branham's healing crusades was "to bring inspiration to the ministry, not to encourage a great number to attempt to conduct vast campaigns but that many with new inspiration will go back to their own churches and begin a real ministry of deliverance."[2] Branham's ministry did inspire many pastors of local churches to seek a ministry of deliverance; nevertheless, many persons were inspired to initiate their own healing campaigns. At the first *The Voice of Healing* convention in 1949, Anna Jeanne Moore reported that Branham's "usefulness in inspiring many of these great ministries was recognized by all."[3] The current existence of many of these ministries reflects Branham's continued influence.

Though less direct, Branham's influence extended to the ministry of the other "giant" of the movement—Oral Roberts. Roberts entered into deliverance evangelism in April 1947, one year after the beginning of Branham's ministry. The ministry of Roberts was not a direct outgrowth of Branham's. The "prophet's" organizational methods, however, probably influenced Roberts' early techniques.

---

[2]Gordon Lindsay, *William Branham: A Man Sent from God* (Jeffersonville IN: William Branham, 1950) 16.

[3]Anna Jeanne Moore, "Historic Conferences of Evangelists Conducting Healing Campaigns Convened in Dallas December 22-23," *TVH* 2 (February 1950): 2. The Latter Rain Movement in Canada, discussed in ch. 1, was also catalyzed in part by the healing campaigns of Branham in Vancouver, during the fall of 1947. Branham condemned the excesses of the movement. See Richard Riss, "The Latter Rain Movement of 1948," *Pneuma* 4 (Spring 1982): 34.

Gordon Lindsay remembered that Roberts had discussions with Branham's team in Tulsa during the summer of 1947. In April 1948, after conducting a small meeting in a local church in Kansas City, Missouri, Roberts attended a Branham crusade in Kansas City, Kansas. Roberts was able to meet Branham backstage and arranged to have his picture taken with the Branham team of Gordon Lindsay, Jack Moore, Young Brown, and Branham.[4] Roberts later recalled that he was "struck at once" with Branham's "quiet humility" and generous spirit.[5] At that time, Roberts had not yet conducted any citywide "union" meetings. After observing Branham's effectiveness, Roberts informed Lindsay that he intended to purchase a tent and initiate "inter-evangelical," citywide campaigns in the near future.[6]

Roberts and Branham were grateful for the positive acknowledgement that each gave to the other's ministry. After the Kansas City meetings, the revival "giants" worked out an agreement that provided for coverage of Branham's schedule in Roberts' *Healing Waters,* and Roberts' itinerary in Branham's *The Voice of Healing.*[7] When Branham left the revival trail for health reasons in late 1948, Roberts requested for the readers of *Healing Waters* to pray that Branham's strength would be restored "for the mighty work that still awaits his labors."[8] After Branham resumed his schedule of revivals, he attended one of Roberts' meetings in Tampa, Florida. In its report of the meeting, *Healing Waters* praised the divinely ordained work of both leaders of the revival and added: "He [Branham] said that Brother Roberts' sermon that night was the greatest sermon he had heard in all his life."[9] A spirit of cooperation between Roberts and Branham was evident again in September 1950, when Roberts' revival tent was destroyed in a storm in Amarillo, Texas. Branham called Roberts and offered the use of his tent. Roberts wanted some time

---

[4]David E. Harrell, Jr., *Oral Roberts: An American Life* (Bloomington: Indiana University Press, 1985) 150.

[5]Statement by Oral Roberts, telephone interview, Tulsa OK, 3 April 1984.

[6]Gordon Lindsay, "The Story of the Great Restoration Revival, Installment II," *WWR* 11 (April 1958): 18.

[7]"The Branham Meetings," *HW* 1 (June 1948): 10.

[8]"Prayer for Rev. William Branham," *HW* 1 (July 1948): 8.

[9]David E. Harrell, Jr., *All Things Are Possible: The Healing and Charismatic Revivals in Modern America* (Bloomington: Indiana University Press, 1975) 42. See also Reg Hanson, "William Branham Attends Roberts Campaign in Tampa, Florida," *HW* 1 (March 1949): 6.

to rest, however, and convinced Branham to substitute for him in some meetings scheduled for the next two months. [10]

Roberts quickly surpassed Branham as the leader of the healing revival. Roberts' business acumen also enabled him to adapt more readily to the transformation of revivalism into a broader charismatic base in the 1960s. According to David E. Harrell, Roberts' ministry was not simply an imitation of the ministry of Branham or of any other deliverance evangelist. The Tulsa evangelist was a leader with the ability to make his own decisions. Consequently, Branham's influence upon Roberts was minimal at best. Perhaps only cynics noted with suspicion that Roberts' ability to detect disease through a vibrating right hand paralleled that of Branham's left hand. [11]

Even while Roberts has remained the most prominent, contemporary charismatic evangelist, he still has fond memories of the early years of the revival and the ministry of William Branham. He described Branham as "a genuine humble prophet of God" whose ministry "certainly impacted my life for good." Roberts elaborated that, after attending one of Branham's services, "you were aware that you had been in the presence of God." Indeed, Roberts concluded that, "had it been God's plan, he [Branham] could have been anything he wanted to in the healing ministry."[12]

In contrast to Roberts, many persons did enter deliverance ministries as a direct result of Branham's influence. Multitudes of lesser-known evangelists paid tribute to Branham for the impact that he had made on their work. *The Voice of Healing* reported how a former Baptist transformed his ministry after sitting "goggle-eyed" in one of Branham's services. [13]

Such well-known healing revivalists as O. L. Jaggers, Gayle Jackson, Velmer Gardner, Richard Vineyard, and Richard Jeffries also received their inspiration or calling while attending Branham's campaigns. Vineyard, for example, testified that he overheard some teenagers in his church discussing Branham's ministry. When Vineyard approached the teenagers, they asked him why he was unable to perform the gifts that

---

[10]Oral Roberts, "My Plans for the Future," *HW* 3 (November 1950): 4.

[11]Harrell, *All Things Are Possible*, 46, 150. The vibration of Roberts' right hand occurred first in the spring of 1948. See Harrell, *Oral Roberts*, 89, 150.

[12]Statement by Oral Roberts.

[13]Leonard Darbee, "A Baptist Scribe Hears a Pentecostal Prophet," *TVH* 9 (September 1956): 20.

Branham did. Subsequently, Vineyard asserted that he prayed for and received the gift of healing.[14]

H. Richard Hall and Tommy L. Osborn, prominent Pentecostal preachers, also claimed influence from Branham. Hall, of Cleveland, Tennessee, was originally a state overseer in the Church of God of Prophecy. He achieved success as a "small revivalist," touring backwater America, and appealing to the social outcasts on the fringe of Pentecostalism.[15]

Hall is currently President of the United Christian Ministerial Association, an interdenominational, full gospel organization that claims a worldwide membership of 8,600 ministers. In addition, the *Shield of Faith* reported that the year 1985 marked the thirty-eighth year of Hall's *"SALVATION—HEALING MINISTRY."*[16] While utilizing television ministry, Hall still travels extensively and preaches to dwindling crowds. Reflecting upon his commitment to the revival trail, however, Hall responded: "I'll be doing this until I die."[17]

An attraction to Branham's early success had a strong influence upon Hall's decision to become a full-time, independent evangelist. Throughout his ministry, Hall has employed the gift of knowledge that paralleled Branham's second sign. At Branham's death, Hall described him as "a major prophet of God."[18] Even today, Hall asserts that Branham "was favored by God in his ministry more than any other [revivalist]." Hall rejected the idea that Branham was the prophet of Malachi 4, noting that others like Billy Graham were also modern day prophets. Yet, Hall could still affirm that there has never been a greater prophet to the Pentecostal world before or since William Branham.[19]

The most famous of Branham's "spiritual sons" was Tommy L. Osborn. Osborn—whose Tulsa-based ministry has achieved worldwide success—received his inspiration to enter deliverance evangelism in

---

[14]Gordon Lindsay, "The Story of the Great Restoration Revival, Part III," *WWR* 11 (May 1958): 4. See also Gordon Lindsay, "The Story of the Great Restoration Revival, Installment IV," *WWR* 11 (June 1958): 18. For Jeffries' testimony, see "Memorial Service #1," eulogy delivered and recorded in Phoenix AZ, 25 January 1966.

[15]Harrell, *All Things Are Possible*, 209-11.

[16]"Healing Ministry . . . Ordained of God," *SOF* 27 (January-February 1985): 5. See also "8,600 Ministers—World-Wide!," *SOF* 27 (January-February, 1985): 7. The United Christian Ministerial Association offered ministerial licenses and ordination that gave as much authority as any church could "to establish churches, missions, and evangelize."

[17]Statement by H. Richard Hall, personal interview, Louisville KY, 22 January 1985.

[18]"Millions Have Reason to Weep," *SOF* 8 (January-February, 1966): 1.

[19]Statement by H. Richard Hall.

Branham's Portland campaign, in 1947. Osborn had just returned from India, disappointed with the results of his mission efforts. At the behest of his wife, Osborn attended one of Branham's services and was captivated by the healing of a young, deaf-mute girl. Upon witnessing what appeared to be an obvious miracle, Osborn remarked, "there seemed to be a thousand voices speaking to me at one time . . . You can do that— that's what God wants you to do."[20]

Osborn embarked on an independent deliverance ministry that was primarily mission-oriented. He reported great success in foreign campaigns. When revivalism expanded its horizons in the 1960s, Osborn remained successful and was quite effective among young people. During the 1970s and 1980s Osborn and his wife, Daisy, continued to travel extensively overseas. In 1982, however, he announced that his itinerary would include more American speaking engagements. Now considered one of the elder statesmen of healing revivalism, Osborn is admired, and even revered, by young Pentecostal evangelists.[21]

Throughout his ministry, Osborn never lost his respect for Branham. At a memorial service just after Branham's death, Osborn showered the deceased leader with ebullient praise. The Tulsa revivalist recalled that, previous to the Portland meeting of 1947, he had never heard the 1933 prophecy about Branham being the forerunner to the second coming of Christ. Upon seeing Branham heal the young deaf-mute, these words came to Osborn: "As John the Baptist was sent as a forerunner of His first coming, William Branham is sent as a forerunner of His second coming." Like H. Richard Hall, Osborn considered Branham to be a prophet. God had sent Branham to awaken the world to the supernatural and miracle-oriented nature of the gospel. The Tulsa evangelist did not judge Branham to be the prophet of Malachi 4. Nevertheless, a deep respect for Branham was apparent in Osborn's willingness to tell a group of "Message" disciples that their leader was "His [God's] prophet for this generation."[22] Indeed, one of Branham's disciples has tried to claim Osborn as a believer in the "message."[23]

---

[20]T. L. Osborn, "My Life and Call to the Ministry," *TVH* 2 (October 1949): 9.

[21]Jim Ernest Hunter, Jr., "A Gathering of Sects: Revivalistic Pluralism in Tulsa, Oklahoma, 1945-1985" (Ph.D. diss., The Southern Baptist Theological Seminary, 1986) 252-62. See also Harrell, *All Things Are Possible*, 64.

[22]"Memorial Service #2," eulogy delivered and recorded in Phoenix AZ, 26 January 1966.

[23]A Baptist minister who became a believer in Branham published Osborn's speech on "Memorial #2" in book form. He changed the text in a few key places to make Osborn look like a "Message" believer. See Tommy L. Osborn, *A Tribute to William Marrion Branham* (Prospect KY: The Grapevine Press, 1983) 1-24.

Throughout the healing revival, other evangelists expressed gratitude for Branham's inspiration for their ministries. Moreover, lesser-
known evangelists could enhance their reputations by appealing to their
relationship with Branham.[24] Even after Branham became controversial,
others could still emphasize Branham's positive contributions as the revival's pacesetter. He could be called a prophet on the basis of his ministry of deliverance and his abilities to function as a seer. Therefore, when
Branham died, the question arose regarding the inheritance of Branham's mantle of leadership.

In his eulogy of Branham, W. V. Grant, Sr. admonished the readers
of his journal:

> The devil killed John the Baptist with a sword, the Lord raised up ten in
> his place. Satan killed Stephen with stones, God raised up one hundred
> in his place. . . . Satan killed William Branham with a drunken driver. God
> will raise up a million in his place: Walk closely to the Lord so that Brother
> Branham's mantle may fall on you in 1966 in the great revival just ahead.[25]

H. Richard Hall's journal also alluded to the issue of successors to Branham's "prophetic" leadership in the arena of deliverance evangelism:
"William Branham, a major prophet of God has now gone on to his re-
ward. Who is left to carry out the prophetic message of one crying in the
wilderness?"[26]

The possession of Branham's "prophetic" mantle was claimed by a
few revivalists outside the "Message." Hall, in an obvious attempt to enhance his ministry, published a photograph of himself with Branham taken
just before the latter died.[27] While Hall claims a prophetic ministry, he
denies that he is a "prophetic" successor or recipient of Branham's mantle.[28]

Two other evangelists, W. V. Grant, Jr. and Neal Frisby, have claimed
to be the direct successors of Branham, and the recipients of his spiritual

---

[24]Roy Davis, Branham's former Baptist pastor, wrote to *The Voice of Healing* to say
that he had become a healing revivalist. He spoke of Branham as his spiritual son, calling
him "my Timothy." See Roy Davis, "Wm. Branham's First Pastor," *TVH* 3 (October
1950): 14.

[25]"Coronation Day," *TVD* 4 (January 1966): 2.

[26]"Millions Have Reason," 1.

[27]"In Memory of a Prophet," *SOF* 11 (November-December, 1969): 4.

[28]Statement by H. Richard Hall. See also H. Richard Hall, "God's Prophets Are Divinely Ordained!," *SOF* 27 (January-February, 1985): 1. While not mentioning Hall, this
feature article revealed the "prophetic" emphasis of his ministry.

power. W. V. Grant, Jr. is the most prominent contemporary charismatic evangelist to claim succession from Branham. He is the son of W. V. Grant, Sr., a contemporary of Branham's during the 1950s and 1960s. Following in his father's footsteps, Grant, Jr. has engaged in a charismatic ministry of deliverance since the mid-1970s. Based in Dallas, Texas, Grant, Jr. holds crusades worldwide and has regular broadcasts on television and radio across the United States and in the West Indies. At the end of 1984, he reported that, for the last eleven years, he has averaged 341 days per year in campaigns.[29]

Grant's spiritual pilgrimage began at an early age. His father wrote that he was saved and baptized with the Holy Spirit when he was four and five years old, respectively. Grant, Sr. had dedicated his son to the Lord and knew that a deliverance ministry was in the future.[30] Grant, Jr. confirmed that, at eight years old, he heard God's call. According to the young evangelist, the call came amidst an accident in which he was hit by a semi-truck, knocked ninety-seven feet, and then hit by a car. Lying on the ground, God revealed to him that none of his bones was broken. As God had healed him, Grant, Jr. testified, he realized that he would later heal others.[31]

Grant described his entrance into deliverance evangelism, however, as integrally related to his inheritance of the "prophetic" mantle of William Branham. According to his testimony, Grant was an all-state high school football player in Texas and had signed a letter of intent to play collegiate ball at UCLA. Just before leaving for college, he met Branham. The evangelist was a guest in the Grant home while preaching a revival in the elder Grant's church. The younger Grant asserted that around 2:30 A.M., he was reading when Branham walked into his room and sat down on the edge of the bed. Grant described the incident: "He took his left hand and laid it on my left shoulder and he looked me right in the eye and he said, 'W. V. even as Elijah's mantle fell upon Elisha, soon my mantle will fall upon you.' "[32] The next day Grant, Jr. told his father about the experience and asked for the meaning of Branham's words. His father

---

[29]W. V. Grant, Jr., "From My Heart to Yours," *New Day* 13 (December 1984-January 1985): 2.

[30]W. V. Grant, Sr., *The Life and Ministry: W. V. Grant, Jr.* (Dallas: Faith Clinic, n.d.) 11-12, 16.

[31]W. V. Grant, Jr., "Four Ways God Speaks to Me," sermon delivered and recorded, n.p. n.d.

[32]Ibid.

advised: "Just pray about it." A few days later, Branham's fatal automobile accident occurred. In a few more days, Grant, Jr. contended, "God began to give me visions." Grant, Jr. was led to enroll in Southwest Bible College rather than UCLA; and he started singing in his father's church. Gradually, a deliverance ministry developed.[33]

Serious discrepancies have arisen regarding the facts of Grant's claim. Branham did preach in the church of Grant, Sr. in March 1964, but not in 1965 just before the tragic accident.[34] The Grant family now acknowledges that the story of Grant, Jr. did not literally occur. They believe that the story reflects a spiritual truth drawn from a vision or "an experience of the Spirit."[35] Grant, however, has preached the event as if it actually happened. He apparently finds no need to distinguish an actual event from a visionary experience. The means justify the end of obtaining spiritual, prophetic authority. Such a methodology is one reason why some other evangelists do not regard Grant, Jr. "in the same ballpark" as those who preceded him like Branham, Jack Coe, Grant, Sr., and even A. A. Allen.[36]

Obviously, the inspiring young evangelist utilized the story about Branham to enhance his ministry. To claim Branham's mantle meant to receive the blessing of the revival's pacesetter and thus to validate one's own "prophetic" claims. Indeed, Grant's followers believe that he is a prophet.[37]

Another evangelist who regards himself as Branham's successor is Neal Frisby of Phoenix, Arizona. Frisby experienced a troubled early adult life. His wife committed suicide; and he later entered a mental institution for treatment of alcoholism. His search for God began while he was still institutionalized; and he received a divine call to be "a prophet in the last days to bring the fullness of Bible deliverance."[38]

After struggling as a revivalist in the early 1960s, Frisby circulated some mystical "prophetic scrolls" and developed an "Elijah company" of followers. By 1972, Frisby had constructed the Capstone Cathedral in Phoenix and was reporting ninety-nine percent accuracy in his healing ministry. Frisby contended that he was able to heal by creating new body

---

[33]Ibid.

[34]See *TSW*, 19:8-12.

[35]Statement by Mrs. W. V. Grant, Sr., telephone interview, Dallas TX, 30 November 1984.

[36]Statement by H. Richard Hall.

[37]Statement by Mrs. W. V. Grant, Sr.

[38]Frisby, quoted in Harrell, *All Things Are Possible*, 221.

parts like eardrums. The radical nature of his ministry was also apparent in the assertion that insanity could be overcome by reading his "prophetic" scrolls. Indeed, Harrell accurately described Frisby as "the most bizarre prophet of the 1970s."[39]

Early in his ministry, Frisby was a devout follower of Branham. Since he was establishing an independent ministry of his own, the Phoenix evangelist was never really a member of the developing "Message."[40] Nevertheless, Frisby's adulation for Branham was unreserved, with Frisby calling him the "Star Prophet" and the "Royal Prophet."[41]

Frisby's early "prophetic" ministry revealed a definite desire to emulate Branham. Frisby prefaced the story of his personal experience with angels by relating Branham's angelic commission of 1946. The ability to create new body parts was like Branham's claim to create *ex nihilo* through the spoken word.

Some of Frisby's doctrinal emphases were also reminiscent of Branham's teachings. The Phoenix revivalist acknowledged Branham's role in advocating the truths about the "oneness" of the Godhead and baptism in the Name of the Lord Jesus Christ. Moreover, Frisby asserted that many Pentecostal denominations were going to enter the demonic confederation of churches. He issued a call to "come out." "The wise will hear [his message] until they are endued with power from reading God's [*sic*] Scrolls," Frisby proclaimed.[42] So devoted was Frisby that he believed Branham's prediction of 1977 as the end of time was accurate. Frisby even seemed to imply that Branham might be uniquely resurrected: "Something very remarkable could happen," Frisby declared, "just before or at the rapture time in union with Christ's return."[43]

In one of his scrolls, Frisby included Branham's seven "prophetic" visions of 1933 to compare the similar content of his own prophecies. He commented, "The Bible says He takes away the first that the second can be established. It says that the matter shall be established in the mouth

---

[39]Harrell, *All Things Are Possible,* 222. See also W. V. Grant, *Creative Miracles* (Dallas: Faith Clinic, n.d.) 15.

[40]Statement by Robert Moore, former follower of Branham, telephone interview, Phoenix AZ, 9 September 1984.

[41]Neal Frisby, *The Revelation of the Written Scrolls and the Word of God* (Phoenix: 20th Century Life Publications, n.d.) 62, 114.

[42]Frisby, quoted in Harrell, *All Things Are Possible,* 223.

[43]Frisby, *Scrolls,* 107. Frisby (62) noted that Branham did not prophesy 1977 as the end of the world, but that the rapture was close to that date. Frisby responded, "The evidence is that he is very close to right."

of two witnesses."[44] In essence, Frisby regarded his "prophetic" ministry as succeeding Branham's. Some of his followers point to the fact that Branham occasionally stated he was looking for another prophet to appear. These disciples do not consider Frisby to be the only prophet alive; yet, he is regarded as the last prophet to the Bride.[45]

The most unique evidence of a claim to Branham's mantle is found in the name and structure of Frisby's current headquarters in Phoenix. Frisby's church is the Capstone Cathedral. Branham frequently preached about the trail of apostolic restoration, justification, sanctification, and Holy Spirit baptism as forming a pyramid. The pyramid would be "capped" by the restoration of the "Word." Significantly, the Capstone Cathedral is a stained glass structure in a pyramid shape. Obviously, the name and structure of Frisby's cathedral are symbols of his ministry being the successor of Branham's work. Indeed, some of Frisby's followers regard the structure as the fulfillment of Branham's tent vision, the symbol of an unparalleled ministry.[46]

As Frisby's ministry grew, the references to Branham in the scrolls diminished. Dependence upon Branham was no longer needed. By claiming Branham's mantle in his earlier ministry, however, Frisby sought to enhance his own reputation as a prophet. Yet, the existence of the Capstone Cathedral still symbolizes Frisby's conviction that he is the last prophet who will succeed Branham.

2.

The most enduring and comprehensive manifestation of Branham's influence is the continued existence of a religious movement based on his teachings. Since Branham's death, his disciples have continued to exist in several feuding groups. This multifarious religious movement, known to its participants as the "Message," is based on the sine qua non doctrine that Branham was the prophet of Malachi 4. The eagle—the biblical

---

[44]Ibid., 62.

[45]Billy Paul Branham concurred that Frisby considered himself to be Branham's successor. Branham's son recalled how Frisby used to correspond with him. Frisby attempted to point out the similarities between his ministry and Branham's. Statement by Billy Paul Branham, son of William Branham, personal interview, Jeffersonville IN, 27 September 1984.

[46]Statement by Robert Moore. See also William Branham, "Restoration of the Bride Tree," *TSW* 3:15 (rpt., 1982): 76.

image of the prophet—is the symbol of the movement.[47] Since Branham condemned denominationalism, "Message" churches are strictly local churches; regional organizations are nonexistent. There are some associations; but their primary purpose is to publish and distribute the sermons of Branham. Some pastors like Pearry Green of Tucson, Arizona, and Ewald Frank of Krefold, Germany, however, do exert various degrees of informal influence upon churches beside their own.[48]

The absence of a denominational structure makes statistics difficult to interpret. In 1973, Pearry Green listed over 300 ministers who regarded Branham as the prophet of Malachi 4.[49] In the early 1980s, it was estimated that "Message" believers totaled 100,000.[50] In 1986, the unofficial estimate had risen to 300,000.[51]

According to "Message" adherents, about 50,000 followers are scattered throughout the United States. The two most significant churches are Green's Tucson Tabernacle and the Branham Tabernacle in Jeffersonville. In 1973, Green had already traveled to over ninety countries to witness about Branham.[52] Billy Paul Branham, the full-time secretary-treasurer of the Branham Tabernacle, also travels extensively to promote his father's "message." The primary medium of evangelization in the "Message" is the publication of Branham's sermons in both taped and written form. In Jeffersonville there are approximately 1,100 sermons available on tape, and over 300 in print.

The "Message" is also a worldwide movement. Churches are scattered throughout Europe. Especially strong churches and publication societies are located in Canada and Germany. The most prominent European leader, Ewald Frank, reported that he has also traveled to over eighty countries in behalf of the "Message." He claims that Branham's sermons are even being read in Russia.[53]

---

[47]The entrance to the Branham Tabernacle in Jeffersonville is identified by no name, only a replica of an eagle and the King's Sword (see 100). A full-size replica of an eagle is perched on top of Branham's pyramid-shaped tombstone.

[48]Moore, letter, 10 October 1983.

[49]Harrell, *All Things Are Possible*, 165.

[50]Statement by Robert Moore.

[51]David Branham, son of Billy Paul Branham, employee of Voice of God Recordings, Inc., personal interview, 6 August 1986.

[52]Harrell, *All Things Are Possible*, 165.

[53]Letter received from Ewald Frank, 28 June 1984. See also Ewald Frank, *The Impact of Revelation* (Krefeld, West Germany: Ewald Frank, n.d.) 28.

Other areas where the "Message" has a significant following include India, Central and South America. Brazil, for example, is said to have 40,000 believers. The area with the most concentrated mission effort, however, is Africa. To date taped sermons have been translated into eight African languages. "Tape libraries" are being established in such countries as Kenya, Nigeria, Ghana, and Zaire. In Zaire, Branham's followers are currently estimated at 25,000—the strongest church totaling 4,000. In fact, "Message" missionary personnel suggest that the "Message" is the fourth largest religious group in Zaire.[54]

Practically all of Branham's followers adhere to the basic tenets that comprised the eschatological "message." The extreme local autonomy of the churches, however, has resulted in diverse interpretations of Branham's teachings. Consequently, the emphases of the churches are often very different.[55] Yet, millennial fervor, the attitude toward Branham and his sermons, and the question of the "prophet's" mantle are three dominant concerns of current "Message" believers.

Since eschatological themes were the major emphases of Branham's later ministry, millennial fervor naturally undergirds the "Message." Specifically, Branham and his disciples have always expected an imminent rapture. When Branham died, this expectation focused upon a hope for his resurrection.

The natural reaction to Branham's death was one of shocking disbelief. In the confusion that immediately ensued, expectations developed that the "prophet" would rise from the dead. Though the funeral was held on 29 December 1965, the burial was delayed indefinitely. The press conjectured that the reason was the belief in Branham's imminent resurrection. A rumor circulated that Branham's body was "embalmed and refrigerated." In reality, the body was being kept in the attic of a Jeffersonville funeral home.[56]

At a memorial service on 26 January 1966, Billy Paul Branham explained the delay in burial. Mrs. Branham had requested it due to the injuries that she received in her husband's fatal automobile accident.

---

[54]Statement by David Branham. South Africa and Trinidad are estimated to have 22,000 and 15,000 respectively. The estimates regarding the size of the "Message" are the unofficial suggestions of the missionary department of Voice of God Recordings, Inc. As of July 1986, there were 120 "tape libraries" in 26 countries. Printed sermons are currently being translated into 28 different languages.

[55]Moore, Letter, 10 October 1983.

[56]Pearry Green, *The Acts of the Prophet* (Tucson: Tucson Tabernacle Books, n.d.) 182-83.

Moreover, in the wake of the tragedy, Mrs. Branham was unable to decide where she would live—Tucson or Jeffersonville—and she wanted her husband buried near her home.[57]

Nevertheless, expectations for Branham's resurrection on Easter increased. Much of the resurrection talk was largely attributed to Pearry Green, though he denied the accusation. Others—even Branham's son, Billy Paul—seemed to be hoping for an Easter resurrection. Giving his testimony to a group of "Message" believers on 27 March 1966, he suggested that the months between his father's death and Easter were the time of "the purification of the Bride." Furthermore, Billy Paul asserted that Easter week, 6-10 April 1966, had been set aside "in the providence of God" for believers in the "message" to listen to some previously unreleased tapes. He affirmed that his father had declared Easter to be the time of year for the Bride's rapture. That Branham would be leading the Bride was an accepted belief among his disciples.[58]

Branham's burial on 11 April 1966 in Jeffersonville was accepted reluctantly by many disciples. The dream of Branham's return did not die, however, and continued to persist in the 1970s. Some "Message" believers felt that Branham had to fulfill literally certain visions—particularly the tent vision and the "third pull"—so that the rapture could occur. The theory developed that Branham and the Bride would be resurrected, and remain on earth for about six months (not less than thirty days). During this time, an unparalleled tent revival would convert so many persons to Branham's Bride that all non-"Message" believers would join the confederation of churches in order to stop the "Message." The rapture would occur after Branham spoke the "Word" and transformed physical bodies to their glorified state.[59]

Much of the excitement of the 1970s dealt with Branham's prediction that 1977 represented the inception of the millennium. Some persons

---

[57]"Memorial #2," recorded.

[58]Green, *Prophet*, 185. See also Billy Paul Branham, "Billy Paul's Testimony #1, eulogy delivered and recorded in Jeffersonville IN, 27 March 1966. Hollenweger commented on the events surrounding Branham's death: "His followers had his body embalmed and refrigerated, because they expected him to rise from the dead on 25 January. When this did not happen, the date was put off until Easter 1966. This postponement of his burial is probably the reason why European Pentecostals heard nothing about Branham's death." See Walter J. Hollenweger, *The Pentecostals,* trans. R. A. Wilson (London: S. C. M. Press, 1972) 355.

[59]Robert Moore , *1977, Circa 1976* (n.p., 1976) 7, 24. See also statement by Billy Paul Branham.

made "important plans" in 1974 because they believed that the rapture would come that year.[60] Moreover, in 1976, Spoken Word Publications of Jeffersonville published a book of Branham's quotes entitled *By 1977*.

After the year 1977 passed, some believers abandoned the "Message." Most explained that Branham's words about 1977 were a prediction rather than an infallible prophecy. When a teenager reported in 1978 that he had seen Branham in a restaurant, the "Message" was temporarily ecstatic. Now, however, some disciples look toward 1988 as the time of Branham's return.[61]

"Message" believers have held various beliefs regarding the second coming of William Branham. Most no longer insist upon the literal fulfillment of the famed "tent campaign." Many of this persuasion contend that the resurrected Branham will spend just thirty days gathering up the Bride. A small minority even believe that the rapture is past and they are already living in the millennium.[62]

The persistence of the belief in Branham's resurrection is still evidenced each Easter. The Branham Tabernacle sponsors an annual Easter revival in which the worshipers listen to Branham's taped sermons. Many disciples come to the revival in anticipation of their "prophet's" resurrection. Billy Paul Branham and Willard Collins, current pastor of the Tabernacle, do not encourage speculation about Branham's resurrection. Yet, a focus of the meetings is the expectation of an imminent rapture.[63]

---

[60]Moore, *1977*, 47. According to dispensational chronology, the rapture will occur three and a half years before the end of the world. Though Branham had predicted 1977, he was always cautious to say the rapture might come at any time. In *The Exposition of the Seven Church Ages* (322) Branham supposedly said: "I predict (I do not prophesy) that these visions will have all come to pass by 1977. And though many may feel that this is an irresponsible statement in view of the fact that Jesus said that 'no man knoweth the day nor the hour,' I still maintain this prediction after thirty years, because Jesus did not say no man could know the year, month, or week in which His coming was to be completed." Not until after 1974 did "Message" believers find out that Lee Vayle, the editor of the book, had put this quote into Branham's mouth. Except for a few other embellishments, however, the book is an accurate summary of Branham's "message."

[61]Statement by Robert Moore. Moore left the "Message" because of the inaccurate prediction of 1977. See also Ewald Frank, *The Time Is at Hand* (Krefeld, West Germany: Ewald Frank, n.d.) 36-39.

[62]Moore, *1977*, 10, 42.

[63]Joel Brinkley, "Many at Easter Vigil in Jeffersonville Hope for Return of Prophet," *The Courier-Journal* (Louisville KY) 12 April 1982, A1:5. I attended a service of the 1984 Easter revival. Billy Paul Branham had a "feeling" that the rapture "might" come in the next year.

Another dominant concern of the "Message" is "Branhamology"—the question of Branham's person. The variegated nature of the "Message," combined with Branham's occasional ambiguity about his identity, has been conducive to doctrinal chaos regarding the true nature and identity of Branham.

Essentially, three different perspectives of "Branhamology" are prevalent. Most disciples simply emphasize that Branham was the prophet of Malachi 4. He was the forerunner of Christ's second coming, his ministry manifested Luke 17:30, and he restored the original apostolic faith.

Many disciples go much further in the description of their prophet and find him mentioned elsewhere in the Bible. They consider Branham to be the messenger of Revelation 22. Moreover, Branham is regarded to be *the* Son of man that Jesus predicted, as opposed to his ministry merely being a manifestation of Luke 17:30.[64] Robert Price explained:

> In this role, Branham is seen as the greatest prophet of all time second only to Christ himself. The second coming of Christ is to be realized primarily through Branham, Jesus himself remaining in heaven till the battle of Armageddon, after the tribulation. In fact, most of the prophecies of the second coming will be fulfilled in Branham.[65]

Those who adhere to this "Branhamological" perspective view their deceased leader as "quasi-divine, possessing the 'fulness of the Godhead bodily,' yet still a sinful man who had to be saved."[66]

A small minority of "Message" believers hold to the most radical view that Branham was God himself, the incarnation of Jesus Christ. He was in all respects like Jesus, including a virgin birth. Consequently, some pray to Branham and baptize in his name.[67]

The different attitudes toward Branham's biblical identity have created tension among the various groups of disciples. One area of tension that erupted soon after Branham's death was the question of his unful-

---

[64]Moore, letter, 10 October 1983. For the suggestion that Branham was the messenger of Rev. 22, see William Branham, *Footprints on the Sands of Time: The Autobiography of William Marrion Branham* (Jeffersonville IN: Spoken Word Publications, 1975) iii.

[65]Robert Price, "Branham's Legacy," unpublished paper, 8.

[66]Ibid.

[67]Moore, letter, 10 October 1983. Felicitas Goodman analyzed a "Branhamist" congregation that developed in 1971 on the Yucatan Peninsula. The group claimed that praying in Branham's name produced miracles. See Felicitas D. Goodman, Jeannette H. Henry and Esther Pressel, *Trance, Healing and Hallucination: Three Field Studies in Religious Experience* (New York: John Wiley & Sons, 1974) 334-36.

filled visions, particularly the tent campaign and its "third pull." Billy Paul Branham was disturbed that other "Message" disciples were so quick to refute the necessity of a literal fulfillment of the tent vision before the rapture. Billy Paul warned, "It is dangerous to say anything against him ["the prophet"]."[68]

The "liberal" "Message" perspective, which primarily emphasizes Branham as the prophet of Malachi 4, is perhaps best represented by Pearry Green and Ewald Frank. Frank wrote concerning the visions of Branham that were never fulfilled: "We must take into consideration that sometimes natural things convey a spiritual meaning."[69] Moreover, Frank cautioned that many "Message" believers were "quickly leaning towards overemphasizing the man. . . . It has reached the point in which the one whom God has used so mightily has become the main object of controversy."[70]

The tension regarding Branham's identity is most acutely manifested in the different attitudes toward his sermons. All disciples regard Branham's teachings as the Word of God for the Bride in this eschatological generation. The authority of the words varies among disciples, however. Some believers accept certain sermons—for example, the revelation of the seven seals—as authoritative.[71] Others, like Pearry Green, assert that all of Branham's sermons are "oral Scripture", yet they are willing to spiritualize some events like the tent vision.[72] Perhaps the most radical view of the "liberal" perspective is the contention that Branham was

---

[68]Billy Paul Branham, "The Messenger," eulogy delivered and recorded in Tucson AZ, 7 May 1967.

[69]Ewald Frank, *Christ and His Church in Prophecy* (Krefeld, West Germany: Ewald Frank, n.d.) 42.

[70]Frank, *Time*, 3.

[71]Moore, letter, 10 October 1983. Branham himself had an exalted view of his taped sermons. In 1962, he had a dream that a famine was approaching. He was instructed to go and store food in the only storehouse in the country. The dream, Branham later related, emphasized the importance of the sermons taped at the Branham Tabernacle. The storehouse was the Tabernacle and the "message" was being stored up on the tapes since the denominations were experiencing a famine of the Holy Spirit. Consequently, Branham always returned to Jeffersonville whenever he preached a new revelation. See William Branham, "The Greatest Battle Ever Fought," *TSW* 3:11 (rpt., 1981): 42-43. See also William Branham, *Conduct*, 2:766. Reminiscent of Rev. 22:18, Branham gave instructions regarding the tapes to his followers: "Just say what is said on those tapes. You do just exactly what the Lord God has commanded to do. Don't add to It." See Branham, *Footprints*, 535.

[72]Green, *Prophet*, 145, 196. See also letter received from Robert Moore, 12 August 1984.

infallibly inspired only when he prefaced his remarks by the prophetic formula, "Thus Saith the Lord." Writing from this perspective, Frank argued that Branham did not give the Bride another Bible. The written Word is preeminent, and is the criterion for judging Branham's sermons. The "Spoken Word" of Branham is necessary to reveal the "Written Word." Frank elaborated: "The end-time message is nothing less and nothing more than the Word of God revealed for this time. It is nothing added to the Bible, but it is the Holy Scripture revealed by the Holy Spirit."[73]

Many "Message" adherents convey a more "fundamentalist" attitude toward Branham's words. They usually admit that Branham could make a mistake in mundane details, but all of his teachings and visions comprised the infallible Word of God to this generation. It follows that Branham's words are literally true; for example, the unparalleled tent campaign and the "third pull" must be literally fulfilled in the future. These believers regard the method of inspiration as essentially plenary verbal dictation.[74] Transforming a popular fundamentalist slogan of the 1980s, Billy Paul Branham testified, "If God thought it, the prophet spoke it, I believe it, and that settles it."[75] Robert Moore reflected upon his rationale for regarding Branham's sermons as infallible:

> Bro. Branham's explication of the Word is declared to be the foundation of our restoration of apostolic days. Yet unhappily, his Message has been subject to nearly as many renderings as has the Bible . . . so we are floundering in a sea of controversy. To rise above this we have pronounced his words to be infallible and this has removed them from the arena of argument.[76]

Commitment to the infallibility of Branham's sermons is evident in the way they are published. When Spoken Word Publications first began to transcribe tapes in the late 1960s, some editing was done. Since many believers objected to any attempt at tampering with their leader's words, the sermons are now printed verbatim, including every stutter. Even misquotations of the Bible are untouched since they might contain hidden meanings. Indeed, some inerrantists also claim absolute literalism regarding every subject that Branham mentioned. Even Branham's offhand

---

[73]Ewald Frank, *Only Believe the "Thus Saith the Lord"* (Krefeld, West Germany: Ewald Frank, n.d.) 25-26. See also Frank, *Time,* 7, 29-30.

[74]Moore, *1977,* 46, 53-54.

[75]Billy Paul Branham, "Personal Testimony," sermon delivered and recorded in Harding AR, 23 June 1984.

[76]Moore, *1977,* 54.

comment that the speed of light was 18,000 miles per hour led one believer to remark, "How could the scientists be so wrong to say it was
186,000 miles per second?"[77]

The "fundamentalist" perspective regards the Bible and Branham's
teachings as equally authoritative. In practice, however, the Bible is
clearly secondary for many believers. Spiritual authority is first and foremost found in Branham's sermons. These sermons, while restoring apostolic doctrine, offer fresh revelation from God.[78]

The dispute over Branham's true nature has also engendered conflict
regarding the inheritance of the "prophet's" mantle. Branham himself
seemed to believe that he was the prophet of Malachi 4. Yet, his occasional ambiguity left the path clear for his disciples to assert messianic
identities of their own, so several "Message" leaders (over a dozen by
one believer's count)[79] have proclaimed that they were "Joshuas" continuing Branham's ministry, or successors inheriting his mantle in a fashion similar to Elijah and Elisha.[80]

Many "Message" believers, of course, deny the possibility of a successor to the "prophet." Ewald Frank, in criticizing the attempt to claim
the "prophetic" mantle, told how certain ministers gained authority by
identifying themselves with Branham's teachings. These ministers then
declared additional revelations required of all who would participate in the
rapture. Such ministers possessed the serpent's seed, Frank concluded.
Other ministers, while not claiming Branham's mantle, envisioned them-

---

[77]Ibid., 53. See also letter received from Robert Moore, 7 January 1984.

[78]Statement by Billy Paul Branham. Branham's sermons, rather than the Bible, are
often used for worship. See Robert Thom, *You and Your Ministry, William Branham:
Prophet Or?* (n.p., n.d.), 87-88.

[79]Donald Derkson, *Who is Joseph Branham?* (Keystone SD: Keystone Press, 1980)
17.

[80]Price, "Branham's," 7. William Podaras, who has an independent ministry in Gas-
tonia, North Carolina, is an example of a minister on the periphery of the "Message." He
accepted Branham as the Laodicean messenger in the early 1960s and left the "error" of
denominationalism. One of Podaras's sermons from 1971 revealed that he also experienced many visions. One of his visions definitely connected his ministry to the "third pull."
See William N. Podaras, "The Vision Speaks," *TSTL* (July-October 1975): 36-38. See
also William N. Podaras, "Tabernacle of God Pays Tribute to Prophet Messenger of the
Age," *TSTL* (July-October 1975) 111-12. Podaras's ministry moved beyond Branham's
shadow. He recently remarked: "You have to consider that Bro. Branham has been dead
almost 24 yrs., and the spirit and move of God is ever moving on. This is why the Word
of God admonishes us in II Peter 1:12 to 'be *established* in the *present truth.*'" See Letter
received from William N. Podaras, 16 October 1984.

selves as his chief interpreter. Frank's evaluation of his own ministry evokes this impression.[81] Pearry Green, who also denies any claim to Branham's mantle,[82] still portrays himself as the disciple closest to Branham during the last days of 1965. According to Green, he was selected by Branham to be the recipient of some private interviews regarding the tent vision and other experiences. These talks would "help the brothers to see which way to look or turn" after Branham's death.[83]

The most bizarre attempt to inherit Branham's mantle involved a deliverance evangelist from India named R. Paulaseer Lawrie. In a campaign tour of America in 1960, Lawrie held some meetings with Lee Vayle, one of Branham's closest advisors. Then Lawrie was rebaptized by Branham and eventually professed belief in Branham as the Laodicean prophet-messenger.[84]

In India, Lawrie gradually built up a band of supporters and began to view Branham as the forerunner to his ministry. Amazingly, Lawrie's disciples believed that the second coming of Christ had arrived in the life of Lawrie on "moonlanding day"—21 July 1969. Thus, Lawrie was the Son of man.[85] Lawrie's emphases were heavily gleaned from the life and "message" of the forerunner. A "pillar of Cloud" reportedly surrounded Lawrie at all times. He also preached the familiar, strict moral code for women and condemned denominationalism.[86] Most important was Lawrie's assertion that his ministry was the "third pull" that was "opening the understanding of the Bride to the many 'secrets' in the Word of God." He used Branham's sermons to show that Branham recognized him as the prophet yet to come.[87]

---

[81]Frank, *Time*, 19-22, 28-29, 48.

[82]Statement by Pearry Green, interview with David E. Harrell, Jr., Tucson AZ, 27 December 1973. Tape was made available by David E. Harrell, Jr., University of Alabama in Birmingham.

[83]Green, *Prophet*, 145, 185.

[84]R. Paulaseer Lawrie, *Heavenly Canaan* (Tirunelveli-8, South India: Paulaseer Lawrie Publications, n.d.) 399.

[85]L. D. Dale and D. E. M. Lawrie, eds., *Gleanings from "The Spoken Word Books"* (Manujothi Ashram South India: Paulaseer Lawrie Publications, n.d.) 1. "Moonlanding day" was the occasion of the first person to ever walk on the moon.

[86]R. Paulaseer Lawrie, *Son of Man: Message to the Bride* (n.p., n.d.), iii. See also R. Paulaseer Lawrie, *Is It Possible to Overcome Death in This Generation or the Feast of the Tabernacles* (Tirunelveli-8, South India: Paulaseer Lawrie Publications, n.d.) 75.

[87]R. Paulaseer Lawrie, *The Hidden Manna* (Tirunelveli-8 South India: Paulaseer Lawrie Publications, n.d.) 44.

The essential element of Lawrie's claim was that his followers were the Bride bound for the rapture. The rapture would occur, as Branham predicted, in 1977. Using a Branham statement that only 700 were saved by Elijah's preaching, Lawrie's group believed that only 700 persons would experience the rapture.[88]

Some of Lawrie's Bride were originally followers of Branham in the United States and Germany. They left their homes, sold their possessions, and went to India. Lawrie promised that they would overcome physical death in the imminent rapture of 1977. "Branhamites" who rejected Lawrie as Branham's successor were constantly chastised for their spiritual blindness.[89]

With the exception of one family, all of the Americans who pilgrimmaged to India returned after 1977.[90] Lawrie's claims of Messiahship were not unique in a nation filled with myriads of religious fortune-seekers. Yet, Lawrie's claim to Branham's mantle was a vivid illustration of the widespread influence of the revival's pacesetter.

The delay in Branham's resurrection has also facilitated the promulgation of the most intriguing theory concerning a successor to Branham. A growing number of "fundamentalist" disciples are now looking to Branham's youngest son, Joseph, to fulfill his father's visions and lead the Bride into the rapture. This group emphasizes that Branham spoke of Joseph as a prophet and his successor. According to Branham, Joseph was just three years old when he had a vision of a friend in a motorcycle wreck. Moreover, Branham made an astounding prophecy the day that Joseph was dedicated to the Lord. The evangelist described the incident:

When I picked up Joseph in my arms, not thinking of what I was saying, I said, "Joseph my son, thou art a prophet." That's my prayer, anyhow, and I believe it'll be someday; God will take everything that He ever gave me, and double it times double, and put on that boy, that when I leave that he'll take my place.[91]

Joseph's role became prominent prior to his father's death.[92] This effort to promote Joseph's leadership was intensified in 1980 when Donald Derkson, a "Message" pastor, published a book entitled *Who Is Joseph Bran-*

---

[88]Dale, *Gleanings*, 52-53.

[89]Lawrie, *Heavenly*, 428.

[90]Letter received from Lee Vayle, 20 June 1984.

[91]William Branham, "Let Us See God," *TSW* 14:2 (n.d.): 3-4.

[92]Moore, Letter, 10 October 1983.

ham? Undaunted by the criticism that Joseph "hangs around hippies" and "drives a hot car," Derkson portrayed him as Branham's successor.[93]

While Derkson accepted Branham as the prophet of Malachi 4, he viewed Branham's ambiguity as a sign that another leader would complete the "prophet's" task. Joseph Branham had to be this successor, Derkson asserted, since he was the only future prophet that the elder Branham identified. Therefore, Joseph would fulfill all the uncompleted visions of his father.[94]

Derkson elaborated that Joseph's ministry would also completely fulfill the prophecy of Malachi 4:5-6. William Branham had only initiated the "prophetic" task of apostolic restoration with his doctrinal "message." Joseph's ministry would "perfect" the restoration of the Bride's fellowship with Christ. Derkson explained with his exegesis of the Malachi passage:

> We should also notice that this leader turns the *hearts* of the children back to the fathers. We have all thought this was Brother Branham exclusively. I think the facts are that Brother Branham restored the mysteries and laid the foundation for that final restoration, but it should be clear that someone must still restore the *hearts.* Our minds are being turned now, but we cannot say our hearts have been turned until we have perfect attitudes, perfect faith, perfect love, etc. The one who restores faith *inside* the children, and turns hearts back to the Word . . . has been promised. All the message points him to be Joseph Branham.[95]

According to Derkson, Joseph was also able to "restore hearts" because he was the lamb of Revelation 5 who would remit sins. Derkson concluded that "Message" believers must follow Joseph in order to be in the rapture.[96]

Joseph Branham did not approve of Derkson's book, nor has he shown any desire to succeed his father. Billy Paul Branham acknowledges that his brother is a prophet though not another church-age messenger. Ambiguously, Billy Paul simply affirms that Joseph's "prophetic" gifts are "a continuation of the ministry, but not a completion."[97] Nevertheless, the hope for a future ministry of Joseph still exists. Many "Message" believ-

---

[93]Derkson, *Who,* 176.

[94]Ibid., 13-14, 49, 59. William Branham frequently used Joseph in the Old Testament as a type of Christ. Derkson took these passages and applied them to Joseph Branham.

[95]Ibid., 61.

[96]Ibid., 114, 147.

[97]Statement by Billy Paul Branham.

THE "PROPHET'S" LEGACY   163

ers have pictures in their homes of Joseph beside those of his father.[98] The splintered "Message" is in need of a leader. Joseph increased his involvement in 1981, becoming the owner of Voice of God Recordings, Inc., the organization in Jeffersonville that sells Branham's taped sermons. In 1986, he assumed the leadership of Spoken Word Publications. Undoubtedly, Joseph's expanding role is a source of hope for many believers. If not the direct successor, then Joseph is the one chosen to preserve the "prophet's" infallible "Word" for the elect Bride.

* * * * *

The most enduring testimony of William Branham's significance to the history of Pentecostal deliverance evangelism is his influence upon other revivalists. As pacesetter of the revival, Branham inspired an untold number of other deliverance ministries with his humble, magnetic personality and legendary success of healings. Many of those inspired by Branham—for example, T. L. Osborn and H. Richard Hall—are still active in deliverance evangelism. Revivalists like Hall consider Branham to be the greatest prophet of the revival. Moreover, Branham's "prophetic" mantle has been claimed by younger evangelists like W. V. Grant, Jr., and Neal Frisby in an attempt to enhance their own ministries.

The "Message," the multifarious religious movement of Branham's disciples, is the most enduring manifestation of Branham's influence. Three dominant emphases of the "Message" are the question of Branham's resurrection, the question of his person—"Branhamology"—and the question of inheritance of the "prophetic" mantle. These issues generate tension among "Message" believers.

Essentially, the "Message" is characterized by a "liberal" and "fundamentalist" perspective. "Liberals" primarily emphasize the sine qua non belief that Branham was the prophet of Malachi 4. The "liberal" attitude toward Branham's words varies. Some select only portions of his sermons—for example, those teachings prefaced by "Thus Saith the Lord"—while others see all the sermonic material as infallible Scripture. "Liberals," however, are more prone to spiritualize Branham's ideas or visions like the tent campaign.

Except for a small minority that regards Branham to be the literal return of Jesus Christ, most "fundamentalists" usually consider Branham to be quasi-divine, possessing the fullness of Christ's Spirit. Therefore, Branham's sermons are infallible, and also literally true, so Branham's return will include a literal tent campaign. Some "fundamentalists" hold

---

[98]Moore, Letter, 10 October 1983.

fast to the belief that Branham will lead the Bride into the rapture. Others have claimed Branham's "prophetic" mantle. These Elijah figures seek to identify themselves with Branham in order to espouse their own spiritual authority. A growing sentiment is to look to Joseph Branham as the inheritor of his father's leadership.

This issue of the inheritance of Branham's mantle, among "Message" believers and independent healing revivalists, reveals the enduring significance of Branham's "prophetic" role within various segments of Pentecostalism. Moreover, Branham's legacy is a primary illustration of how American religious sectarianism develops. One entity, a mother church, develops under the inspirational guidance of a charismatic-prophet. Consequently, the prophet's death often gives rise to additional entities led by prophets who attract followers with the promise to fill the vacuum of spiritual authority and assurance.

CONCLUSION

The significance of the ministry of William Branham for a better understanding of the Revivalistic/Pentecostal tradition is readily apparent; a study of his ministry reveals the important role that he held in postwar healing revivalism. The revival first erupted in his ministry; and subsequently he influenced many others to initiate deliverance ministries. Along with Oral Roberts, he was a "giant" of healing revivalism. Thus a study of Branham's ministry is important for a better understanding of contemporary revivalism. His theology of healing—particularly his requirement that the sick recognize his role as God's prophet before deliverance could occur—highlighted the role of the evangelist as mediator between Christ and the afflicted.

The study of Branham's ministry also reveals much about the healing methodology of deliverance evangelists, past and present. Some of the methods that Branham used effectively are popular elements of current healing methodology. W. V. Grant, Jr., for example, asks each person who desires healing if they had previously talked with him or any of his staff. After confirming that the sick person is a stranger, Grant occasionally selects the persons to be healed by seeing a light hovering over their heads. This heavenly light indicates that the candidate has sufficient faith.[1] Moreover, Neal Frisby heightens the miraculous nature of his ministry by claiming to have photographs of angelic lights hovering about him.[2]

---

[1]I attended one of Grant's services at Calvary Cathedral, Louisville KY, 17 November 1984.

[2]J. Gordon Melton, "Miracle of Life Revival, Inc.," *The Encyclopedia of American Religions*, 3 vols. (Wilmington NC: McGrath Publishing Company) 3:284.

The most significant influence of Branham's healing methodology was his second sign—the use of visionary discernment. The evangelist's ability to tell people the secrets of the heart, their names, addresses, and the nature of their illnesses became one of the most common elements of the healing repertoire of many evangelists. The European Pentecostal, Donald Gee, noted the frequency of such a gift among evangelists. He cautiously acknowledged that the gift was "very often . . . startling in its accuracy." At the same time, he feared "a too frequent repetition of the item" and repudiated the contention that the gift was the biblical "word of knowledge" (1 Cor. 12:8).[3] Nevertheless, the use of visionary discernment is still popular today. Old school revivalists like H. Richard Hall and charismatic "stars" of the electronic church like W. V. Grant, Jr., Richard Roberts, and Pat Robertson employ the method that Branham popularized in the postwar revival.[4]

A study of William Branham is more than an illustration of a full gospel, healing evangelist, however. Though "always outside the mainstream of pentecostalism,"[5] Branham's full gospel ministry was representative of several characteristics of the Pentecostal tradition. First, Branham was representative of the Pentecostal "holy-man," the charismatic-authoritarian leader prominent throughout the movement's history. His life story was a tale of the miraculous, of one foreordained for a divine task. The early life paralleled that of C. H. Mason, the leader of the Church of God in Christ, who claimed that since his youth "God had endowed him with supernatural characteristics which were manifested in dreams and visions."[6] Branham often told about his mysterious birth and its accompanying divine light. Indeed, his early life was reportedly filled with infallible visions and signs.

Alongside the supernatural perspective of his early life, Branham's background illustrated another common characteristic of the lives of many Pentecostal leaders: economic, cultural, social, and physical deprivation. As a child, he lived in abject poverty and only received a seventh grade education. He blamed his father's alcoholism for the family's hardships.

---

[3]Donald Gee, "The 'Word of Knowledge,' " *TVH* 5 (March 1953): 14.

[4]Oral Roberts occasionally used the gift of knowledge in his early healing ministry. Besides Branham, Katherine Kuhlman is also known for popularizing visionary discernment. See David E. Harrell, Jr., *Oral Roberts: An American Life* (Bloomington: Indiana University Press, 1985) 450.

[5]Harrell, *All Things Are Possible*, 41.

[6]Klaude Kendrick, *The Promise Fulfilled: A History of the Modern Pentecostal Movement* (Springfield MO: Gospel Publishing House, 1961) 197.

Moreover, he claimed that his spiritual experiences and moral purity alienated friends and family alike. Branham's ministry was also deeply affected by personal tragedy. He interpreted the loss of his wife and daughter in the Ohio River flood of 1937 as God's punishment for his refusal to minister to Oneness Pentecostals.[7]

Harrell noted that the "unusual emotional strength of many evangelists" was often derived from "tortured childhoods." "In the more militant ministers," Harrell added, "their sense of rejection and persecution seemed clearly linked with the insecurity of their early lives. It also appeared to be their chief source of personal magnetism."[8] Indeed, some of Branham's most touching sermons during the revival were the stories of his sense of rejection. This sense of rejection was even present after Branham had achieved ministerial prominence. Recalling the effect of his father's alcoholism upon his adolescence, Branham exclaimed: "People didn't love me at all, nobody had any use for me. And now, by the help of God, I believe that I'm directing the Bride of Jesus Christ."[9]

Another characteristic of the Pentecostal, charismatic-authoritarian leader was the claim to a direct call from God, often in an audible voice or vision, to enter the ministry or initiate a new work. The earliest Pentecostal leaders formed their Pentecostal subgroups in response to divine calls. A. J. Tomlinson received his famed apocalyptic vision upon Burger Mountain outside Cleveland, Tennessee, regarding *the* true Church of God. Moreover, Aimee Semple McPherson's vision of the Foursquare Gospel was the inspiration for the International Church of the Foursquare Gospel.

The experience of the postwar healing revivalists often conformed to this pattern.[10] Branham claimed that an angel instructed him to take a message of healing to the masses. Throughout his ministry, Branham had direct confrontations with God. In 1955, the angel revitalized the evangelist's declining ministry with the tent vision and its promise of a ministry that no one could imitate. The most significant event of the 1960s—

---

[7]These characteristics were part of the profile of an early Pentecostal leader that was outlined by Robert Mapes Anderson. See Robert Mapes Anderson, *Vision of the Disinherited: The Making of American Pentecostalism* (New York: Oxford University Press, 1979) 93-113.

[8]Harrell, *All Things Are Possible*, 236-37.

[9]William Branham, *Conduct, Order, Doctrine of the Church*, 2 vols. (Jeffersonville IN: Spoken Word Publications, 1973-1974) 2:1053.

[10]Harrell, *All Things Are Possible*, 237.

the opening of the seven seals of Revelation—was a result of Branham's claim to have witnessed angels in the guise of an Arizona cloud.

Perhaps the most important element of the Pentecostal "holy-man" lies in the claim that he is God's selected vessel of continuing revelation. In light of their supernatural callings and miracle-oriented ministries, the earliest Pentecostal leaders were spiritual autocrats. The disciples of W. H. Durham, for example, considered his words to be law. New revelations flourished and often resulted in the establishment of new sects. As the Pentecostal movement grew, the more mature believers became less dependent upon revelatory pronouncements. Nevertheless, the mentality of the Pentecostal/charismatic masses still grants an aura of infallibility to the words of contemporary charismatic leaders. [11]

Branham was an extreme personification of the Pentecostal emphasis on spiritual autocracy. His hermeneutic rested on a doctrine of continuing revelation pronounced through selected vessels. Like other "holymen" he functioned as a mediator of continuing revelation through infallible visions. By virtue of the anointing, Branham regarded himself as the mouthpiece of the angel. His words were not his own.

After the peak years of the revival, Branham expanded the role of continuing revelation. He continued to utilize visions and dreams for revelatory purposes. The interpretations of his dreams were given prominent spiritual authority. Indeed, the dreams of his more credulous disciples often helped produce some of Branham's most grandiose messages. It was after a series of dreams by close supporters that Branham headed west and became convinced of a divine mandate to open the "seven seals."

Branham did not promote the interpretation of tongues and prophecy to validate his spiritual authority as readily as did many Pentecostal leaders. When his disciples used these gifts, however, the revelatory messages confirmed Branham's leadership as the eschatological prophet. At the conclusion of a 1961 service, Branham's co-pastor at the Branham Tabernacle prophesied: "Yea, I say this night that thou hast well done that thou hast heard My Voice and heeded My servant as he hath spoken unto thee; for this night again I have vindicated the office of his ministry . . . the office of My prophet in this day." [12]

---

[11]Larry Douglas Hart, "Problems of Authority in Pentecostalism," *Review and Expositor* 75 (Spring 1978): 257.

[12]Orman Neville, quoted in William Branham, *Respects to God's Servants* (Hendersonville NC: True Vine Memorial Library, 1962) 32. Neville was the resident pastor of the Branham Tabernacle since Branham's ministry involved so much travel.

Branham's transition to more "prophetic" doctrinal teaching, however, was the impetus for his most extreme use of continuing revelation through selected vessels. Earlier Pentecostal leaders had appealed to continuing revelation for doctrinal viewpoints. Oneness Pentecostals considered their views on the "oneness" of the Godhead and rebaptism in the Name of Jesus Christ as a revelation that restored New Testament practices. Branham and his disciples affirmed that God had revealed the eschatological mysteries in Branham's "message." Indeed, Branham appealed to revelation for his most controversial doctrines—the serpent's seed and the identity of the prophet of Malachi 4.

Like all Pentecostal "holy-men," Branham believed in principle that the Bible was the infallible Word of God, and that no one should add to the Scripture. Yet, his emphasis on the "Word" coming afresh to each church age permitted his followers to accept his pronouncements as fresh revelation from God. Furthermore, Branham's belief that prophets were the sole revealers of the "Word," and that he was such a prophet, has encouraged his disciples to consider his taped sermons as Scripture. Indeed, Branham himself asserted that God's eschatological "message" was being stored on his tapes due to a "famine" of the presence of the Holy Spirit in the denominations.

By implying that he was the end-time prophet, Branham carried the Pentecostal emphasis on continuing revelation to its most radical and logical conclusion. Branham undermined the priesthood of the believer in his assertion that God only spoke to one prophet in a generation, that is, only the interpretations of the charismatic-authoritarian leaders have spiritual authority. As this prophet, Branham's claims of infallibility manifested the dangerous excesses of subjective, authoritarian revelation. Though Branham did not intend it, the result of his "prophetic" revelations is a religious movement that has partially or totally deified him and his words.

To label Branham's hermeneutic of "prophetic" revelations a logical conclusion of the Pentecostal emphasis on continuing revelation is not to denigrate the entire Pentecostal movement. It is simply to affirm that Pentecostals, more than most Christian traditions, are particularly vulnerable to the tension between individualism and subjectivism and the canonical authority of the biblical revelation. For those full gospel believers who emphasize the revelatory nature of the spiritual gifts alongside the Scripture, and grant their leaders spiritual autocracy, radical excesses will always be possible.[13]

---

[13]Recall the statement of Charles Farah, "Wherever the Spirit bursts forth in new power there is always the danger that continuing revelation will take precedence over Scripture." See Charles Farah, "A Critical Analysis: The 'Roots and Fruits' of Faith-Formula Theology," *Pneuma* 3 (Spring 1981): 17.

Another issue in the Pentecostal tradition to which William Branham speaks is the question of prophecy versus order. Jeffrey Burton Russell described medieval Christianity in terms of "the tension within the Church between the spirit of prophecy and the spirit of order."[14] These two dynamics both seek the Kingdom of God. The spirit of prophecy uncompromisingly demands a radical transformation of the world, places earthly institutions under judgment, and seeks the end of the world. The approach of the spirit of order is more patient and moderate, attempting to reform institutions and the world. Russell demonstrated that during the medieval period the two forces cooperated and experienced conflict. While the search for order was necessary for the Church to exist, the process often frustrated the spirit of prophecy.[15]

Pentecostalism, like all movements within Christendom, can be seen from the perspective of prophecy versus order. Incipient Pentecostalism was a prophetic reaction, in part, against the absence of the Spirit within dead institutionalism. The early Pentecostals believed they were restoring primitive spirituality to the church. Nevertheless, new institutions were formed around these restored doctrinal emphases. The formation of subgroups by Aimee Semple McPherson and A. J. Tomlinson—both of whom functioned as prophets to their disciples—represented the institutionalization of the prophetic in early Pentecostalism.[16]

The ministry of William Branham is a contemporary illustration of the tension between prophecy and order in the Pentecostal tradition. During the peak years of the revival, he functioned within the Pentecostal institutional structure. In healing campaigns, he emphasized ecumenical "union" meetings of the various Pentecostal subgroups. His "prophetic" message stressed the unity of Spirit-filled Christians through the medium of divine healing.

With the decline of the revival and the rejection of the healing evangelists by the Pentecostal denominational hierarchies, tension increased between the spirits of prophecy and order. Oral Roberts is an excellent example of one who kept his ministry within the institutional context. His ability to adapt to a broader charismatic revivalism and his subsequent entrance into the Methodist denomination dramatically revealed how the

---

[14]Jeffrey Burton Russell, *A History of Medieval Christianity: Prophecy and Order* (Arlington Heights IL: AHM Publishing Corporation, 1968) v.

[15]Ibid., 1-5.

[16]See Charles H. Barfoot and Gerald T. Sheppard, "Prophetic vs. Priestly Religion: The Changing Role of Women Clergy in Classical Pentecostal Churches," *Review of Religious Research* 22 (September 1980): 2-17.

Pentecostal tradition had spread its influence within other institutional contexts.

Branham's later years, however, illustrate the danger of fanaticism produced by an unrestrained spirit of prophecy. Too unsophisticated to adapt to the age of television evangelism and the modish charismatic movement of the 1960s, Branham's "prophetic" identity became more exaggerated. He rejected the growing institutionalization of Pentecostalism. Moreover, he increasingly condemned denominationalism as the mark of the beast and insisted that the Pentecostals' loss of the Spirit was due to their acceptance of creeds. In essence, the rejection of the spirit of order became an integral element of the eschatological "message" of the "prophet" of Malachi 4. Branham's long-standing desire for a unique ministry was expressed in dogmatic, "prophetic" revelations that ultimately resulted in the exclusivistic idea that his followers were the elect Bride of Christ.

All branches of Christendom will continue to live with the tension of the spirits of prophecy and order. Prophecy is needed to guard the Church from worldly compromise and the weakening of the Spirit's presence in excessive institutionalism. Segments of the Pentecostal tradition, however, are more readily susceptible to the fanaticism and exclusivism generated by an unrestrained spirit of prophecy. With its potential to generate an excessive emphasis on continuing revelation through selected vessels, the Pentecostal tradition will continue to have more than its fair share of Elijah figures.

Branham's ministry must also be considered, at least in part, as a precursor of the Faith/Confession movement that is currently the fastest growing phenomenon in the charismatic movement. Kenneth Hagin is called the founder, and is the self-acknowledged "prophet" of the movement. Other prominent voices—all who consider Hagin their spiritual father—include Kenneth Copeland, John Osteen, Kenneth Hagin, Jr., Fred Price, and Charles Capps.[17]

Recent studies have demonstrated that Hagin's teaching on faith and confession is derived primarily from the work of the early Pentecostal

---

[17]Daniel Ray McConnell, "The Kenyon Connection: A Theological and Historical Analysis of the Cultic Origins of the Faith Movement" (M.A. Thesis, Oral Roberts University, 1982) 8-9. For a recent study of the ministries of Kenneth Hagin, Kenneth Copeland, and Fred Price see Jim Ernest Hunter, Jr., "A Gathering of Sects: Revivalistic Pluralism in Tulsa, Oklahoma, 1945-1985" (Ph.D. diss., The Southern Baptist Theological Seminary, 1986).

faith healer, E. W. Kenyon.[18] Hagin was also influenced by the teachings of F. F. Bosworth, the famous healing evangelist of the 1920s who participated in the post-World War II revival as a member of the Branham party.[19]

Faith-formula theology is built around the cornerstone of Mark 11:23, "Whatosever you say, believe that what you say shall come to pass, and you can have what you say." Faith, using proper confession, is believing that God's promises are already your possession. Faith is acting upon God's Word. "Hope is always future tense. . . . But faith is always now. Faith says, 'I'll receive right now. I have it now,' " according to Hagin.[20]

The certainties of faith are based upon "Revelation Knowledge," an infallible spiritual knowledge (continuing revelation) that is given to the believer directly from God. Faith teachers assert, consequently, that believers with illnesses should confess they are healed, despite physical symptoms to the contrary. God is obligated to heal those who claim their healings. Loss of healing indicates a loss of faith. In addition to health, the use of faith/confession formulas will bring material wealth, success, and prosperity.[21]

Several of the themes of the Faith/Confession movement can be found in the teachings of Branham. Influenced by F. F. Bosworth, Branham emphasized the "obligation" of God to heal those who have demonstrated proper faith. The absence of healing indicated a lack of faith; and sick persons should possess their healing despite the contradictory physical evidence. Though Branham did not use the term "Revelation Knowledge," he preached that faith was solely obtained by divine revelation. According to Branham, "Faith is believing what God reveals to you."[22]

---

[18]See McConnell, "Kenyon," passim. See also Farah, "Faith,"6-7, 14. Farah also discusses Faith teaching in Charles Farah, Jr., *From the Pinnacle of the Temple* (Plainfield NJ: Logos International, n.d.).

[19]McConnell, "Kenyon," 19-20. For the teachings of Bosworth see F. F. Bosworth, *Christ the Healer* (Miami: Mrs. Florence N. Bosworth, 1948). See also F. F. Bosworth, "The Faith That Takes," *TVH 1* (June 1948): 11-12.

[20]Kenneth Hagin, *What Faith Is* (Tulsa: Kenneth Hagin Ministries, 1978) 3-4. According to Hagin, he was healed after reading and believing Mark 11:23. See Kenneth Hagin, "How God Raised Me From a Deathbed," in *Kenneth E. Hagin's 50 Years in the Ministry: 1934-84* (Tulsa: Kenneth Hagin Ministries, 1984) 23.

[21]Farah, "Faith," 13-15. See also E. W. Kenyon, *Jesus the Healer* (Lynnwood WA: Kenyon Gospel Publishing Society, 1968). In this volume, Kenyon speaks of Revelation knowledge (1), hope as future and faith as believing now (14, 76) and right and wrong confessions (92-93).

[22]See above, 63-65.

On the other hand, Branham did not adhere to some of the key elements of faith-formula theology that current Pentecostal scholars view to be heretical. The healer-prophet denounced the gospel of wealth and prosperity that became a dominant theme of many revivalists in the 1960s. Moreover, he never preached the intense dislike of adversity that characterizes some current Faith teachers. On the contrary, sickness could occur as a test of one's faith. In addition, Branham believed that his elect Bride would be persecuted for its "message."

Branham's ministry should be considered a precursor to the Faith/Confession movement, however. The evangelist taught that all things were possible with faith. Rather than seeking materialistic prosperity, Branham utilized Mark 11:23 to speak the "Word" —a gift of perfect faith. In the process, he gained spiritual fame from his disciples—a relief from ambiguity far superior to the fleeting riches of this world.

In evaluating Branham's career as a Pentecostal healing evangelist, the hallmarks of his character—a personal magnetism of sincerity, humility, and unassuming manner—are a tribute to his enduring legacy as a giant of healing revivalism. His healing gift and the power of his services are still held in awe by participants in the tradition of divine healing in America. On the other hand, Branham's later ministry is aptly described as "eccentric." With the certainty of "Thus Saith the Lord," he prophesied that Los Angeles would fall into the Pacific Ocean. His ability to speak the "Word" reportedly eventuated in the resurrection of a fish, the calming of a Colorado storm, and the *creatio ex nihilo* of squirrels. He believed that the final manifestation of his gift would transform physical bodies into the glorified bodies necessary for the rapture. His eccentricity climaxed in his identification with the eschatological prophet of Malachi 4.

In the tradition of divine healing, Branham's later ministry is like that of the earlier giant of the late nineteenth century—John Alexander Dowie. Dowie became increasingly dependent on divine revelations and visions and finally regarded himself as Elijah, the Prophet foretold by Moses (Deuteronomy 18:18-19), and the First Apostle of the Church with "the right to speak as the instructor of the nations."[23] Like Dowie, Branham was the victim of his own illusions.

Evaluating Branham beyond the parameters of the Pentecostal movement, his ministry must be seen as part of the broader prophetic tradition of American religious history. Figures in this tradition abound like Mary Baker Eddy of the Christian Scientists, Charles Webster

---

[23]Gordon Lindsay, *The Life of John Alexander Dowie* (Shreveport LA: The Voice of Healing Publishing Co., 1951) 170-72, 234-40.

Leadbetter of the Theosophists, and Joseph Smith of the Mormons. These leaders, and others, acted as God's selected vessels of revelation for their followers and proclaimed authoritative divine teachings. Eddy, for example, insisted that her *Science and Health with Key to the Scriptures* (1875) provided the true, revealed meaning of Scripture. By claiming that the book's message was of divine origin, she had proclaimed an authoritative interpretation of the Bible that her followers must accept. Leadbetter is a second representative of the broader prophetic tradition. A bishop in the Liberal Catholic Church in the 1920s, he advocated an eclectic philosophy that contained Christian and Hindu elements. Consequently, he became a spokesperson of the "Masters," who were in constant touch with him on the astral plane and gave him messages of spiritual authority.[24]

The remarkable parallels between Branham and prophet figures outside the Pentecostal tradition are especially seen in the life of the Mormon prophet, Joseph Smith. Similar to Branham, Smith experienced a vision from God at the age of fourteen in which a pillar of light appeared and a divine voice spoke to him. As Branham's ministerial colleagues had done, the religious persons of Smith's community remarked that his visions were demonic. Perhaps the most obvious parallel in the lives of the two prophet figures is the role of an angel. Moroni, the heavenly messenger who visited Smith—and later directed him to the golden tablets from which the *Book of Mormon* would be translated—is reminiscent of Branham's man-like angel who gave the evangelist the divine commission to heal the sick. Finally, the spiritual authority of both leaders was based on continuing revelation.[25] These parallels do not suggest a linkage between Branham and Smith; nevertheless, the fascinating similarities point out some basic elements in the making of radical prophetic identities.

In contextualizing Branham's "Message" disciples, the movement might best be described as an extremist Pentecostal expression of Protestant fundamentalism. Fundamentalists assert that the Bible is inerrant and argue for the literal fulfillment of eschatological biblical prophecies. Fundamentalists differ, however, over the question of spiritual author-

---

[24]Sydney E. Ahlstrom, *A Religious History of the American People* (New Haven: Yale University Press, 1972) 1021-26, 1038-43. See also Peter F. Anson, *Bishops at Large* (New York: October House, Inc., 1964) 347-51.

[25]Joseph Smith, *Joseph Smith Tells His Own Story* (St. Louis: Zion's Printing and Publishing Co., 1838) 3-13. Smith has been called "pre-eminently the American prophet" by his followers. See Brigham H. Roberts, *Joseph Smith: The Prophet-Teacher* (Princeton NJ: Club of Princeton University, 1967) 66. See also Ahlstrom, *Religious*, 501-508.

ity. Non-Pentecostals achieve certainty in an uncertain and confused world by arguing for the propositional authority of the Bible. Biblical statements about God can be rationally proven through common sense realism.[26] In contrast, Pentecostal piety emphasizes the authority of the present experience of the Spirit as well as the written biblical revelation. Consequently, spiritual certainty is potentially available through the Spirit's continuing revelation in the spiritual gifts and the authoritative pronouncements of selected vessels.

The "Message" extended Pentecostal fundamentalism to its most radical conclusion. The sermons of Branham were deemed infallible in order to implement the fundamentalist abhorrence of ambiguity in life. Since the organized church was apostate, divine revelations were needed for the assurance and guidance of God's presence. The presence of the Spirit, Branham's disciples came to affirm, was mediated through the "Word" of the Malachi prophet. As Billy Paul Branham testified, "We are just following a one man "Message" with the voice of God for this day."[27]

* * * * *

There is no doubt that William Branham was a sincere practitioner of an increasingly "eccentric" expression of American Pentecostalism. Throughout his ministry he reflected a prophetic office that shaped, and was shaped by, the Pentecostal "vision of the disinherited."[28] Though little known outside the Pentecostal subculture, Branham was a powerful influence in the "prophetic" identity claimed by later healing revivalists and the whole of Pentecostalism itself. In the end, as Robert Moore said, Branham "got a sort of fame, a kind congenial to his lone wolf personality and his followers got what they sought too—the absolute assurance of 'Thus Saith the Lord' in a world confusing and uncertain."[29]

---

[26]George Marsden described how fundamentalists utilized Baconian common sense realism. See George M. Marsden, *Fundamentalism and American Culture: The Shaping of Twentieth-Century Evangelicalism: 1870-1925* (New York: Oxford University Press, 1980) 55-62.

[27]Billy Paul Branham, "Personal Testimony," sermon delivered and recorded in Harding AR, 23 June 1984.

[28]This phrase is taken from the title of Anderson's history of Pentecostalism. Interpreting the movement from a sociological theory of deprivation, he suggested that the adherents of Pentecostalism were drawn from the social, economic, and cultural "disinherited" segment of American life. See Anderson, *Vision,* 228-29.

[29]Letter received from Robert Moore, 10 October 1983.

A
BIBLIOGRAPHICAL
NOTE

Scholarly work on the history of divine healing in America is increasing. David E. Harrell's *All Things Are Possible: The Healing and Charismatic Revivals in Modern America* (Bloomington: Indiana University Press, 1975) is the best survey of the post-World War II healing revival in America. Harrell's work contains an excellent bibliography on the revival, including several books written by each of the major evangelists. The bibliography also gives sources on earlier twentieth-century revivalists like F. F. Bosworth and Aimee Semple McPherson. Harrell's most recent work, *Oral Roberts: An American Life* (Bloomington: Indiana University Press, 1985), is not only an in-depth study of Roberts' ministry but has a wealth of information about healing and charismatic revivalism in general. Another bibliographical source that contains some entries on the Pentecostal faith healers is J. Gordon Melton, *A Reader's Guide to the Churches Ministry of Healing* (Evanston IL: The Academy of Religion and Psychical Research, 1973).

The "faith cure" movement in the nineteenth-century Holiness tradition is surveyed in several works. An early important article was Raymond J. Cunningham's "From Holiness to Healing: The Faith Cure in America, 1872-1892," *Church History* 43 (December 1974): 499-513. Donald Dayton has contributed three fine articles that discuss the beliefs of several prominent Holiness teachers who advocated divine healing, and that demonstrate the thorough theological preparation for Pentecostalism in the Holiness tradition. These include "From Christian Perfection to the 'Baptism of the Holy Ghost' " in Vinson Synan, ed., *Aspects of Pentecostal/Charismatic Origins* (Plainfield NJ: Logos International, 1975),

"The Rise of the Evangelical Healing Movement in 19th Century America," *Pneuma* 4 (Summer 1982): 1-18, and "Theological Roots of Pentecostalism," *Pneuma* 2 (Spring 1980): 3-21. The latter article summarizes Dayton's University of Chicago dissertation (1983) by the same name. *The Theological Roots of Pentecostalism* is also a forthcoming book to be published by Scarecrow Press, Metuchen NJ. Another dissertation on the nineteenth-century Holiness tradition is Paul Chappel's "The Divine Healing Movement in America" (Ph.D. diss., Drew University, 1982). Chappel's work is the most thorough survey of the thought of the major faith healers of the Holiness tradition. Chappel also includes a discussion of the pivotal transitional figure between the Holiness and Pentecostal movements—John Alexander Dowie.

Further work needs to be done in the period between the Holiness movement and the post-World War II revival. Theses and dissertations are now being written on different facets of the healing emphasis of the contemporary charismatic revival. Daniel Ray McConnell's "The Kenyon Connection: A Theological and Historical Analysis of the Cultic Origins of the Faith Movement" (M.A. thesis, Oral Roberts University, 1982) deals with the Faith/Confession movement, specifically the dependence of the current leader Kenneth Hagin upon the early Pentecostal healer, E. W. Kenyon. Jim Ernest Hunter, Jr., in his study, "A Gathering of Sects: Revivalistic Pluralism in Tulsa, Oklahoma, 1945-1985" (Ph.D. diss., The Southern Baptist Theological Seminary, 1986) discusses the work of Kenneth Hagin, Oral Roberts, Kenneth Copeland, Tommy L. Osborn, and other revivalists who have roots in the Tulsa area.

Numerous journal articles are being published on the Faith/Confession movement. These include Sherry Andrews, "The Controversy over Faith," *Charisma* 7 (January 1982): 44-49, Stephen Board, "Is Faith a High Wire Act?," *Eternity* 32 (July-August 1981): 12-16, 26, and the observations of a leading participant, Kenneth Hagin, Jr., "Trend Toward Faith Movement," *Charisma* 11 (August 1985): 67-70. Some of the most vocal opposition to the movement has come from Charles Farah, Jr., of Oral Roberts University. His works include *From the Pinnacle of the Temple* (Plainfield NJ: Logos International, n.d.) and "A Critical Analysis: The 'Roots and Fruits' of Faith-Formula Theology," *Pneuma* 3 (Spring 1981): 3-21.

Scholarly research on William Branham is not extensive. Harrell's work, *All Things Are Possible,* contains an excellent section on Branham. Harrell elucidates the fact of Branham's role as pacesetter of the healing revival. Harrell's *Oral Roberts: An American Life* also includes a few pages on Roberts' relationship to Branham. Some standard Pentecostal histories make brief mention of Branham. These include W. J. Hollenweger, *The Pente-costals* (London: S. C. M. Press, 1972), Nils Bloch-Hoell, *The Pentecostal Movement: Its Origin, Development, and Distinctive Character* (New York: Humanities Press, 1964) and John Thomas Nichol, *Pentecostalism* (New York: Harper & Row, Publishers, 1966).

Recent efforts that analyze the Pentecostal tradition in light of its spread into mainstream Protestant bodies do not usually mention Branham. Two exceptions, Prudencio Damboriena's *Tongues as of Fire: Pentecostalism in Contemporary Christianity* (Washington: Corpus Books, 1969) and Steve Durasoff's *Bright Wind of the Spirit: Pentecostalism Today* (Englewood NJ: Prentice-Hall, 1972), do briefly acknowledge the role of Branham in healing revivalism. Durasoff is particularly sympathetic, having experienced the gift of tongues for the first time in a Branham service. The lack of knowledge regarding Branham's importance in the Pentecostal tradition by non-Pentecostals is especially apparent in Wade H. Boggs's *Faith Healing and the Christian Faith* (Richmond: John Knox Press, 1956). Boggs incorrectly identifies Branham as Henry Branham.

The few non-Pentecostal works that mention Branham are critical of him. They utilize the presupposition that the practice of faith healing is not acceptable to orthodox Christianity today. Consequently, some authors dismiss Branham as being associated with the demonic. Two works of Kurt Koch, *Occult Bondage and Deliverance* (Grand Rapids MI: Kregel Publications, 1970) and *Between Christ and Satan* (Grand Rapids MI: Kregel Publications, 1972), describe Branham as a deceived Satanic medium.

Other writers point to Branham as the originator of a religious cult. The only reference to Branham in the multitudinous new encyclopedias on cults is found in Bob Larson's *Larson's Book of Cults* (Wheaton IL: Tyndale House Publishers, Inc., 1982). He briefly describes "Branhamism" as a "personality cult." Some anti-cult organizations, however, are beginning to take notice of the continued existence of Branham's followers. Cal Beisner wrote a short tract, entitled *William Branham,* for the Christian Research Institute of San Juan Capistrano, California.

The most extensive anti-Branham material, however, is published by the Western Tract Mission, Inc., of Saskatoon, Saskatchewan, Canada. In addition to tracts, this organization has recently published a book about Branham. This work by Carl Dyck is entitled, *William Branham: The Man and His Message* (1984). Dyck is motivated by an apologetic fervor of warning Christians against the errors of Branham's beliefs. He offered a theological critique of several Branham distinctives. Similar to Kurt Koch, the author asserted that Branham's gift of healing "was the work of a man under satanic influence and not a ministry of healing from God.

. . ." He concluded that "Branhamites" were going to hell for following a perverted gospel. Characteristic of most cultic groups, these misguided persons were brainwashed and must be freed from their potentially disastrous faith.

Most of the secondary journal material that deals with Branham and healing revivalism is located in the Holy Spirit Research Center of the library of Oral Roberts University, Tulsa, Oklahoma. *The Voice of Healing,* edited by Gordon Lindsay, was begun in 1948 as the publicity organ of Branham's ministry during the healing revival. In the late 1950s and 1960s, the *Herald of Faith,* which later became the charismatic *Logos* journal, publicized Branham's ministry. The editor, Joseph Mattsson-Boze, was never a member of Branham's developing "Message." Nevertheless, Mattsson-Boze remained close friends with Branham until the latter's death. A third journal source is *Voice,* the official publication of the Full Gospel Business Men's Fellowship International. Throughout the 1950s and 1960s *Voice* included numerous glowing reports of Branham's extensive meetings with the businessmen's organization.

A few secondary books about Branham, written from an apologetic and hagiographical perspective, are also available. A heavily colored description of Branham's last years is Pearry Green's *The Acts of the Prophet* (Tucson: Tucson Tabernacle Books, n.d.). Other apologetic works include Julius Stadsklev's *The Prophet Visits South Africa* (Minneapolis: Julius Stadsklev, 1952) and Lee Vayle's *Twentieth Century Prophet* (Jeffersonville IN: Spoken Word Publications, n.d.). The best secondary source of Branham's early ministry in the healing revival is Gordon Lindsay's *William Branham: A Man Sent from God* (Jeffersonville IN: William Branham, 1950). Some information on Gordon Lindsay's involvement with Branham can be found in Lindsay's *The Gordon Lindsay Story* (Dallas: The Voice of Healing Publishing Co., n.d.).

The primary source material for a study of Branham is a voluminous collection of taped sermons (1100 +). More than 300 have currently been printed as *The Spoken Word.* These materials are available through the Voice of God Recordings, Inc., and Spoken Word Publications, both located in Jeffersonville, Indiana. An *Index of Messages* places the sermons in alphabetical and chronological order. My dissertation, "William Marrion Branham, 1909-1965: A Paradigm of the Prophetic in American Pentecostalism" (Ph.D. diss., The Southern Baptist Theological Seminary, 1985) contains the most complete listing of the primary and secondary sources about Branham.

INDEX
OF NAMES AND SUBJECTS

SCRIPTURE INDEX

Lightning Source UK Ltd.
Milton Keynes UK
UKOW04f0337091117
312413UK00001B/98/P